Transforming the Role of the SENCo

Transforming the Role of the SENCo

Achieving the National Award for
SEN Coordination

Second edition

Fiona Hallett and Graham Hallett

Open University Press

Open University Press
McGraw-Hill Education
8th Floor, 338 Euston Road
London
England
NW1 3BH

email: enquiries@openup.co.uk
world wide web: www.openup.co.uk

and Two Penn Plaza, New York, NY 10121-2289, USA

First published 2010
First published in this second edition 2017

A catalogue record of this book is available from the British Library

ISBN-13: 978-0-335-26360-8
ISBN-10: 0-33-52360-7
eISBN: 978-0-335-26361-5

Library of Congress Cataloging-in-Publication Data
CIP data applied for

Typeset by Transforma Pvt. Ltd., Chennai, India

Printed and bound by CPI Group (UK) Ltd, Croydon, CR0 4YY

Fictitious names of companies, products, people, characters and/or data that may be used
herein (in case studies or in examples) are not intended to represent any real individual,
company, product or event.

Praise for this book

"This timely, much needed book will be a valuable resource for all SENCos, including those currently engaging with the National Award for SEN Coordination. As a second edition, Fiona and Graham Hallett, working with contributing authors who are known experts in the world of special and inclusive education, have produced a volume which moves the original anticipatory discussions forward and fully reflects the current educational and political context.

Some really important discussions are included which raise awareness of tensions embedded in policy and practice and which challenge accepted ways of thinking about special educational needs and the role of the SENCo.

Throughout the book, there is an excellent balance of critical review of policy, drawing on wider conceptual frameworks relevant to discussions about the role of the SENCo, with grounded examples of the experiences of the SENCos that have been shared with the contributing authors.

This is a well-written and engaging book which will be a valuable resource for the reflective, forward-thinking SENCo."

Dr Alison Ekins, Canterbury Christ Church University, UK

"This new edition provides a very valuable resource for all those involved in provision for special educational needs and disabilities in schools and colleges, and in particular for those studying for the National Award for Special Educational Needs (and Disability) Co-ordination. It offers an interesting overview of the evolution, development and current expectations of the role of the SENCo. There is an important consideration of issues pertinent to those employed to carry out this role viewed through discussions in the SENCo Forum, and a critical examination of the contested and changing nature of the role of the SENCo as change agent with the potential to support inclusive policy and practice that should be at the heart of the school or setting."

Professor Janice Wearmouth, Faculty of Education
and Sport, University of Bedfordshire, UK

Contents

About the authors

Professor Lani Florian is Bell Chair of Education at the University of Edinburgh and Fellow of the Academy of Social Sciences (FAcSS). She is editor of the *Sage Handbook of Special Education*, now in its second edition, and co-author of *Achievement and Inclusion in Schools*, also in its second edition.

Fiona Hallett is a Reader in Education at Edge Hill University. Her research interests focus around social injustice and she is also interested in the ways in which research methodologies position the researcher and the researched.

Graham Hallett is a Senior Lecturer at the University of Cumbria, specialising in Special Educational Needs and Inclusion. His research interests include child and adolescent behaviour and innovative pedagogic practices.

Fiona and Graham Hallett are joint Editors of the *British Journal of Special Education*.

Brahm Norwich is Professor of Educational Psychology and Special Educational Needs, Graduate School of Education, University of Exeter. His on-going research is in the areas of lesson study, targeted inclusive models of early intervention and analysing the trends for special school and alternative setting placements for students with SEN.

From 2004–2013, **Lorraine Petersen** was the CEO of nasen and prior to that held a number of teaching posts within mainstream schools, including two headships. Since November 2013 Lorraine has worked as an Independent Consultant. She is a Governor at Chadsgrove School and is currently the Director of the Chadsgrove Teaching School Alliance. Lorraine was awarded an OBE for services to education in 2009.

Dr Artemi Sakellariadis is director of the Centre for Studies on Inclusive Education (CSIE), a national charity that works to promote equality and eliminate discrimination in education, and Honorary Research Associate at the University of Bristol. She is a teacher who worked in special schools for many years before devoting her time and energy to the development of more inclusive education.

Klaus Wedell was the first holder of the chair in Special Needs Education at the Institute of Education, University of London. On his retirement in 1995 from national and international academic work, one of his activities involved jointly setting up and maintaining an email support network for special needs coordinators in UK schools.

Acknowledgements

We would like to acknowledge the invaluable contributions of all those with whom we had conversations during the preparation of this book.

Introduction

Fiona and Graham Hallett

The preparation of a second edition of *Transforming the Role of the SENCo* has offered a timely opportunity for a reconsideration of the education landscape surrounding the role, and the National Award for SEN Coordination. The passage and implementation of the Children and Families Act (DfE, 2014a) have led to fundamental changes in the way that procedures to identify, assess, and provide for, children and young people with special educational needs and/or disability are operationalised. The introduction of the third SEN(+D) Code of Practice (DfE/DoH, 2015) has provided an extended requirement for what 'should' and 'must' be done by stakeholders within special needs education.

Of course, these changes, although focussed on the needs of children and young people who experience specific educational difficulties, do not stand outside of a much broader system, which has also undergone significant alteration. Changes include the introduction of a revised, more knowledge-based, National Curriculum in 2014, the introduction of assessment without levels in 2015, the opening of Free schools since 2010, the extension of the Academies programme between 2010 and 2017, and the proliferation of routes into teaching, culminating in proposed changes to the validation of Qualified Teacher Status (QTS).

The National Award for SEN Coordination has not been exempt from these changes. It is certainly of value to see a number of sections in the SEND Code of Practice (DfE/DoH, 2015) emphasising the importance of the National Award, perhaps providing future-proofing for the qualification in the medium term. Although the Award remains a compulsory requirement for all new SENCos, with three years being allowed for completion, government funding is no longer available for the training programme. Since the demise of the National Professional Qualification for Headship in 2012, the National Award is the only mandatory qualification required of a teacher and therefore the only qualification requiring mandatory study at Level 7, Master's level, something that might seem to reflect a genuine aspiration to embody academic rigour and quality within the Award.

The role of the SENCo would also have appeared to have matured and developed over the same period, based on both published research (Rosen-Webb, 2011; Griffiths and Dubsky, 2012; Brown and Doveston, 2014; Pearson, Mitchell and Rapti, 2015) and on the conversations held with stakeholders in the preparation of this book. It would now seem to be certain that every one of the 24000 or so schools in England (DfE, 2016) not only has a full or shared SENCo in post, but that all of these are qualified teachers, rather than also including TAs and head teachers as SENCos, as has been suggested was the case.

Of course, the ways in which this role has developed in schools since its inception following the publication of the first SEN Code of Practice (DfE, 1994) are as varied as the schools and settings in which the post holders are employed and the role is delivered. This variety is to be welcomed, as the last thing that should happen is that the role becomes reduced to a series of prescribed activities following externally imposed protocols. What is seemingly obvious is that the scope of the role has widened in a way that suggests an increasing importance in the development of good practice for a broader group of pupils than might be expected within the label, SEND.

It is clear that best practice has the role of the SENCo at the heart of the educational processes occurring within a setting, exerting an influence on teaching and learning for all. However, it is equally clear that the SENCo is not always able to implement significant change within those processes. Certainly, situations still exist where the role is focussed solely on administrative and bureaucratic procedures, in fulfilling the guidance laid down in the SEND Code of Practice, or in meeting requirements that ensure the effective gatekeeping of funds delegated to SEN provision.

That the SENCo is ideally placed to champion changes in schools as places of teaching and learning for all might seem obvious. However, it might be equally clear that such a transformation, through a process of innovation, is in the hands of all practitioners, whether teaching or support, who work in a setting. The idea that all teachers are teachers of all children has gained increased traction in the recent past (DfE/DoH, 2015). Where this idea has become part of the culture of a school, it is much more likely that class teachers will be working directly with pupils with SEND, rather than this being seen as a support role, or part of the role of the SENCo. Another example here is the development of support models based on collaborative approaches planned by teaching and support staff, supported by the SENCo, rather than the model often found in larger schools, of a learning support department led by the SENCo meeting the needs of marginalised children separately from those not in this category.

Changing approaches to support, such as this, seem to have enabled post holders to embrace a much more strategic function, for example, in questioning how these approaches are configured within broader structures of school development and improvement for all learners, by questioning or problematising that practice. Adopting a more strategic role is not without difficulties, of course, besides the obvious problem that might arise from poorly defined role expectations in a complex managerial system. Significant among these difficulties is the frequent lack of knowledge found among SENCos of the funding mechanisms that operate within their school; or those that arise in ensuring liaison and shared planning between the SENCo and the Governor responsible for SEN provision.

There would seem to be parallels here with other facets of school development. There is an extensive literature, for example, that addresses issues of school effectiveness, frequently constituted as increased competency in attainment tests. Often this has led to a concentration on school measures that promote performativity within national testing regimes. Although this process seems to deliver steadily increasing standards of attainment for many, it often seems to be at the expense of those for whom the educational experience is marked by a seemingly intractable failure to provide successful outcomes.

And yet the successive National Curriculum Inclusion Statements (DfEE, 1999; DCSF, 2010; DfE, 2014b) all place emphasis on the need to meet the learning needs of *all* pupils. The most recent version, admittedly somewhat more brief than previous iterations, states that 'a wide range of pupils have special educational needs, many of whom also have disabilities. Lessons should be planned to ensure that there are no barriers to every pupil achieving' (DfE/DoH, 2015: 8). There is also a very clear requirement that the provisions contained within the Equality Act 2010 are met.

At the centre of this debate lies an argument that can be stated as a tussle between those who advocate measures designed to raise standards, often through a concentration on a narrowed curriculum of properly 'academic' subjects, and those who contend that current practice is driving out the entitlement to a broad, balanced, relevant and differentiated curriculum that informed the premise on which the National Curriculum rests, one that might be seen to raise the achievements of all pupils.

That this is a current and relevant debate is suggested by several things. Evaluations of the previous version of the National Curriculum (DCSF, 2009a; Alexander, 2009) suggested the need to provide a better curriculum balance in terms of creativity, relevance and breadth, although this seems to have had little impact on policy makers, judging by the more narrowly prescriptive nature of the 2014 National Curriculum. At the same time, however, the change in perception of the role, described above, seems to have produced a situation where the SENCo is less of an agent of change for specific pupils, and more a change agent for all pupils; that is, a much more strategic pedagogical role. This would seem to place the SENCo at the centre of the school development process, able to meet the needs of all pupils, while providing a specialist focus for those with additional needs.

That a sense of a developing and emerging role for the SENCo gave us our title was acknowledged in the first edition of this book. That decision now seems prescient, as the changes of the intervening years seem to have brought about a significant degree of change; the themes identified in this edition have the potential to carry this transformation still further.

The structure of the book is seen as consisting of two related, but independent parts. The first three chapters in Part I provide a sense of the evolution and development of the role of the SENCo through a series of perspectives, including an historical overview, an examination of the SENCo Forum, and a consideration of the expectations and requirements of the role. The last three chapters offer a view of the role of the SENCo drawn from a series of conversations held with stakeholders during the summer of 2016. Each of these three chapters addresses one of the sections of the Learning Outcomes for National Award for SEN Coordination (NCTL, 2014).

Part II is intended to examine the contested and changing nature of the role of the SENCo; in this sense, it might echo the theme outlined above, of the SENCo as a change agent, placed at the heart of the school or setting, and driving an agenda that seeks to move practice in the direction of meeting the many, diverse, needs of the whole teaching and learning community of that setting.

In Chapter 1, Lorraine Petersen, an educational consultant and former Chief Executive Officer of NASEN (National Association of Special Educational Needs) gives an overview of the genesis of the SENCo role and how it has developed since the first SEN Code of Practice (DfE, 1994), outlining the national context of training for SENCos. In tracking the processes that have been influential in the development of the role, Lorraine draws attention to two main points. Firstly, she notes that responses in schools to the first SEN Code of Practice were varied because of the need to only 'have regard' to its recommendations, leading to little uniformity in the way that the role of SENCo became formalised.

Secondly, Lorraine draws attention to the parallel demands to enhance the scope and effectiveness of the role of the SENCo, including the need to promote greater Inclusion, to raise expectations for all young people, and to extend and develop best practice in teaching and learning, as well as meet the requirements of regulatory frameworks. In 2009, regulations were introduced that specified mandatory training for SENCos, that all SENCos must be qualified teachers, and that places the SENCo in a much more strategic and central position within schools and settings.

This new emphasis, from a role bounded by a non-regulatory framework to one operating within statutory limits, required a fundamental element of change in practice, as Lorraine notes; schools and governing bodies now had the dual responsibility of ensuring that their school met the standards laid down for them in the regulations, and for providing their SENCo with the 'training, time and resources to carry out their role effectively'.

Three further issues of importance to the role are then addressed. The issue of the changing nature of the school's workforce is considered, with the attendant development of the role and responsibilities of the SENCo in managing and training this workforce. The second issue, of facilitating a greater level of inter-agency working and collaboration, is seen as challenging. By drawing on legislation and reports such as the Lamb Inquiry Report (DCSF, 2009b), Lorraine highlights the third issue, the need to ensure the development of the SENCo role through effective training and development.

In new material provided for this edition, Lorraine examines the significant changes to the SEND landscape that followed the election of the Coalition government in 2010. As a precursor to intended legislation, the over-identification of SEND described by Ofsted in 2010 is noted, and this is seen as the catalyst for change as new policy emerged. The processes involved in proposing, legislating and implementing the changes associated with the Children and Families Act (DfE, 2014) are examined, and related to the way that the responsibilities and working practices of the SENCo are likely to change. The need to be increasingly involved in whole-school strategic development is discussed, and this is aligned to changes in the role of the SENCo specified in the SEND Code of Practice (DfE/DoH, 2015).

In concluding the chapter, Lorraine looks ahead at the challenges that are likely to face the emerging role, citing a number of difficulties that are likely to be significant. While these might be seen as offering a major threat to the continuity of good practice, Lorraine prefers a much more positive analysis of the challenge, suggesting that the opportunity exists to place well-trained and motivated SENCos at the heart of change leadership in our schools.

In Chapter 2, Klaus Wedell, who is Emeritus Professor at UCL Institute of Education, discusses the SENCo Forum, which he convened for many years, focussing on perceptions of transparency and accountability. The chapter opens by exploring the background to the Forum in providing support for newly appointed SENCos, who were often isolated and lacked relevant experience or expertise. The evolution of the Forum is mapped, with some idea of the current size and scope of the Forum being given. An outline of the four sections of the chapter follows.

Klaus introduces the first of these sections by linking the title of this book to discussions from the Forum that focus on extending the capacity of schools to meet the learning needs of all pupils. The interpretation of terms that appear in the SEND Code of Practice (DfE/DoH, 2015), such as 'must' and 'should', is discussed and this leads to an extended consideration of the role of the SENCo as a school leader. Here, practices that are central to the development of school-wide inclusive practices are contrasted with those that constrain the role, for example, workload demands and a narrowed remit. The need to provide a systemic lead in staff training and development is acknowledged alongside that of monitoring and deploying support staff.

The second section of the chapter deals with the role of the SENCo in assessing pupil engagement with the teaching provided, including difficulties that might arise from the way the task is presented; the development of collaborative working is suggested here, illustrated with material drawn from a Forum discussion. A discussion on Quality First teaching follows, linked to the presumption that all teachers are teachers of pupils with special educational needs, and this is linked to the need to change the perception of teachers towards their role in assessing learning needs; the example given here, relating to homework, is thought-provoking.

In the third section of the chapter, Klaus turns his attention to broader aspects of assessment related to 'special' educational needs, through an exploration of the interaction between factors 'within' the child and those within the child's environment. Material is drawn from a Forum discussion that suggests how difficult it is to determine when the threshold is reached that makes a need 'special', despite the use of tests that offer scores said to identify the existence of a particular labelled difficulty.

The final section of Klaus's chapter deals with provision, identifying three issues frequently addressed in the Forum. The first concerns the operationalisation of support, to avoid the stigmatisation of recipients in the eyes of other pupils and adults, offering some relevant and interesting thoughts about the efficacy and utility of both in-class and withdrawal approaches. The second issue considers how interventions can provide evidence of achievements that attainment-led testing cannot, particularly where this impacts on the appraisal of the SENCo within a school's accountability structures. The final issue identified in this section considers school/parent relationships, and the use of 'equivalent expertise' in co-constructing assessments and interventions.

Klaus concludes the chapter by offering some remarks about the degree to which SENCos possess the necessary agency to direct, manage and implement changes in the capacity of schools to be inclusive. He also acknowledges that the Forum has provided SENCos with a platform to share views, frustrations, and concerns that illustrate perceptions of accountability and transparency within their role.

The editors of the book, Fiona and Graham Hallett have contributed the third chapter, which considers the role of the SENCo as a leader. An essential element of the current agenda to transform the role of the SENCo surrounds changes to the leadership and management functions of the role. This focusses on the SENCo as an agent of change in the learning and achievements of those with barriers to learning, and as a change agent promoting improvements to teaching and learning for all within schools, where all is seen to include both pupils and adults within the setting.

The chapter develops three standpoints from which the role of the SENCo as an agent of change, and as a change agent, can be examined and evaluated. In the first of these, the current situation is examined, through a discussion of the requirements of the role, and the necessary attributes of role holders, set out in legislation and the most recent version of the SEND Code of Practice (DfE/DoH, 2015). The leadership potential of the SENCo is seen to be shaped by the current policy agenda, and the practices that have developed in response, both in implementing that agenda, and in undermining its efficacy. Where the perceived policy message is ambiguous or contradictory, for example, around Inclusion, the response is likely to mirror this uncertainty, giving rise to role definitions that entrench practice. Some significance is given to the difficulties that surround the positioning of the SENCo as a member of the senior leadership team within a setting, which seems to be seen as a precursor of change, although practice suggests that this might not be the best way of promoting whole-school developments. The chapter then considers the implications of the Learning Outcomes of the National Award for SEN Coordination (NCTL, 2014), and the way that these can be seen to influence the personal development of post holders and, in turn, the way that they discharge their responsibilities. This discussion is set against the typology developed by Kearns (2005) based on five metaphors that are seen as representative of the underpinning rationale of those post holders; at the end of this discussion, an alternative explanation of the typology is offered, as a nested hierarchy bounded by the possibilities offered within the structure of a setting, rather than a continuum of discrete philosophical positions The outcome of personal responses to the demands of fulfilling the role of SENCo, and balancing the often contradictory expectations of policy makers and senior managers, is examined through the concept of the street-level bureaucrat.

A second standpoint is then outlined; this is characterised as an interim position and is derived from the national policy aspiration that sees the role of SENCo being placed at the heart of school development, with the post holder being a member of the Senior Leadership or Management Team. This is seen as engendering two possible responses. In the first, the assimilation of the SENCo into the management hierarchy of the setting does not always lead to change, particularly in organisations where entrenched structures inhibit school development and promote subversive responses that work against collegiality. In an extended examination of social capital, it is suggested that the benefits of making connections between people with differing degrees of power and authority can be overstated unless linked to a willingness to embed autonomy in a core moral purpose that extends throughout the setting. It may also require a significant and disturbing reorganisation of roles and responsibilities, which in the end serves only to preserve a narrow hierarchy that sustains bureaucratic process management.

In proposing an interim model, a more positive response can also be suggested. Here, the positioning of the SENCo role within the senior leadership team is seen as capable of unlocking the potential of a school to engage with raising the achievement and attainment of all pupils. While this will offer short-term benefits, the sustainability of such change is challenged, as it does not require the fundamental development of practice that moving to other models of leadership might bring to an organisation.

This opens the possibility of a third standpoint. Drawing on work connected to distributive leadership, it is argued that a community of practice model would best serve the aim of moving the SENCo to a transformative position as a change agent. This embraces the concept of legitimate peripheral participation, where all members of the school community are 'leaders for learning and learning to lead' (MacBeath, 2009). The standpoint is developed through an examination of 'bridging' social capital, as a way in which community members, including pupils and parents, can express their agency, in the establishment of these communities of practice.

Three conditions are identified and developed as being prerequisites for the development of a distributive model of SEN Coordination: shared leadership; balanced accountability, both internal and external; and the removal of structures that atomise the role of the SENCo. With these in place, it is suggested that the opportunities offered by the National Award for SEN Coordination could find expression in a distributive model of leadership that promotes the role of the SENCo as serving the aims and aspirations of all learners, rather than only meeting the needs of those deemed to have special educational needs.

Chapters 4, 5 and 6 form a sub-section of the book that reports the conversations held by the editors of this book with those who have a direct interest in SEND, as SENCos, parents, governors or through being Statemented. The first of these, Chapter 4, both opens and ends with some thoughts on how gathering evidence to meet the Learning Outcomes for the National Award might be approached. It is our view that the outcomes should not be viewed as a list of competencies to be demonstrated one by one, but should emerge as part of a continuing reflective engagement that involves the synthesis of practice with the principles that underpin the Learning Outcomes.

In Chapter 4, Part A of the Learning Outcomes, the four themes of professional knowledge and understanding are addressed. In the first, dealing with the statutory and regulatory context, our conversations identified a significant level of tension; this was evidenced both at the strategic level, with perceived conflicts between legislative and regulatory frameworks, and at the operational level, where practice was not always seen to align with these frameworks.

This first theme, focussing on knowledge, is seen as being different to the remaining themes, which relate more clearly to understanding. The second theme links to the development of leadership and management processes, and continuing professional development, while the third theme, the most widely discussed overall in our conversations, focussed on enhancing the degree to which working practices meet the needs of those with SEN and/or disabilities. The fourth theme, about improved outcomes, also formed the basis of many conversations; issues discussed here included interventions, evidence-based practice, inspections, staff knowledge and expertise, and school vision.

Chapter 5 deals with Part B of the Learning Outcomes, leading and co-ordinating provision, which has five themes, the first three dealing with aspects of leadership, the fourth drawing on external support and the last about coordinating systems. There was a very strong thread in conversations on the first three themes, about the balance between strategic and process leadership expressed in terms of workload, resources, spheres of influence and staff training. This is an area where changes, although expected and often seen, do not always meet the expectations of practitioners.

One aspect of the conversations concerned the response to the inclusion of the word challenge in the second theme. A number of conversations focussed on this aspect, as the sense of empowerment provided by this usage allowed staff to challenge current practice; examples given include aspects of Quality First teaching, pupil voice and leading staff meetings. The third theme, on the use of evidence, is also reported, particularly where this relates to evidence-based practice.

The fourth theme dealt with here, on external support, produced a number of interesting conversations. One important discussion thread related to a perceived decrease in support available from local authorities; this was balanced by the opening up of other, collaborative networks. The final theme dealt with in this chapter considers system coordination; this is seen as an emerging area of expertise, moving away from what has been possible in the past to considering what could be provided in a changing educational arena. The chapter concludes with a consideration of opportunities for moving the role of the SENCo from one of limited coordination to one of leading on Inclusion.

The final chapter in this sub-section, Chapter 6, deals with Part C of the Learning Outcomes, Personal and Professional Qualities. The first quality noted suggests the need to create an ethos and culture that place the child at the heart of all that takes place and this is illustrated in a number of conversations that illustrate inclusive initiatives moving from the SEND arena into whole-school practice.

The need for attitudinal change is recognised in comments about the first theme; there was a clear sense of the SENCo being a change 'champion', for example, in battling for equality and identity for pupils, evidenced by an appetite in stakeholders to embrace positive change for the whole-school community.

The second theme deals with pupil-centred processes, and this was an area of the conversations that produced an extensive and varied response; that this supported such processes is to be expected, although a significant number of examples of the difficulties that arise in operationalising this concept were also discussed. The third theme extends ideas introduced in the second, focussing on pupil voice and how this can be heard. Two divergent themes are discussed; difficulties in hearing puplis' voice, for example, in a pupil without verbal communication, were acknowledged, but there was also a sense of disquiet stemming from the difficulty in enacting what is said by children and young people, even when their voice is heard. Some suggestions for strategies are given, in particular to secure best practice in transitions.

The final theme in this section concerns the co-construction of provision through a recognition of family leadership. This is recognised as a potentially difficult area within the expected expertise of the SENCo, if only because of views and practices that tend to currently exist within schools and settings concerning power relationships. The section gives examples of these difficulties, but ends on a positive note, encouraging of good practice in this area, based on the extended reflection possible in meeting the Learning Outcomes of the National Award for SEN Coordination.

Chapter 7 is contributed by Artemi Sakellariadis, the Director of the Centre for Studies on Inclusive Education (CSIE), who offers a thoughtful and provocative chapter that expresses a sense of disquiet about how Inclusion, disability and special educational needs are viewed in current discourses in education. In particular, Artemi offers a convincing argument about the need to revisit arguments about Inclusion that seem to have almost been dismissed as untenable, or at least unobtainable, in current policy pronouncements.

The chapter departs from conventional approaches to academic writing by offering a reflective and analytical account of a conversation between Artemi and Sophia, her 'trusted writing partner'. The opening section contextualises the conversation by offering some thoughts on definitions offered for the term Inclusion, and the way that it has developed and been challenged over time. The conversation then goes on to explore a much broader conceptualisation of Inclusion, that of 'processes that make everyone feel welcome, visible and respected in schools', developing this further to suggest that the context of Inclusion should encompass equality issues in education for all, of whatever age. This is linked to identity, in the sense that identity can be seen as multi-faceted, and inequality can affect individuals in one, some or all of these facets.

The way that schools or other settings deal with these issues forms the next section of the conversation, introducing ideas around the role of the SENCo and how that role has evolved, in some settings, to include a brief covering equality for all learners, rather than only those with the label of special educational needs, locating this debate in an examination of the way that schools have or have not developed to meet the learning needs of pupils at the margins.

Having considered the difficulties inherent in providing such opportunities, the discussion between Artemi and Sophia moves to a sustained, well-supported argument examining the very clear assumptions in legislation that Inclusion represents current policy within the UK, linking this to perceptions of disability among those who are not disabled, citing the narrowness of governmental responses to this issue in comparison to what those who are disabled are saying, using the 2012 Paralympics as an example of this difference.

An examination of the difficulty of implementing social change follows, with an acknowledgement that major changes rarely happen suddenly, but usually occur as a gradual evolution often including periods where progress appears to be temporarily reversed. This develops into a passage that examines ways to reconcile varying views on Inclusion, in what otherwise appears to be a contradictory argument. An examination of the need for a position on Inclusion that offers genuine choice within schools that are enabled to meet the needs of all learners follows, leading to a discussion about the often unnecessarily disabling language used within debates on this subject. This discussion, about terminology, is extended to include some thoughts on the seemingly inadequate definition of special educational needs in current usage and to consider the use of labels in the special needs arena.

The chapter concludes by offering an insight into the relationship between Artemi and Sophia, based on the reflective nature of their musings, linking this to the need for SENCos to engage in a similar process.

In the eighth chapter, Brahm Norwich, who is Professor of Educational Psychology and Special Educational Needs, at the University of Exeter, identifies and discusses 'some of the key dimensions and tensions associated with the SENCo role'.

The chapter begins with an overview of developments that have occurred since the introduction of the role, including the continuing uncertainty of what the role should be called that suggests an equal uncertainty about the scope of the role. Among the key themes outlined is the failure to properly address the needs of pupils with SEN and/or disabilities when the National Curriculum was introduced, the rise in exclusions that followed the introduction of a market-driven curriculum, and the increased demand for funded support for SEN that followed the introduction of school league tables.

The uncertainty surrounding the role of the SENCO and an increasing sense of the unmanageability of the demands of the role are then examined. In particular, a shift of focus resulting from the SEN Code of Practice (DfE, 1994) is noted, from meeting the needs of pupils with Statements of SEN to meeting the needs of those with SEN but without Statements. The extension of these responsibilities, firstly to include a more strategic role in management and leadership, and latterly to a position of centrality in managing change is then discussed. The section ends with an examination of the Learning Outcomes for NASC (National Award for SEN Coordination), which are summed up as showing a 'dual focus on the operational and strategic aspects' of the role.

In the main part of his chapter, Brahm identifies four interrelated aspects of the role, namely function versus role; justification and boundary of specialism; coverage of the function / role; and focus of coordination activities. In relation to the first aspect, it is noted that the set of functions of the role outlined in the National Award for SEN Coordination 'might be better distributed across various staff roles'. Following an examination of the TTA Standards for middle managers in schools (TTA, 1998), which make only limited reference to functions associated with the needs of pupils with SEN, Brahm goes on to examine recent material published by the National College for Teaching and Leadership (NCTL, 2014). These are not standards; however, it is argued that standards can be inferred from the requirements contained within qualifications for middle or senior leadership. The overall conclusion is that there is very little here that refers specifically to SEND, and that which is mentioned is often optional.

In considering the second aspect, that of 'justification and boundary of specialism', Brahm questions whether a distinct function for SEN coordination can be justified. In questioning whether others in a school might accept these responsibilities as part of their already defined management roles, the argument is developed to consider whether this distribution of function could render the role of SEN Coordination obsolete. In an interesting examination of the nature and degree of SEND, and how these needs can be met within generic and/or specific teaching strategies, the section concludes that 'some specialist or specific knowledge will continue to be required', as a form of 'connective specialisation'.

The third aspect identified is that of the coverage of the role/function. Building on the analysis explored in the previous section, Brahm suggests that, rather than creating a role with many functions that others might better discharge, a more inclusive role such as learning support/consultancy might be suggested. This would involve questioning whether the role should be broadened to include what is described as 'additional needs', something that is seen as increasingly unlikely in England, given recent legislation. The section ends with a note of caution, to ensure both that pupils are not defined only by their additional need, and that expertise beyond the setting should not be overlooked.

The final aspect concerns the focus of the coordination activities. Here Brahm acknowledges the variety of ways in which the role of the SENCo has been configured, and suggests that the role, as currently defined, is beyond the effective capacity of a single person, unless the argument returns to the first issue, of function versus role.

In conclusion, Professor Norwich makes the case for the distribution of most coordination functions to middle and senior management, leaving only specialist residual activities that reflect a concept of additional needs as a 'connective specialization'. The chapter ends with a challenge; a major re-examination of management roles will be needed in schools if an inclusive concept of coordination for those with additional needs is to be realised.

The ninth chapter develops the concept of inclusive pedagogy, and is contributed by Lani Florian, Bell Professor of Education at the University of Edinburgh. The chapter opens with a discussion of the problematic nature of the variability in 'educational reform policies' that has arisen in the UK, partly as a result of the divergence in policy consequent on the 'devolution of political power', and partly because of the advent of 'new types of schools'. In endorsing approaches that continue to offer separate support for those assessed with identifiable needs while also valuing personal choice, it is argued that the fragmentation implicit in variability, while welcome, is not always positive.

In defining 'the inclusive pedagogical approach', Lani makes reference to research that studied the practice of classroom teachers; in particular, this focussed on classrooms with diverse learners where a commitment to raising *achievement* for all learners coexisted with inclusive practices to prevent marginalisation or exclusion. The representation of 'teachers' craft knowledge of inclusive practice' (rigorously defined) in a way that is of use to the 'professional learning and practice of others' is seen as 'a key driver for this research'.

In developing this theme, Lani argues that a focus on meeting individual need as a way of promoting more inclusive practice can be challenged by examining five interrelated themes. The first suggests that such a focus serves to reinforce difference rather than lead to a resolution of it; it is suggested that this occurs because what is offered as 'inclusive education' does not rely on any significant change in practice, but simply replicates what was offered as 'special needs education'. This leads to a second theme which questions whether practice based on matching interventions to child characteristics is effective, drawing on research that suggests that 'different teaching strategies are not differentially effective with different types of learner'.

The third theme questions whether teaching strategies that are commonly used are consistent with those suggested in the literature on Inclusion, and notes that teachers report that they differentiate as a response to a variety of individual differences, but that these were not 'dependent on, or specific to, the identification of special educational need'.

In the remaining themes, the complexity associated with meeting the learning needs of all children through the identification of difference is examined. The fourth theme notes the increasing use of categorisations in schools. It is suggested that the many sources of variation and difference within these groups makes this problematic and unhelpful. The fifth theme develops this point, by considering the degree to which membership of a group produces an intractable cycle which is difficult to escape. It is suggested that this often leads to the assumption that learners 'possess all of the characteristics of group membership to the same degree'.

In proposing a theoretical framework for inclusive pedagogy, Lani argues for an approach that subsumes the complexities associated with learner difference within a set of ideas about children, learning, teaching, curriculum, and the school and policy contexts in which these ideas are acted out, asserting that 'learning occurs in shared activity in shared contexts'.

This is characterised as taking place in the 'community of the classroom' to avoid connotations that inclusive pedagogy is simply whole class teaching. It is argued that the distinguishing characteristics of the inclusive pedagogical approach are marked by 'the ways in which teachers respond to individual difference, the choices they make about group work, and how they utilise specialist knowledge'. This difference is illustrated in an extended example from practice.

The chapter concludes by arguing that it is only through 'accepting the notion of individual differences among learners without relying on individualised approaches to responding to them' that the needs of the community of learners in the classroom can be extended to include all pupils.

Chapter 10 offers a discussion of some of the tensions and challenges that can be seen to exist in the development of best practice for pupils with SEND through the operationalisation of the role of the SENCO. The chapter, by Fiona and Graham Hallett, reflects on the conversations with stakeholders in the role of the SENCo reported more fully in Chapters, 4, 5, and 6. It became increasingly clear in these conversations that the tensions derive both from the complexity stemming from conflicting policy and ideological positions experienced by the respondents but also from how these positions are operationalised by those respondents within the spaces in which they experience special educational needs.

The first part of the chapter offers an extended discussion of the fracturing of the school system in the period in which the National Award for SEN coordination has operated, and suggests ways in which continued changes in these structure will impact on practice in settings, and in the role of the SENCo. Consideration is given to how these changes have had an impact on the way we view special educational needs and Inclusion within a context in which other agendas have emerged, have gained importance, and have become dominant. It is suggested that the sort of binary thinking that develops within this sort of conflictual arena has served to embed practices that best embrace the interests of many children and young people but do not meet the needs of all, particularly those at the margins.

Moving beyond what might be described as system issues, the chapter then examines a series of broader challenges to the role of the SENCo, both within the personal development of post holders through engagement with the National Award, and in the systems and structures that bound that development. Areas examined include the perceived medicalisation of assessment procedures within

SEND, the impact of funding mechanisms on schools, the development of the curriculum model required of schools and the use of support staff. The chapter concludes with a consideration of the extent to which an individual SENCo can have an impact on practice, through a discussion of the sphere(s) of influence open to post holders and the degree to which the 'permitting circumstances' available in a setting allow the extension of practice, or simply serve to protect orthodoxy.

In a short conclusion, Chapter 11, Fiona and Graham Hallett consider the academic nature of the National Award for SEN Coordination, given suggestions that apprenticeship models of training are more appropriate within the teaching profession, a view that is repudiated in the chapter.

In concluding this Introduction, some thought is given to generic themes that seem to emerge from the chapters. It is clear that there is a changing landscape surrounding the role of the SENCo and the meeting of special or additional needs in schools. This is linked in the chapters to moves to make schools more inclusive; to the ambition to raise achievement and attainment, particularly for those pupils who are marginalised by current educational practice; and to make the best use of the resources, both physical and, most importantly, human, that are brought to bear on the school improvement agenda. There is also a recurring focus on the need to examine the use of language, and the concepts that lie beneath this usage, in the debate surrounding special educational needs, disability, and Inclusion, and the teaching and learning that occur in meeting these needs.

The purpose of the SENCo role has also been placed under scrutiny. A conflict can be suggested, between the role in enhancing outcomes for individual pupils, and that as an agent of change for all, where existing management structures may inhibit the possibilities of the SENCo making a difference. Arguably, this is the biggest challenge in the field; it would seem that there are a significant number of SENCos who either do not see the need for structural change, or are not in a position to instigate and manage the process of change. In some cases, this might be because they lack influence within their settings, perhaps because of their place in the management structure or because there is a lack of congruence in the vision for the school, between the SENCo, and other managers. It can be suggested that instead of seeing the SENCo, in a somewhat limited way, as the lead practitioner for SEND in a school, it would be better if the role could be situated within a community of practitioners committed to whole-school improvement. In such a structure, where management and leadership are vested in all, the SENCo, by offering expertise, knowledge and practical wisdom derived from the special education field, could arguably make the greatest transformative contribution to the enhancement of achievement and attainment for all learners, in a whole-school community of learners.

References

Alexander, R. (ed.) (2009) *Children, their World, their Education: Final Report and Recommendations of the Cambridge Primary Review.* London: Routledge.

Brown, J. and Doveston, M. (2014) Short sprint or an endurance test: the perceived impact of the National Award for Special Educational Needs Coordination. *Teacher Development,* 18(4): 495–510.

DCSF (2009a) *The Independent Review of the Primary Curriculum [The Rose Review]*. London: DCSF.

DCSF (2009b) *Lamb Inquiry: Special Educational Needs and Parental Confidence*. Nottingham: DCSF Publications.

DCSF (2010) *The National Curriculum 2010*. London: DCSF.

DfE (2014a) *Children and Families Act*. London: TSO.

DfE (2014b) *The National Curriculum in England*. London: TSO.

DfE (2016) *Statistical First Release 20/2016 Schools, Pupils and Their Characteristics*. Retrieved 27 October 2016 from: https://www.gov.uk/government/uploads/system/uploads/attachment_data/file/552342/SFR20_2016_Main_Text.pdf.

DfEE/QCA (1999) *National Curriculum: Statutory Inclusion Statement*. London: DfES.

DfE/DoH (2015) *Special Educational Needs and Disability Code of Practice: 0 to 25 Years*. London: TSO.

DfES (1994) *Code of Practice on the Identification and Assessment of Special Educational Needs*. Nottingham: DfE.

DfES (2001) *Special Educational Needs: Code of Practice*. Nottingham: DfES Publications.

Griffiths, D. and Dubsky, R. (2012) Evaluating the impact of the new National Award for SENCos: Transforming landscapes or gardening in a gale? *British Journal of Special Education*, 39(4): 164–172.

Kearns, H. (2005) Exploring the experiential learning of special educational needs coordinators. *Journal of In-Service Education*, 31(1): 131–150.

MacBeath, J. (2009) A focus on learning, in: J. MacBeath and N. Dempster (eds) *Connecting Leadership and Learning: Principles for Practice*. London: Routledge.

National College for Teaching and Leadership [NCTL] (2014) *National Award for SEN Co-ordination: Learning Outcomes*. London: DfE.

Pearson, S., Mitchell, R. and Rapti, M. (2015) 'I will be "fighting" even more for pupils with SEN': SENCOs' role predictions in the changing English policy context. *Journal of Research in Special Educational Needs [JORSEN]*, 15(1): 48–56.

Rosen-Webb, S. (2011) Nobody tells you how to be a SENCo. *British Journal of Special Education*, 38(4): 159–168.

Teacher Training Agency [TTA] (1998) *National Standards for Special Educational Needs Coordinators*. London: HMSO.

1 A national perspective on the training of SENCos

Lorraine Petersen

Introduction

Up until the early 1990s the teaching of pupils with special educational needs (SEN) had been isolated from mainstream schooling with the majority of children identified as having SEN being withdrawn from their classrooms by an SEN teacher. They would be taught basic, specific skills which had little connection to the curriculum that was being taught to the other children in their classroom and when returned to work alongside their peers were often given 'holding' work rather than being included in the wider classroom activities.

The 1993 Education Act promoted the requirement for all children to have the opportunity to access their education in a mainstream school and this was supported, in 1994, by the introduction of the *Code of Practice on the Identification and Assessment of Special Educational Needs*. This document gave schools guidance on how to make provision for children with SEN.

It was acknowledged that if a school was to be able to manage the process of integration in an effective way, there needed to be a managerial post in every school that would lead and support teachers in this process. The special educational needs coordinator (SENCo) was to be the key person given the responsibility for implementing the *Code of Practice*.

There was no recognition at this time that the role and responsibility of this post would be diverse and demanding and would need a teacher with a high level of training to ensure they had the skills, experience and knowledge to support the children effectively.

For many schools the appointment of the SENCo was made internally, a willing volunteer being sought from existing staff members. Many had full-time teaching commitments and were given very little time, resources or training to undertake the role effectively. Local education authorities would offer SENCo training sessions but these were often about raising awareness of local issues rather than professional development opportunities to meet the very individual needs in schools.

By the mid-1990s the Inclusion agenda was well embedded in our schools, with the emphasis on the achievement of all children including those identified with special educational needs. *The SENCO Guide* (DfEE, 1997) offered best practice examples on how the role was carried out in schools, how individual education plans (IEPs) were being used and how schools were developing and embedding their SEN policies.

The SENCo's role was becoming onerous and in many instances untenable with far too much time being spent on excessive paperwork, (completion of IEPs) and taking sole responsibility for all aspects of SEN provision in a school.

The Government's Action Programme: Meeting Special Education Needs (DfEE, 1998) set out a broad agenda to ensure that the needs of all pupils with SEN were met through greater access to the curriculum and specific training for teachers.

The programme aimed to achieve successful Inclusion of pupils with SEN by securing better training for teachers working with SEN pupils, and deploying teachers with specialist knowledge of SEN more effectively across schools, units and services, in order to:

- raise expectations for pupils with SEN;
- promote their greater Inclusion within mainstream schooling;
- encourage effective partnerships between special and mainstream schools in support of Inclusion;
- develop the role of special schools to meet the continuing needs of some pupils with severe and/or complex difficulties; and
- promote stronger consortia arrangements in SEN provision.

The reality was that individual schools were trying to embed inclusive practice with very little, training, support or advice.

The publication of the *National Standards for Special Educational Needs Coordinators* (TTA, 1998) offered structure and reinforced the key roles and responsibilities that this important post would have in the implementation of the action programme within schools.

These national standards set out:

- the main responsibilities of the SENCo role;
- the particular knowledge, understanding, skills, attributes and expertise needed by those coordinating SEN provision; and
- a definition of the context in which the coordination of SEN provision within a school is likely to be successful.

Their main aim was to:

- set out clear expectations for teachers at key points in the profession;
- help teachers to plan and monitor their development, training and performance effectively and to set clear, relevant targets for improving their effectiveness;
- ensure that the focus at every point was on improving the achievement of pupils and the quality of their education;
- provide a basis for the professional recognition of teachers' expertise and achievements;
- help providers of professional development to plan and provide high quality, relevant training.

Using the National Standards for Special Educational Needs Coordinators (TTA, 1998) offered help to professionals such as head teachers and teachers on how to make more informed decisions about SEN in educational settings.

In theory these standards should have offered a real opportunity for SENCos and aspiring SENCos to develop, through training, their skills, knowledge and understanding, enabling them to be more effective in their role. A lack of time, budget and training opportunities meant that many SENCos meandered along with very little high quality professional development to support them in this ever-demanding role.

The *National Special Educational Needs Specialist Standards* (TTA, 1999) quickly followed the SENCo standards and offered an audit tool to help teachers and headteachers to identify specific training and development needs in relation to the effective teaching of pupils with severe and/or complex SEN.

Both the *National Standards for Special Educational Needs Coordinators* (TTA 1998) and The *National Special Educational Needs Specialist Standards* (TTA 1999) have never been revised or superseded and much of their content is still applicable to the role of the SENCo today.

In 1998 the Government, in their Action Programme (DfEE, 1998), stated that they are

> committed to ensuring that all teachers have the training and support they need to do their job well and are confident to deal with a wide range of special educational needs.

By the end of the twentieth century there was still very little evidence that this training and support were available to SENCos let alone all teachers.

Twenty-first-century schools

The role of the SENCo has never been easy to define and has always been open to interpretation. It is a role that has had to move with the times and has evolved in schools, based on the needs of the individuals within each establishment.

The dawn of the new century brought with it a glimmer of hope in the form of the revised *Special Educational Needs Code of Practice* (DfES, 2001). This was to become the SENCo's most thumbed document. Although not legislative, only guidance, a school should 'have due regard' to it for all their students with SEN.

Section 6.2 of the 2001 Code of Practice states:

> Provision for students with special educational needs is a matter for the school as a whole. In addition to the governing body, the school's headteacher, SENCo and learning support teams and all other members of staff have important operational responsibilities.

> All teachers are teachers of pupils with special educational needs. Teaching such students is therefore, a whole school responsibility, requiring whole-school response. In practice the way in which this responsibility is exercised by individual staff is a matter for schools.

It is only now that we begin to finally see the role of the SENCo acknowledged as being one that should be closely involved in the strategic development of the SEN policy and provision, taking responsibility for the day-to-day operation of the school's SEN policy and for the coordination of the provision for students with SEN, particularly through School Action and School Action Plus.

Definitions of their role at each phase of education can be found in Sections 4.14, 5.30 and 6.32 of the *SEN Code of Practice* (DFES, 2001) where it clearly states that the SENCo should be taking the lead in providing professional guidance to colleagues to ensure high quality teaching for all children but especially for those with SEN. It was also assumed, but not explicit, that the SENCo would be a qualified teacher, although with the increasing changes that were taking place within the school workforce it has to be acknowledged that some schools did not always appoint qualified teachers to this role.

The *SEN Code of Practice* (DFES, 2001) is also very clear in Sections 5.33 to 5.36 and 6.36 to 6.40 that the SENCo needed significant non-contact time to carry out their duties.

This was the ideal opportunity for schools to begin to raise the status of this key role within their school and offer training, pay and conditions that would support the SENCo in managing high quality educational opportunity for all children identified as having a special educational need. Unfortunately, this happened in a very piecemeal fashion. Some schools took the guidance from the Code of Practice and implemented changes in their organisational practices with the SENCo being offered training, time and resources to manage the role effectively. Others saw it as only guidance and made very few changes at all. The financial constraints on schools meant that budgets did not take into account the need for a non-teaching SENCo to be able to meet the needs of the increasing number of vulnerable children within mainstream settings.

Changes to the school workforce including the appointment of a large number of teaching assistants had a significant impact on the role and responsibilities of the SENCo as it introduced a large number of non-teaching staff into classrooms to support children, many of these supporting pupils with SEN. The SENCos became the line manager of this ever increasing group and found themselves organising timetables, planning work, holding meetings and often trying to broker collaboration between class teachers and support staff.

The *Every Child Matters* (HMSO, 2003) Green Paper and subsequent *Every Child Matters; Change for Children* (DfES, 2004a) introduced a much wider remit for schools in ensuring that opportunities and outcomes for all children were co-ordinated through a multi-professional approach with collaboration, information sharing and joined up service provision. For the SENCo this meant not only additional responsibilities but an increased workload often leaving them frustrated due to lack of co-operation from para-professionals from other agencies.

Removing Barriers to Achievement: The Government's Strategy for SEN (DfES, 2004b) outlined the current and future policies for SEN provision in England. This strategy clearly recognised that SENCos should be a member of school leadership teams.

> SENCOs play a pivotal role, co-ordinating provision across the school and linking class and subject teachers with SEN specialists to improve the quality of teaching and learning. We want schools to see the SENCO as a key member

of the senior leadership team, able to influence the development of policies for whole school improvement.

(3.14)

Despite the plethora of references to the roles and responsibilities of a SENCo being key to the raising of standards through supporting teachers in providing high quality teaching and learning experiences for their children, it was no surprise that when the *House of Commons Education and Skills Select Committee Report on SEN* (HMSO, 2006a) was published, it offered a very adverse commentary on the role of the SENCo. This report, based on an overwhelming amount of written and oral evidence as well as research, highlighted that there was a very large gap between policy and practice in terms of the ever-increasing role of the SENCo. The Select Committee noted that the DfES had not ensured

> . . . that SENCOs are always given the appropriate training – or the appropriate authority – to be able to undertake these significant responsibilities. Despite the recommendation in the Code of Practice that SENCOs should be part of the Senior Management this is not often the case. . .

(para 319)

The report recognised that many schools had in fact appointed teaching assistants to the role of SENCo, thus, not only were they not part of the leadership team, but in many cases they were carrying out administrative and peripheral duties and not the strategic role that had been envisaged.

It was also at this time that Planning, Preparation and Assessment time (PPA) was introduced and schools found themselves having to manage the need for all teaching staff to have their agreed time outside the classroom.

The Introduction of Teaching and Learning Responsibilities (TLR) to replace responsibility points also gave rise to a great deal of anecdotal evidence that SENCos had lost out both in terms of the time they had to carry out their SENCo duties, and also on status and pay due to loss of responsibility points without acknowledgement through the introduction of TLR.

There was a very clear view taken by the House of Commons Education and Skills Select Committee in their Report on SEN (HMSO, 2006a) in regard to the future role of the SENCo and what the government should do to address the disparity across England.

> Special Educational Needs Co-ordinators (SENCos) should in all cases be qualified teachers and in a senior management position in the school as recommended in the SEN Code of Practice. Firmer guidelines are required rather than Government asking schools to 'have regard' to the SEN Code of Practice. The role and position of a SENCo must reflect the central priority that SEN should hold within schools.

(Recommendation 84)

> Special Educational Needs Co-ordinators (SENCos) should be given ongoing training to enable them to keep their knowledge up to date as well as sufficient non-teaching time to reflect the number of children with SEN in their school. These baseline standards for SENCos to be given training both on and off the

job should apply to all schools, including academy and trust schools. Schools should set out in their SEN policy action to ensure that all SENCOs are adequately monitored and supported in their vital roles.

(Recommendation 85)

For the first time there was a very clear, prescriptive understanding of what a SENCo in a twenty-first-century school should be:

- They should in all cases be qualified teachers.
- They should be members of the senior leadership team.
- Stronger guidance from the government about the SEN Code of Practice to ensure that schools paid more than 'due regard' to its contents.
- The SENCo role should reflect the central priority that SEN should have within every school.
- SENCos should be given on-going training to enable them to keep their knowledge up to date.
- SENCos should have sufficient non-teaching time to reflect the number of children with SEN in school.
- Academy and Trust schools should embed the same standards to SENCos in their schools.
- Schools should set out in their SEN policy, action to ensure that all SENCOs are adequately monitored and supported in their vital role.

The government's response on this issue (HMSO, 2006b) was welcomed by many within the profession, since at last there was a very clear commitment to enhancing the role of the SENCo. It stated:

Special Educational Needs Co-ordinators (SENCos) play a key role in building schools' capacity and skills in meeting children's SEN because of their crucial role in advising other members of staff on SEN matters and linking with parents. Each school is required, by regulations, to publish the name of the person with the role of co-ordinating the provision of education for children with SEN. In making the appointment, we would expect the head and governing body to take into account:

- The skills and experience required in connection with the role, and extent to which the candidate has demonstrated these or could acquire them
- The range and complexity of SEN represented within the school; and
- Practical issues such as authority(credibility)in relation to members of the teaching staff, parents and external parties.

The response continued by emphasising three very specific aspects.

- We have reflected carefully on the Select Committee's comments on SENCos. We share their view as to their importance and believe that the person taking on the lead responsibility should be a teacher and a member of the senior leadership team in a school (para 21).
- We will be introducing an amendment to the Education and Inspections Bill to require governing bodies to make such an appointment for the purpose of co-ordinating the provision of education for children with SEN and to give the

Secretary of State a power to make regulations relating to the role, responsibilities, experience and training required (para 21).

- We have commissioned TDA to develop, in conjunction with interested parties, an accreditation system for SENCos which will have at its heart an agreed training curriculum for co-ordinating staff covering both generic aspects such as implementing an SEN policy and securing help for pupils from external agencies, and knowledge of key areas such as autistic spectrum disorders. We will require all SENCOs to undertake nationally accredited training (para 22).

In September 2008 the SENCo regulations came into force. All schools (community, foundation, voluntary schools and maintained nursery schools, in England had to comply with:

- Regulation 3 requiring the SENCo to be either a qualified teacher, the Head Teacher or appointed acting head teacher or a person carrying out the role for at least six months prior to the regulations coming into force, who has shown reasonable prospect for gaining Qualified Teacher Status (QTS) within a period of two years from the date the regulations come into force.
- Regulation 4 requiring SENCos to be employed, i.e. not volunteers, and employed as teachers, not members of support staff.
- Regulation 5 requiring the governing body to define the role of the SENCo in relation to the leadership and management of the school.
- Regulation 6 requiring the governing body to monitor the actions of the SENCo in relation to key areas of the role.

The draft regulations had also required SENCos to be a member of the Leadership Team but after consultation this was amended to recommend that, where the SENCo was not a member of the team, a member should be designated as champion of SEN and disability issues within the school.

Finally, to strengthen the role of the SENCo, the DCSF required all newly appointed SENCos (September 2008) to undertake nationally accredited training and commissioned the TDA to manage this process. The first cohort of these newly appointed SENCos began their training in September 2009; to be followed by further cohorts of new SENCos as this training programme continues. The advent of the National Award at the beginning of the second decade of the twenty-first century means that we finally have high quality, professional development opportunities for the next generation of SENCos, and for their successors.

The National Award for SEN Coordination was a long time coming but was nevertheless very welcome and represents the first step in the raised status that SENCos deserve. The basic principles of the twenty-first-century SENCo as underpinned by the National Award are:

- Senior leadership
- Strategic
- Relevant skills, knowledge, understanding and attributes
- Raising standards
- School improvement
- Lead teaching and learning.

Not a great deal different from those outlined in the SEN Code of Practice (DfES, 2001), but they are now statutory and schools and governing bodies have to ensure that the SENCo in their school is meeting these exacting standards while providing them with the training, time and resources to carry out their role effectively.

It must be acknowledged that supporting children and young people with special educational needs has never been more important and as many of these learners are in our mainstream schools, the SENCo's role has become more challenging than ever. The number of new initiatives, guidance documents and legislation plus intervention programmes and training materials that were bombarding our schools up to 2010 is testament to the increased impetus of government support for vulnerable children.

Removing Barriers to Achievement (DfES, 2004b) highlighted that all teachers were responsible for teaching children and young people with special educational needs and therefore there needed to be high quality professional development available to ensure that all staff had the necessary knowledge, skills and understanding to meet the individual needs of learners.

In 2008 the National Strategies launched the first phase of the *Inclusion Development Programme* (DCSF, 2008), a professional development programme for all those working in *schools*.

The aim of the *Inclusion Development Programme* was to support schools and Early Years settings through the use of web-based materials, including teaching and learning resources, training materials, guidance on effective classroom strategies, models of good practice for multi-disciplinary teams, and information about sources of more specialist advice.

Covering the topics of Dyslexia, Speech, Language and Communication, the programme was intended to be disseminated through local authorities for individual schools to share with their staff. In many instances, the SENCo became the key person in a school to disseminate this information, attempting to engage all teaching and non-teaching staff in the professional development activities within the programme.

This first programme was followed in 2008 with Supporting the Needs of Children on the Autism Spectrum and in 2010 with Supporting Pupils with Behavioural, Social and Emotional Difficulties. The practicalities of trying to ensure all staff engage in all three programmes have been an immense challenge for many SENCos and just one of the many new responsibilities they have had to take on.

In March 2008 Brian Lamb was asked by the Secretary of State to look at how parental confidence in the special educational needs systems could be improved. The Lamb Inquiry was set up and emerging issues during the course of the inquiry expanded the remit by looking at SEN and disability information, the quality and clarity of Statements, inspection and accountability, and what impact changes in the Tribunal system were having on parental confidence.

The final report, *The Lamb Inquiry: Special Educational Needs and Parental Confidence* (DCSF, 2009a) made 51 recommendations. All of these were agreed by the Secretary of State and reinforced in the implementation plan published by the DSCF, *Improving Confidence in the Special Educational Needs System* (DCSF, 2010).

Many of the 51 recommendations have had an impact on schools and have added a further range of challenges for the SENCo as schools responded and began to implement them. The following examples reflect just six of these.

- The principles of Achievement for All were to be embedded within school leadership, continuing professional development and initial teacher training to ensure that as wide a range of children, parents and schools as possible benefitted from the effective practices developed. SENCos would need to be aware of the good practice examples from the 10 local authority pilot projects and begin to embed them within their school practice.
- SENCos would be able to access specialist support and advice from the additional 4000 specialist dyslexia teachers being trained to support schools.
- New specialist SEN and disability resources were to be introduced to support Initial Teacher Training. This would result in student and newly qualified teachers requiring additional support and guidance during their early teaching careers. The SENCo was to guide, direct and support new teachers in their schools.
- SENCos would be required to play a crucial role in leading the teaching and learning of pupils with SEN, and advising other staff within the school on effective approaches and interventions.
- New guidance would be issued on the effective deployment of teaching assistants. As the majority of SENCos line-managed TAs, this would directly impact on the work and support that they gave.
- New governor training was to give a high profile to governors' responsibility for SEN and disability, with a particular focus on progress and outcomes. It was seen as vital that SENCos were to be involved in the training of their governing body and develop a strong relationship with the governor/s responsible for SEN.

The White Paper: *Your Child, Your Schools, Our Future: Building a Twenty-first Century Schools System* (DCSF, 2009b) outlined the key challenges that faced us.

- Families becoming more diverse with some families under more pressure, so there was a need to ensure our response was tailored to their needs.
- The need to keep the most vulnerable children and young people safe, especially in the face of greater-than-ever pressure on children's social care, and for them to develop the resilience and knowledge necessary to avoid risky behaviours.
- Increasing demand for higher skills with very few jobs available for people with low or no skills; and
- Increasing numbers of children and young people using our services while resources were tighter.

These challenges demanded an increase in the voice of both parents and pupils, a stronger link between all the professionals working with families, schools ensuring good behaviour, strong discipline and safety, and an effective personalisation of teaching that will meet the needs of all pupils.

There was a need for increased collaboration between schools, taking expertise, experience and models of good practice and sharing these with local schools to ensure the best outcomes for all children. Special schools were to become centres of excellence offering support, guidance and specialist training to mainstream schools.

There was increased pressure to reduce the number of young people who are Not in Education, Employment or Training (NEETS) by ensuring that those individuals who are disaffected and/or at risk of exclusion are able to access an education that is appropriate and accessible to meet their individual needs.

It was felt that SENCos would have to play a pivotal role in all of these challenges, by engaging with parents, pupils, external agencies, colleagues from other schools and both Early Years and Further Education practitioners to ensure smooth transition through the educational journey of an individual.

As a result of the election in 2010, the beginning of the second decade of the twenty-first century found the country with a new Coalition government with an education agenda that many feared would lessen the prominence of special educational needs in policy making.

However, Ofsted, in their report, *A Statement Is not enough* (2010) reported that there was an over-identification of children and young people with special educational needs. The report suggested that this over-identification was actually due to poor teaching and with better teachers many of these pupils would no longer be on SEN lists. This was to become a key catalyst for change as new policy emerged.

The newly appointed Minister of State for Children and Families, Sarah Teather, launched the Green Paper *Support and Aspiration: A New Approach to Special Educational Needs and Disability* (DfE, 2011, 2012). This Green Paper incorporated many of the recommendations from the Lamb Inquiry Report including putting children, young people and their families at the heart of the system; it also included key recommendations designed to ensure that every teacher took responsibility for the teaching and learning of all pupils, including those with SEN. A number of local authorities became Pathfinders, testing out the proposals from the Green Paper, prior to the finalisation of the policy direction.

Following the consultation period, the DfE published their response, introducing it in the Queen's Speech on 9 May 2012 as part of the Children and Families Bill which was going to result in the biggest reform of SEN for 30 years. At this stage, the key measures were:

- A single assessment process (0–25) which was to be more streamlined, and better involve children, young people and families and was to be completed quickly
- An Education, Health and Care Plan (replacing the Statement) to bring services together and be focussed on improving outcomes
- An offer of a personal budget for families with an Education, Health and Care Plan
- A requirement for local authorities and health services to jointly plan and commission services that children, young people and their families need
- A requirement on local authorities to publish a local offer indicating the support available to those with special educational needs and disabilities and their families
- The introduction of mediation opportunities for disputes and a trial giving children the right to appeal if they are unhappy with their support.

What followed instead was two years of more consultation, the Pathfinder testing of the proposals and a huge hiatus within the SEN system for many children, young people and their families as they waited for the reforms to be implemented.

The Children and Families Act received Royal Assent in May 2014; Part 3 of the Act related to special educational needs and disabilities. Due to the number of major reforms that the Act outlined, the DfE decided that there would be transitional arrangements for implementation, beginning in September 2014, becoming finally embedded by March 2018.

One of the key elements of the reform was the publication of a new *SEND Code of Practice: 0 to 25 years* (Dfe/DoH, 2014) which was later revised and republished in January 2015. The whole of Chapter 6 is dedicated to the role and responsibilities of schools, with paragraphs 6.84–6.94 outlining the role of the SENCo. Although very little had changed from the 2001 Code of Practice, there was far more emphasis on the strategic role that the SENCo now needed to undertake. The key message of every teacher being responsible and accountable for all pupils meant that the SENCo should be more engaged in advice, support and management of SEN within a school, rather than actually being involved in working with the pupils.

The key responsibilities of the SENCo were clearly set out:

- overseeing the day-to-day operation of the school's SEN policy
- coordinating provision for children with SEN
- liaising with the relevant Designated Teacher where a looked-after pupil has SEN
- advising on the graduated approach to providing SEN support
- advising on the deployment of the school's delegated budget and other resources to meet pupils' needs effectively
- liaising with parents of pupils with SEN
- liaising with early years providers, other schools, educational psychologists, health and social care professionals, and independent or voluntary bodies
- being a key point of contact with external agencies, especially the local authority and its support services
- liaising with potential next providers of education to ensure a pupil and their parents are informed about options and a smooth transition is planned
- working with the headteacher and school governors to ensure that the school meets its responsibilities under the Equality Act (HMSO, 2010) with regard to reasonable adjustments and access arrangements
- ensuring that the school keeps the records of all pupils with SEN up to date.

There was also reference (for the first time) that the SENCo would be more effective if they were part of the school leadership team. These reforms have added a great deal of additional challenge to the role of SENCo but they have also raised the profile of the post within schools.

The major changes that this reform brought about will continue to be implemented until March 2018. The includes the transfer of Statements to Education, Health and Care Plans, ensuring that all those pupils identified as SEN Support are receiving their full entitlement of additional and/or different provision through the Graduated Approach, and bringing health, social care and education together to support children, young people and their families.

At the same time as SEN reforms are being implemented, the education sector has seen a massive growth in academy and free schools and a consequence of this is the decline in local authority support and services. The introduction of a new National Curriculum and extensive assessment reform has added to the challenges that schools face.

Looking ahead, the proposed changes to the distribution of funding to schools will have a major impact on school budgets and funding for SEN pupils. It is really important that SENCos have a full understanding of the delegated school budget and the specific amounts available to support children and young people with special educational needs. The proposed introduction of a national funding formula will ensure that every pupil across the country is in receipt of the same amount of funding but it is likely that SEN funding will still be allocated via a local authority formula.

It is widely acknowledged that this funding is not ring-fenced and can be used for other purposes. The SENCo must take responsibility for this funding and work with the leadership team and governing body to ensure that the most vulnerable children in their school receive the resources not only allocated to them but also additional provision if necessary.

The SENCo must also ensure that children and young people with an Education, Health and Care Plan receive the full provision highlighted within that plan. There is a legal responsibility to ensure that the individual has adequate support to meet the needs of the plan, providing another challenge for the SENCo if the funding arrangements that supports this are not a transparent part of the school budget.

In the last six years we have seen a decrease in the number of pupils identified as SEN, from 21% in 2010 to 14.4% in 2016 (DfE, 2016). This reduction is partly due to the changes in categorisation that have removed School Action and School Action Plus but it would also seem that SENCos and schools have got much better at identifying SEN as opposed to underachievement.

In contrast, what we have seen is a significant increase in children and young people with very complex needs including those with mental health problems, thus requiring the SENCo to offer support and advice to staff in areas that once would have been seen as a 'health' issue. This is a major concern for SENCos and schools as extensive training is required to support teachers in both identifying and supporting individual needs of this type.

Due to the diversity of need identified in mainstream schools coupled with the loss of local authority specialist services, it is clear that SENCos need to be building a resilient and extended workforce that meets the needs of all pupils. The days when teachers and teaching assistants were able to meet the needs of all pupils through the support that could be offered from within the setting have gone, with schools now having a social care and health responsibility in addition to their educational responsibilities, if they are to meet those needs.

Further changes to come include further growth in the number of academy and free schools, the possible introduction of more selective schools, and an increased pressure for all pupils to achieve at national standards, adding further pressures to those already experienced by children and young people with SEN; all of this will have a significant impact on the role of the SENCo in the future.

It is clear that well-trained, flexible and experienced leaders will be needed, who are able to challenge, support and collaborate to ensure that the teaching and learning in every school are meeting the needs of all children. Twenty-first-century SENCos need to have the time, status and support to enable them to be able to react and meet the demanding and challenging responsibilities that are now central to the role. It will no longer be sufficient to have a willing volunteer or a caring friend to carry out this extensive and diverse role. The SENCo has to be at the centre of change, if schools want to raise standards and improve their overall performance in meeting the needs of all pupils.

References

DCSF (2008) *Inclusion Development Programme.* Nottingham: DCSF Publications.

DCSF (2009a) *The Lamb Inquiry: Special Educational Needs and Parental Confidence.* London: DCSF Publications.

DCSF (2009b) *Your Child, Your Schools, Our Future: Building a Twenty-first Century Schools System.* London: DCSF Publications.

DCSF (2010) *Improving Parental Confidence in the Special Educational Needs System: An Implementation Plan.* London: DCSF Publications.

DfE (1994) *Code of Practice on the Identification and Assessment of Pupils with Special Educational Needs.* Nottingham: DfE.

DfE (2011) *Support and Aspiration: A New Approach to Special Educational Needs and Disability.* London: DfE.

DfE (2012) *Support and Aspiration: A New Approach to Special Educational Needs and Disability – Progress and Next Steps.* London: DfE.

DfE (2014) *Children and Families Act.* London: TSO.

DfE (2016) *Statistical First Release 29/2016 Special Educational Needs in England.* Retrieved July 2016 from: https://www.gov.uk/government/uploads/system/uploads/attachment_data/file/539158/SFR29_2016_Main_T.pdf.

DfE/DoH (2015) *Special Educational Needs and Disability Code of Practice: 0 to 25 Years.* London: DfE and DoH.

DfEE (1997) *The SENCO Guide.* London: DfEE.

DfEE (1998) *The Government's Action Programme: Meeting Special Educational Needs.* London: DfEE.

DfES (2001) *Special Educational Needs Code of Practice.* London DfES Publications.

DfES (2004a) *Every Child Matters: Changes for Children.* London: DfES Publications.

DfES (2004b) *Removing Barriers to Achievement: The Government's Strategy for SEN.* London: DfES Publications.

HMSO (1993) *The Education Act.* London: TSO.

HMSO (2003) *Every Child Matters, Green Paper.* Norwich: TSO.

HMSO (2006a) *House of Commons Education and Skills Select Committee Report on Special Educational Needs.* London: TSO.

HMSO (2006b) *Government Response to the Select Committee Report on Special Educational Needs.* London: TSO.

HMSO (2010) *Equality Act.* London: TSO.

Ofsted (2010) *The Special Educational Needs and Disability Review: A Statement Is not enough.* London: Ofsted.

TTA (1998) *National Standards for Special Educational Needs Co-ordinators.* London: TTA.

TTA (1999) *National Special Educational Needs Specialist Standards.* London: TTA.

Accountability and transparency – SENCos' perceptions

Klaus Wedell

Introduction

The editors have asked me to contribute a chapter on issues of accountability and transparency that SENCos have discussed on the SENCo Forum.[1] This is a mutual support group based on an electronic mailing list. The ideas for a Forum originally started in 1994, when the first SEN Code of Practice (DfE, 1994) was introduced. It was evident that those teachers who took on the role of SENCo would need support. The aim of the Forum was to enable SENCos to share problems and solutions in their work, so that they would not each have to 're-invent the wheel' in the course of their day-to-day work. Many SENCos were appointed to these roles with little relevant background experience or expertise. Inevitably they were likely to be working in a lone position, in contrast to other teachers who might be part of a 'year' or subject group of teachers. The mailing list was originally set up by the then National Council for Educational Technology (NCET) as an evaluated project funded by the Department for Education. The technical services for it are provided by the current Department for Education (http://lists.education.gov.uk/mailman/listinfo/SENCo-forum).

Research on the Forum (NCET, 1997; Lewis and Ogilvie, 2002) has shown that the membership is representative of SENCos in general, apart from fact that they are willing to operate the mailing list system. The Forum membership rapidly accumulated to over 1000, and currently stands at slightly over 2000 in April 2016 (Waller, pers. comm., 2016). An average of 300 messages a month are sent or responded to, although members differ in the number of messages they contribute. The Forum exists within an ethos of mutual support which itself reflects accountability for members' professional development. It is also founded on transparency in so far as members are willing to acknowledge their need for help. When a colleague and I first proposed the Forum in 1994, some claimed that SENCos would never admit to this need, but the success of the Forum over the years has shown this charge to be unfounded. The value of the Forum was acknowledged in the second Code (DfES, 2001) which enjoined head teachers to enable SENCos to have access to it (5.36 and 6.39). SENCos are now working within the provisions of the third Code, which came into force in September 2014 following the Children and Families Act of that year. The Third Code follows the main principles of the previous ones, but made some further significant proposals – for example, the extension of provision to age 25. I will deal with relevant details in the rest of this chapter. It is reassuring that the Code is explicit in emphasising the importance of the SENCo's role.

Accountability and transparency are considered in four sections: SENCos in their schools; identifying children and young people's special educational needs; assessment; and making provision. I will not be dealing with issues about record keeping and other administrative bureaucratic duties – although these feature extensively in the Forum messages. This would require a further chapter, but I should mention that SENCos often report that their administrative duties frequently have to be fitted in after the school day, and at weekends. The SENCos in the Forum work mainly in the primary and secondary education phases and this is reflected in the chapter's coverage. Finally – one last explanation – in order to avoid reference to the lengthy phrase 'children and young people' I will, as relevant, be referring to them as 'pupils' regardless of their age.

SENCos in their schools

The editors target this book at considering how the role of SENCos might be transformed. In this chapter, I have focussed on discussions in the SENCo Forum that have indicated how SENCos aim their accountability at extending the margins of their schools' capacity to be more inclusive and to offer their pupils greater entitlement to a broad and balanced curriculum. SENCos, in common with many educators, are aware that provision for pupils with special educational needs is determined by the current state of the education system as a whole (Norwich, 2014). The system is widely regarded as lacking the flexibility to respond to the individual learning needs of pupils or preparing them for the twenty-first century (Alexander, 2009; Institute of Directors, 2016; Wedell, 2008). The recent and present (in 2016) modifications in the governance of schools such as the development of 'academies' and 'free' schools are claimed to have increased schools' 'autonomy', but the current government's over-riding 'standards' agenda and the new curriculum specifications seem, in general, to be constraining schools' scope for flexibility. The Education White Paper (DfE, 2016) now proposes that all schools should become DfE-funded academies grouped into Multi-Academy Trusts (MATs) with executive head teachers, under the overall control of centrally appointed Regional Schools Commissioners, thus drastically reducing local authorities' role in the provision of education. A House of Commons Library Briefing Paper (House of Commons Library, 2016) has reported 'the proposals have proved highly controversial' – and so it remains to be seen whether or how far they will be implemented.

The main aim of most SENCos' work has been to explore ways of extending their schools' capacity for flexibility by internal systemic 'patching' up, as a means of realising their accountability to individual pupils and their families. The systems' parameters have been set by the three successive SEN Codes of Practice. The establishment and formulation of the first Code occurred as the result of intensive lobbying to ensure that mainstream schools attended to the diverse needs of their pupils. Forum members made a joint response to the consultation on the second Code and this demonstrated that a professional group such as the Forum can offer a sounding board in the development of policy changes. In the consultation on the proposals for the third Code, members responded individually and their critiques were the subject of much discussion on the Forum.

The statutory compliance demands in the first section of the third Code (DfE/ DoH, 2015), start with an explanation about how the words 'must' and 'should' are to be distinguished. The section states:

> The listed bodies (to whom the Code applies) '*must*' [my emphasis] be able to demonstrate . . . . that they are fulfilling their statutory duty to have regard to the Code.
>
> (page 12)

The 'listed bodies' of course include schools. The section goes on to define the use of the word 'should':

> where the text uses the word '*should*' [my emphasis] . . . . those who must have regard to it will be expected to explain any departure from it.
>
> (page 12)

The interpretation of this distinction is inevitably taking some time – particularly in relation to SENCos' 'patching up' endeavours. SENCos' messages on the Forum have already shown up points where the Code's aspirations fall short of matching real life, and thus present SENCos with dilemmas about compliance.

With regard to the formulation of the intended roles for SENCos, the governing bodies of schools are required to note that:

> The SENCo has an important role to play with the head teacher and governing body in determining the strategic development of the special needs policy and provision in the school. They will be most effective in that role if they are part of the leadership team.
>
> (para 6.87)

Some SENCos have in fact been accorded such a status, and they have been able to extend their schools' capability in outstanding ways – even in the judgement of the inspectors of the Office for Standards in Education (Ofsted). Indeed, some Forum SENCos have demonstrated a level of entrepreneurial initiative that has raised their school's inclusive support for pupils to remarkable levels. This has been evident from the titles that some SENCos are given in their schools. The following were recently listed on the Forum: Additional Educational Needs Coordinator, Learning Support Coordinator, Inclusion Manager, Vulnerable Groups Coordinator, Director of Curriculum Support. The conferring of such titles often implies extending SENCos' responsibilities to pupils not necessarily regarded as having special educational needs, such as those receiving help for English as an additional language.

However, these status levels are definitely not the norm. For many SENCos the scope for accountability to which they aspire has been constrained to varying degrees. Often the arrangements about the status of the SENCo reflect the nature of the school's ethos in relation to its commitment to pupils with special educational needs. It has to be acknowledged that some schools would rather not be known for their success in serving such pupils. Discussions on the Forum evidenced the pressure on schools emanating from the current government's 'Standards Agenda' which focusses on 'outcomes' in terms of attainment in National Curriculum subjects at the primary and secondary phases. Consequently some

schools are wary of staffing support for pupils with special educational needs –
an example of how government policies can be mutually conflicting. The problem
particularly impinges on smaller primary schools, where the SENCo role may just
be added to staff appointed as class teachers. The third Code has acknowledged
an arrangement that has in fact existed for many years (Evans et al., 1999)
whereby some small schools collaborate to share a SENCo (DfE/DoH, 2015, 6.92):

> It may be appropriate for a number of smaller primary schools to share a
> SENCo employed to work across the individual schools, . . . Schools can con-
> sider this arrangement where it secures sufficient time away from teaching
> and sufficient administrative support to enable the SENCo to fulfil the role
> effectively for the total registered pupil population across all the schools
> involved.

These kinds of arrangements have the advantage that the collaborating schools
can appoint someone devoted to the SENCo role, and so offer a greater level of
expertise and accountability – both for school systems in general, and in serving
the needs of individual pupils and their families. In addition, they can have greater
familiarity with the relevant local authority, health, social and voluntary services.
These advantages have, however, to be balanced by the likelihood that the SENCo
may have lesser scope to influence the day-to-day special needs provision within
the individual schools. It is clear that the above differences in the deployment of
SENCos have a significant impact on the ways in which their potential can be
realised, and the discussions on the Forum clearly indicate that SENCos are frequently faced with dilemmas in the accountability decisions which face them in
their duties.

The Codes have all mentioned SENCos' wider systemic contributions to the
in-service training for teaching staff and Teaching Assistants (TAs). Forum
members frequently exchange ideas about how and when it is most strategic to
provide this training. Some are able to book a session at the beginning of each
school year to brief teachers about how support is arranged within their schools.
The purpose of such regular training is not only to remind teachers about the
prevailing support arrangements, but also to ensure that any new staff are familiar
with them. SENCos used the Forum to share ideas about the content of such training, and also about effective styles of delivery. Needless to say, there is always a
particularly great demand for in-service training when a new Code is issued, and
SENCos may also be required to update governors.

Deploying TAs can be another school-wide responsibility for SENCos. In
schools with higher numbers of pupils with special educational needs a larger
number of TAs may have been taken on to cover the funded 'hours' allocated to
pupils under the 'Statement' or now the Education, Health and Care Plan (EHCP)
procedure. The third Code stipulates that EHCPs should stress accountability
through specifying the outcomes to be achieved by allocated TA time. Forum
members have often discussed how TAs can be deployed in a way that ensures
the effectiveness of their support. The training offered by SENCos is directed at
ensuring closer collaboration between teachers and their allocated TAs (Russell,
Webster, and Blatchford, 2013). Without such planned collaboration pupils may
spend the bulk of their time at school being attended by someone who has less

understanding of their individual learning needs than their teacher. In many schools, SENCos have responsibility for appointing TAs working with these pupils, and there are frequent discussions about how best to select appropriate candidates for this work. In the current financial constraints on schools, SENCos are now starting to be held accountable for monitoring the cost of TAs' deployment.

Identification

The second Code identified the significance of the point at which the teacher or the parent of a pupil has a 'concern' that a pupil is not making expected progress. For teachers, the concern is that they feel their normal range of responses to a pupil's learning needs are not proving to be effective. This point of course differs according to the teacher's own further professional development and experience. Ofsted, in a report (Ofsted, 2010), claimed that schools were identifying too many pupils as having 'special needs' just because teachers were not 'personalising' their teaching to meet pupils' individual learning needs – failing to practise 'Quality First' teaching. This reflects a point made in the third Code (6.19):

> the class or subject teacher, working with the SENCo, should assess whether the child has SEN.

SENCos have long seen themselves as working in consultation with teachers at the point of their 'concern' in the light of their own experience and further professional training (e.g. through the National Award for SEN Coordination) and so are able to offer 'added value' to teachers' own understanding of their pupils.

SENCos feel that one of the first ways in which they offer support to teachers, is to help them to see the particular task that is proving difficult though the eyes of the pupil him or herself. A simple instance of this was raised in one of the Forum discussions. A teacher was described as puzzled about a pupil's spelling performance in a primary school. The pupil successfully spelt certain words correctly in a spelling test, but made errors in a free-writing task. The teacher wondered whether this was an indication of a spelling 'disability'. The SENCo pointed out that, in the spelling test, the pupil's attention was directed at the accurate spelling of the individual words, but in the free-writing task, her attention was mainly on the meaning of the content of what she was writing. Consequently, the apparent discrepancy in the spelling performance did not indicate a 'disability', but needed to be understood in terms of the component functions of the task. For the SENCo, the situation involved both the responsibility of representing the pupil to the teacher, but also providing the teacher with a conceptual framework of task analysis as a means of supporting the pupil's learning (Wedell, 1995). The third Code places much emphasis on teachers' capacity for 'Quality First' teaching so that they can be expected to take responsibility for the necessary understanding demanded. SENCos on the Forum pointed out that this was more practicable for primary teachers who have the opportunity to get to know individual pupils in a class. For secondary subject teachers the demand could become quite Herculean, considering the number of pupils they teach within any one week due to the prevailing ways in which most secondary schools deploy teachers.

Elkins, et al. (2016) found that teachers in the secondary phase felt less 'self-efficacy' in serving pupils with SENs.

Another discussion on the Forum concerned the experience of a SENCo who was helping a teacher with a quandary about quality teaching. A young pupil – again in a primary school – did not seem to be responding to the emphasis on synthetic phonics promoted by the current government. The teacher felt that the particular pupil seemed to be more interested in reading for meaning and would thus respond better at this stage to a 'whole word' approach. The teacher was thus caught in a dilemma between following the third Code's encouragement to 'personalise' her teaching approach, and the same Code's equally strong claim that 'quality' teaching was characterised by a synthetic phonics approach. SENCos commented that children come into school at a wide variety of stages in their development of oral communication, and of learning to read – the issue is how to synchronise teaching methods with the particular acquisition stage of the individual. There was no claim that learning sound–symbol association is irrelevant to reading acquisition, but it is a case of getting the synchronising right. The danger is that following a rigid pedagogic 'doctrine' may potentially impede a particular pupil's progress in literacy, and thus actually curtail a school's scope for being inclusive. This instance shows how the SENCo's accountability to the pupil is linked also to an accountability to the teacher, in supporting her wish to personalise her teaching – and this has implications for transparency in interpreting the compliance demands of the 'must' and 'should' formulations of the third Code.

These examples illustrate a SENCo's role in making decisions about whether a pupil's learning difficulty represents a 'special' need. But SENCos also evaluate how far the school's system might itself need 'patching' to avoid a pupil's failure to achieve. SENCos discussed pupils who were failing to produce their required homework in secondary schools. In schools which run on the basis of a sequence of timed teaching 'periods' during a day, SENCos recognised that teachers are made to feel that a set amount of the curriculum has to be delivered during such time constraints, and so often end up by rushing out their pupils' homework instructions at the end of a lesson. Those who are slower writers may then have difficulty in copying out all the homework details, with the result that they are vulnerable to misunderstanding what is required, and to producing faulty work. The discussion then explored how schools considered the role of homework within the curriculum, and the circumstances in which it might be pedagogically beneficial. The point was made that it can provide a pupil with the opportunity to explore and extend an aspect of meaningful learning about a topic if it is spread progressively over a succession of periods. In this case, the pupil is already able to understand what is required at successive points, and the task is not imposed primarily as disconnected 'busy work'. At a practical level, SENCos also pointed out that schools which make constructive use of electronic communication – as for example – through a 'virtual learning environment' can disseminate the task on the website. Teachers can disseminate homework information in a form which allows pupils to access it whenever convenient. SENCos also recognised that one cannot assume that all pupils have access to the internet at home. They referred to schools that arranged homework facilities on site, particularly for pupils who do not have quiet places to study at home.

Assessing 'special' educational needs

The previous section explored the SENCo's role in consulting with teachers when they have a concern about a pupil's progress, and suggesting how they can extend their responsiveness within their 'Quality First' teaching. This section deals with the next stage when it becomes necessary to go on to assess the degree and possible nature of a pupil's difficulty. All three Codes have recommended that this further exploration should involve asking pupils, and possibly their parents, how they perceive a learning difficulty. The third Code, in its list of SENCos' responsibilities, describes this phase as advising on the 'graduated approach' to providing SEN support, consisting of an 'Assess, Plan, Do, Review' cycle, in which the evidence from successive outcomes is used to arrive at an incremental understanding of the degree and nature of a pupil's difficulties. Not surprisingly, absolute criteria for assessing when educational needs should be regarded as 'special' have never been achieved. The third Code provides definitions that hark back to the initial 1981 Education Act:

> A child or young person has special educational needs if they have a learning difficulty or disability which calls for special educational provision . . .
>
> (p. 15)

and:

> a child has a learning difficulty if he or she has a significantly greater difficulty in learning than the majority of others of the same age . . . or has a disability which prevents or hinders him or her from making use of facilities . . . generally provided . . . .
>
> (p. 15)

In other words these definitions are inevitably relative. The third Code continues the challenge to SENCos, by stating (as a 'should' requirement) that:

> in deciding whether to make special educational provision, the teacher and SENCO should consider all the information gathered from within the school about the pupil's progress.
>
> (6.38)

The fundamental issues for teachers and for SENCos in this decision making then form the context of their respective accountability in assessing 'special' educational needs. As the above relative definitions have existed for so many years, it is not surprising that the conceptual challenge they pose has been a continuing topic of Forum discussions. The definitions reflect the way causation works out in reality. The Warnock Report in 1978 (DES, 1978) proposed that special educational needs occur in a continuum of degrees of severity, resulting from the interaction between individual children's and young people's relative levels of vulnerability and resilience as they grow up – the interaction between factors 'within' the child and factors in the child's environment. Consequently it is difficult to state any fixed threshold point where a need becomes 'special'. Some discussions on the Forum have focussed on the claims made about tests of 'within-child' functioning which offer threshold scores for establishing the presence of specific difficulties (e.g. of labelled difficulties such as 'dyslexia'). SENCos in secondary schools have been faced with this issue in applying for allowances (such as extra exam time) to be to be allocated to pupils in GCSE exams. These are determined by Joint Council for Qualifications criteria aimed at the principles underlying the Equality Act of 2010. Discussion on the Forum has shown the accountability dilemmas that SENCos face in balancing the requirement to make 'reasonable adjustments' for pupils, without affecting the integrity of the assessment. An analogous issue has arisen with recently published guidance in which the government recommends the use of a rating scale to indicate thresholds in assessing a pupil's mental health (DfE, 2014). These recommendations all illustrate the understandable administrative attempt to superimpose 'objective' criteria on the 'continuum' of special needs. SENCos' discussions indicate that in reality, relevant information has to be derived from the 'graduated approach' to the interactive processes described above, but this constitutes a continuing dilemma in SENCos' response to demands for accountability and transparency.

Making provision

In this section I will focus on three of the most common issues that have come up in Forum discussions relating to making provision. The first issue concerns SENCos' role to support the aim of including pupils with learning needs within the classroom and so avoiding stigmatising the pupil. SENCos found that some schools have a blanket policy of Inclusion, which proscribes any form of withdrawal of pupils from the classroom. However, the majority of SENCos felt that the priority is to make arrangements that ensure the particular goals of intervention (Ireson et al., 1989). The context in primary schools normally differs from that in secondary schools. In primary schools pupils are commonly arranged in lessons in a variety of small groups, and these may be formed according to the foci of pupils' learning. The groups may even be located in different areas of the school during a lesson session. In such a context, offering support for learning difficulties for an individual or a group of pupils does not signify 'withdrawal'. Similarly in good classroom practice, the teacher may decide to give intensive support to a group of pupils with special needs, while a TA ensures that the rest of the class are remaining on task for set work. In other words, the focus on specific intervention for learning needs does not necessarily convey stigmatisation. SENCos also made the important distinction between the objectives of intensive help for particular aspects of basic attainments such as literacy, and of whole group learning of subject content, intended as part of the 'broad and balanced' curriculum. In the latter, the aim of support is to enable the pupil to benefit optimally from participating effectively as a member of the class. This is the kind of situation where a TA becomes a mediator of communication between the teacher and the pupils by helping them to by-pass any disabling aspects of their particular difficulties. Needless to say, this requires skill on the part of the supporting TAs, so that the help for learning is in fact enabling – rather than interfering with the pupil's opportunity to be as autonomous as possible (Bosanquet, Radford and Webster, 2016).

SENCos have recognised that, in secondary schools, applying these kinds of strategies for implementing Inclusion and curriculum entitlement may constitute a greater challenge, depending on the flexibility with which teaching and learning are offered. Primary and secondary SENCos often collaborate in supporting pupils to make a smooth transfer between the phases. Some secondary schools even arrange for the teaching and learning in year 7 to be offered in ways that are more similar to primary schools. However, SENCos also described schools where this kind of ethos is not promoted, and where their efforts on behalf of pupils are greatly circumscribed. SENCos deploy TAs to carry out the 'enabling' strategy in subject departments, including promoting effective briefing between class teachers and the allocated TAs. However, focussed intensive support most commonly takes place in dedicated 'resource' bases. SENCos are very aware that this does constitute 'withdrawal', and so has the potential of making pupils feel stigmatised. They recently discussed which names for these bases might avoid the problem. The following names were offered – 'additional learning', 'curriculum support faculty', 'learning support', 'support for learning'. All agreed that these are better than the traditional 'SEN Department' title. SENCos felt that whatever the title, it was likely to acquire stigma over time, but this could depend on the countervailing inclusive ethos of the school.

The second issue in this section relates to how the outcomes of intervention for pupils are accredited within schools' own systems and in relation to Ofsted inspection criteria. The latter tend to determine the former in the light of the current national overriding 'standards agenda' which evaluates achievement (and progress) within the framework of National Curriculum subject attainment. SENCos were concerned that these criteria do not give a corresponding recognition to pupils' progress in other dimensions of achievement such as improvement in approaches to learning; adjustment to the behavioural demands of schooling; or emotional adjustment to personal stress. All of these dimensions may be recognised in schools' own general evaluation of pupils, but there is wide concern that the considerable individual efforts by teachers are not adequately acknowledged. Furthermore, there is plenty of evidence that progress in these areas often has to take place before it is manifested in national curriculum attainment. SENCos are particularly affected by this unbalanced evaluation of the efforts that they and their staff colleagues make, and how this redounds on their perceived accountability. SENCos have felt let down if this impacts on their appraisal by schools' senior management.

The third issue relates to how SENCos consult the pupils and their parents about the form of intervention proposed for them. This 'co-construction' process was emphasised in the first two Codes, but the third Code's strong emphasis was stimulated by the findings of a government-sponsored report (The Lamb Inquiry) (DCSF, 2009). Parental involvement has been a recurring theme in the Forum discussions. A number of SENCos went into this work because they themselves have or had children with special needs. The Lamb Report's findings confirmed the experience of SENCos that some parents are dissatisfied either because the provision offered their children is inadequate, or that they were not appropriately involved in the decisions made. Many years ago Professor Wolfendale pointed out that education professionals have to acknowledge that parents have 'equivalent expertise' through their long-term knowledge of their children – and consequently have an important contribution to make (Wolfendale, 1999). SENCos on the Forum have supported this view – and have usually built up a positive relationship from initial contact. If and when there is a problem, it usually reflects parents' unfortunate experiences in other situations, where they felt the need to be assertive. The difficulty for SENCos occurs when, because of resource limits, they are not able to offer the level of provision parents feel necessary. For SENCos who are parents themselves, this raises a serious dilemma through their own commitment to acknowledging the limits of available resources in a transparent way. Paradoxically, SENCos might be grateful to parents who subsequently direct their protest to higher levels of school management, to which SENCos themselves may not have access. By contrast, SENCos' concerns about equitable sharing of limited resources applies similarly to parents who demand provision for their child, when others have greater needs. This places SENCos in a dilemma about accountability, although they may acknowledge parents' justified concern for their own child. The issue applies at all degrees of need because of the current financial constraints on schools' 'notional budgets' for special needs, and the limited access to the Education, Health and Care Plans (EHCPs) from local authorities' 'High Needs' funding (DfE and GSR, 2016).

Conclusion

As mentioned in the first section of this chapter, this is being written at a time when the present government is proposing major structural changes in the education system. There is also uncertainty whether or how far these proposals might come to be implemented. Over the twenty-one years of the SENCo Forum the role of SENCos has been to extend schools' capacity to be inclusive and to further the curricular entitlement for children and young people with special educational needs and disabilities. The successive Codes of Practice have maintained these principles and the third Code has confirmed SENCos' role in promoting them, particularly through its requirement that SENCos should be able to offer 'added value' through their designated further professional training. So while structural changes in the school system may change, and the 'musts' and 'shoulds' of the details of the Code may alter, the basic educational charge to SENCos remains that they have to be agents of change within whatever particular educational context they find themselves. The account of SENCos' perceptions of their work in this chapter has shown the wide range of circumstances within which this 'agency' may have to be realised. It has also illustrated how SENCos are applying their developing understanding of children's and young people's special needs to improving provision even in times of financial constraints. It is also apparent that prevailing circumstances face SENCos with dilemmas in carrying out their role – and this challenge in decision making has been a feature of current educational systems in general (Levinson and Fay, 2016). The SENCo Forum has enabled SENCos to air their frustrations, and to know that there are colleagues who understand their feelings and empathise. Many have commented that this has been important in helping them to carry on, and in renewing their commitment to the pupils and the families they serve. Hopefully this chapter has offered an acknowledgement of SENCos' awareness of their accountability, and an illustration of the transparency of their attempts to fulfil it.

Note

1 The references to SENCos' discussions on the SENCo Forum are derived from the SENCo Forum archives (http://lists.education.gov.uk/pipermail/SENCo-forum) and from my regular 'Points from the SENCo Forum' column which has appeared in each issue of the *British Journal of Special Educational Needs* from 1998 onwards.

References

Alexander, R. (ed.) (2009) *The Cambridge Primary Review: Children, Their World, Their Education.* London: Routledge.

Bosanquet, P., Radford, J. and Webster, R. (2016) *The Teaching Assistant's Guide to Effective Interaction.* London: Routledge.

DCSF (2009) *The Lamb Inquiry: Special Educational Needs and Parental Confidence.* Annesley: DCSF.

DES (1978) *Report of the Committee of Enquiry into the Education of Handicapped Children and Young People [Warnock Report].* London: HMSO.

DfE (1994) *Code of Practice on the Identification and Assessment of Special Educational Needs.* London: DfE.

DfE (2014) *Mental Health and Behaviour in Schools: Departmental Advice for School Staff.* London: DfE.

DfE (2016) *Educational Excellence Everywhere.* London: HMSO.

DfE/DoH (2015) *Special Educational Needs and Disability Code of Practice: 0 to 25 Years.* London: DfE and DoH.

DfE and GSR [Department for Education and Government Social Research] (2016) *Mapping User Experience of the Education Health and Care Process: A Qualitative Study, Research Report DFE-RR523.* London: DfE and GSR.

DfES (2001) *Special Educational Needs Code of Practice.* Annesley: Department for Education and Skills.

Elkins, A., Savolainen, H. and Engelbrecht, P. (2016) An analysis of English teachers' self-efficacy in relation to SEN and disability and its implications in a SEN policy context. *European Journal of Special Needs Education*, 31(2): 236–249.

Evans, J., Lunt, I., Wedell, K. and Dyson, A. (1999) *Collaborating for Effectiveness: Empowering Schools to Be More Inclusive.* Buckingham: Open University Press.

House of Commons Library (2016) *Every School an Academy: The White Paper Proposals, Briefing Paper 07549.* London: House of Commons.

Institute of Directors (2016) *Lifelong Learning: Reforming Education in an Age of Technological and Demographic Change, IoD Policy Report.* London: Institute of Directors.

Ireson, J., Evans, P., Redmond, P. and Wedell, K. (1989) Developing curriculum for children with learning difficulties: towards a grounded model. *British Educational Research Journal*, 15(2): 141–154.

Levinson, M. and Fay, J. (eds) (2016) *Dilemmas of Educational Ethics.* Cambridge, MA: Harvard Education Press.

Lewis, A. and Ogilvie, M. (2002) *The Impact on Users of the National Grid for Learning, SENCo-forum mail list.* Birmingham, UK: Research report to BECTA/DfES.

NCET [National Council for Educational Technology] (1997) *SENCos Sharing Solutions: An Evaluation of the SENCo Electronic Communications Project.* Coventry: NCET.

Norwich, B. (2014) Changing policy and legislation and its radical effects on inclusive special education in England. *British Journal of Special Education*, 42(2): 128–151.

Ofsted (2010) *The Special Educational Needs and Disability Review,* Reference 090221. London: Ofsted.

Russell, A., Webster, R. and Blatchford, P. (2013) *Maximising the Impact of Teaching Assistants.* London: Routledge.

Wedell, K. (1995) *Putting the Code of Practice into Practice.* London: Institute of Education.

Wedell, K. (2008) Confusion about Inclusion: patching up or system change? *British Journal of Special Education*, 35(3): 127–135.

Wolfendale, S. (1999) Parents as partners. *British Journal of Special Education*, 26(3): 164–169.

3 Leading Learning: the role of the SENCo

Fiona and Graham Hallett

Introduction

The creation of the SENCo role was undoubtedly viewed by many as an imaginative and progressive move. To nominate an agent who would coordinate provision for learners with all forms of special educational need and/or disability appears to have been seen as a means for school practices, parental views and government policy to come together to ensure that children experiencing these difficulties would be given equal opportunities for educational success. The original SEN Code of Practice (DfE, 1994) and subsequent revision (DfES, 2001) define the role largely within a description of areas of responsibility; these were predominantly phrased in terms of 'maintaining' records, 'liaising' with stakeholders and 'contributing' to staff development. In the 2001 SEN Code of Practice (DfES, 2001) mention is made of the SENCo, in collaboration with the head teacher and governing body of the setting, playing a key role in the strategic development of policy and provision (section 5.30, page 50, for example), rather than in terms of strategic leadership. However, it is also suggested that where the SENCo is a member of the senior leadership team (SLT) (section 5.34 and section 6.37) or the senior management team (SMT) (section 4.17) 'many schools find (this) effective' (ibid.).

Following the changes made by the Children and Families Act 2014 (DfE, 2014), a new Code became necessary, resulting in the SEND Code of Practice: 0–25 years (DfE/DoH, 2015). This deals much more robustly with the role of the SENCo; no doubt in part due to the introduction, and continued implementation, of the National Award for SEN Coordination, now increasingly abbreviated as NASENCo. A number of points are made about the role that suggest the importance attached to it within government policy. It is clear that the responsibilities and duties of the role are seen as requiring the appointment of a post holder with the qualifications, resources and authority to carry out the role effectively and with a suitable degree of independence. Firstly, the SENCo must be a qualified teacher, working at the school for which they fulfil the role (section 6.84/5), with one exception to be discussed later, where a collaborative appointment is arranged between small schools. The SENCo must, on first appointment to the role, achieve the National Award within three years of appointment (section 6.85), where the award is accredited through a recognised Higher Education provider and where the award is at least equivalent to 60 credits of postgraduate study (section 6.86).

The SENCo is seen as having an important role in the strategic development of SEN policy and practice within the school, and it is stated much more strongly than previously that the post holder will be most effective 'if they are part of the school leadership team' (DfE/DoH 2015, section 6.87). The description of the key responsibilities that follows offers a view of the strategic nature of the work to be carried out; all of the eleven specified roles can be best described as strategic, rather than process roles. For example, four of the roles are qualified by the word 'liaising', two with the word 'advising', one with 'overseeing', and so on. There can be little doubt that it is envisaged that the role requires a considerable degree of strategic vision and leadership in bringing the best out of the varying stakeholders within a school setting to produce the best outcomes for pupils designated as having a special educational need or disability. To allow this to happen, schools are expected to ensure that the SENCo will be provided with both the time and resources needed to properly fulfil the role requirements, including 'sufficient administrative support and time away from teaching' (section 6.91) and notably, in a way similar 'to other strategic roles within a school' (section 6.91).

As mentioned previously, small schools can appoint a shared SENCo, providing that sufficient time and resources are provided for the post holder to carry out the role in an effective way for all pupils with special needs across the sharing schools (section 6.92); to reinforce the importance of the role, it is then stated that the SENCo in such a circumstance 'should not normally have a significant teaching commitment' and, perhaps most interestingly in leadership terms, this shared role should not be carried out by the head teacher at any of the schools.

Reviews of practice conducted over the last ten years or so have, somewhat unsurprisingly, reported that the reality of the role is clearly varied (Kearns, 2005; Layton, 2005; McKenzie, 2007; Fisher, 2012; Griffiths and Dubsky, 2012; Robertson, 2012; Pearson, Mitchell and Rapti, 2015) and very much dependent upon context and interpretation of sometimes contradictory legislation. These findings are largely replicated in the material gathered for this book, which form the substance of the material covered in the next three chapters on the Learning Outcomes for the National Award. It is certainly the case that the status and significance of the role have developed and strengthened, both in practice and within the new regulatory framework described above, with no current evidence of the discharge of the role being placed in the hands of anybody other than a qualified teacher, suggesting that the advocacy of the *House of Commons Education and Skills Select Committee Report on SEN* (HMSO, 2006) in urging the government to address the unanticipated appointment of TAs as SENCos has been successful.

That the status, significance and intent of the role are being seen differently is strengthened when the most recent iteration of the Learning Outcomes (DfE/DoH, 2015) are considered, that providers of the National Award are expected to deliver and which participants are expected to meet. When preparing bids for Inclusion in the first group of providers for the Award, in 2009, providers were expected to deliver programmes congruent with a set of 55 learning outcomes. In many ways these were both instrumental and reductionist, inviting a competence/compliance response that demonstrated personal attributes. One section of the outcomes, out of five, focussed on leadership, in what might be seen as a process orientation; for example, under a general heading of providing professional direction, the SENCo is seen as promoting improvements in teaching and learning, or leading the development of a whole-school culture of best practice; under the heading of leadership and development of staff, there is an expectation to provide support and feedback to colleagues on effective practice. In both of these cases, the responsibility of the SENCo can be interpreted as a monitoring or accountability function of leadership, rather than one of setting an expectation that the leadership element of the role is one of promoting change, and challenging practice within existing structures.

The Learning Outcomes that are currently expected (NCTL, 2014) appear to be directed much more at a conception of the SENCo acting as an agent of change. There are fewer outcomes, divided into only three categories, dealing with Professional Knowledge and Understanding, Leading and Coordinating Provision, and Personal and Professional Qualities. While it is certainly the case that some of the 2014 Learning Outcomes can be mapped directly on to the Learning Outcomes set out previously, it is equally clear that a change of emphasis has occurred. This is exemplified in the introduction to the outcomes, where it is made clear that these are not standards. It is stated that those undertaking further, specialist training

> will already be skilled teachers who have demonstrated the professional attributes, professional knowledge and understanding, and professional skills set out in the Qualified Teacher Status and Teachers' Standards as a minimum.
>
> (NCTL, 2014: 4)

This would appear to align with a view that the acquisition of Qualified Teacher Status (QTS), by whatever route, should prepare all teachers to meet the challenges offered by all pupils echoing the aspiration included in the SEN/D Codes of Practice (DfES, 2001; DfES, 2015) that 'all teachers are teachers of children with SEND'. It goes on to say that meeting 'these learning outcomes should enable new SENCos to fulfil the leadership role set out in the SEND Code of Practice' (DfE/DoH, 2015: 4), firmly aligning the National Award with the precepts contained in the Code, suggesting a thought-through application of common principles guiding the legislative framework and the role most associated with their implementation.

The Learning Outcomes go on to explore the way that leadership is conceptualised in some detail, using language that locates expectations firmly within a strategic and challenging view of what is entailed in leadership. Part B, Leading and Coordinating Provision, following a general strapline about completing the Award, contains five subsections containing a total of 24 statements outlining specific functions relating to the broad pattern set by the introduction to each of the subsections. It is noticeable that these sections are hierarchical in moving from what might be characterised as strategic leadership or change management in the first two subsections to a much more process view of leadership in the latter subsections. The first section refers to the ability to: 'Work strategically with senior colleagues and governors', the second refers to the ability to: 'Lead, develop, and, where necessary, challenge senior leaders, colleagues and governors', suggesting a proactive stance in relation to change. By contrast, the fourth subsection refers to the ability to: 'Draw on external sources of support and expertise', and the fifth to: 'Develop, implement, monitor and evaluate systems', suggesting a more bureaucratic, and perhaps more familiar, stance in relation to the work involved in the role of the SENCo.

It is perhaps worth considering some of the statements contained within these subsections in more detail, particularly given the perceived shift in policy direction in the Green Paper, *Support and Aspiration,* where the stated aim, although quietly and quickly removed from further documentation, suggested an end to the 'bias towards inclusive education' (DfE, 2011). For example, it is suggested in the first subsection that the SENCo should: 'advise on and influence the strategic development of a person-centred and inclusive ethos, policies, priorities and practices' while the last point in this subsection requires the SENCo to: 'Commission, secure and deploy appropriate resources . . . and evaluate and report upon their impact on progress, outcomes and cost-effectiveness.' In the second subsection, two statements are of particular interest in relation to the scope and focus of the role; the first, within the general expectation to lead, develop and challenge senior leaders, is to: 'model effective practice, coach and mentor colleagues', and this is immediately followed by: 'lead the professional development of staff so that all staff improve their practice and take responsibility for removing barriers to participation and learning'. It can, of course, be argued that these statements contain a great many words that are conceptually ambiguous or are poorly defined, but there would seem to be both an opportunity and an expectation here that, in completing the National Award, participants will become skilled in the language, structure and theory of leadership but will also be confronted with the implications of carrying out a role enhanced by this knowledge within their settings.

By contrast, the language used in the latter subsections of Section B outcomes seems much more familiar in relation to those provided in previous published Learning Outcomes (for example, from 2009). The last section, on systems, requires a newly qualified SENCo 'to develop, implement, monitor and evaluate systems to: identify pupils who may have SEN and/or disabilities; record and review the progress of children and young people with SEN and/or disabilities'; and 'ensure appropriate arrangements are put in place . . . [for] . . . national tests and examinations or undertaking other forms of accreditation'.

It is also worth noting that in addition to Section B, there is also a leadership outcome within Section A, Professional Knowledge and Understanding. The second subsection, on: 'the principles and practices of leadership in different contexts' is clearly intended to provide detailed expectations of what can be seen as the theoretical basis for leadership within a school setting, as the precursor for the enactment and implementation of these principles within the Learning Outcomes outlined in Section B. This means that of the nine subsections in Parts A and B of the Learning Outcomes, six deal specifically with elements of leadership. Section C, dealing with Personal and Professional Qualities, while not having any bulleted points relating to the subject, does mention 'the personal; and professional qualities and leadership' that are needed in the role.

The remainder of this chapter will explore what this might, and should, mean in terms of 'leadership for learning', described by John MacBeath as 'the capacity for leadership to arise out of powerful learning experiences and opportunities to exercise leadership to enhance learning' (MacBeath, 2009: 83). There can be little doubt that 'leadership for learning' can be seen to inform the practice of most, if not all, SENCos, if a narrow interpretation of the phrase is used; that is, where this leadership is exercised in the context of support, rather than in developing whole-school policies. However, applying this in a broader sense, where an enhanced learning environment meeting the needs of all pupils is seen as what is meant by the term, it is suggested that leadership for learning only occurs when an existing school culture and the core beliefs of the SENCo align.

That is, it happens in spite of current legislation and initiatives, rather than as a result of them, suggesting that where practices embodying a narrowly prescriptive view of learning are embedded in the culture and ethos of a setting, simply requiring a SENCo to adopt a leadership role may do little to enable them to exercise that leadership, to enhance learning. Further, there is little evidence to support the notion that this sort of leadership is, of itself, an artefact of membership of the senior leadership team in a school; rather the positioning that facilitates this sort of alignment seems to be much more related to the personal qualities of the SENCo, and to a large degree, those of the head teacher or pedagogical lead in the setting, than to role occupancy.

Kearns suggested the following five metaphors for ways in which the SENCo role was practised: 'auditor', 'rescue', 'expert', 'collaborator' and 'arbiter', any of which can dominate, overlap and co-exist (Kearns, 2005). Given the legislative structure in which the 'first' SEN Code of Practice (DfE, 1994) operated, it is perhaps not surprising that a typology such as this could be identified. The Code offered non-statutory guidance; that is, a school had to pay regard to the Code without necessarily adopting all of the processes that it advocated. The 'auditor' role, identified by Kearns, stressed the bureaucratic and procedural management that dominated the lives of many SENCos at the time, often leading to role anxiety and overload (McKenzie, 2007) due to the time demands associated with these procedures. The 'auditor' SENCo focussed on legalities and administration, asserting that a critical phase of their personal growth towards this type of working was 'the introduction in the school of the official Code of Practice' (Kearns, 2005: 141); it might well be that neither the 'second' SEN Code of Practice (DfES, 2001) or the 2009 Learning Outcomes for the National Award (TDA, 2009) did much to change this view.

Here, the leadership implications had the tendency to lead to 'single loop learning' (Argyris and Schön, 1978), caught up in a self-perpetuating loop of targets, strategies, implementation and evaluation; in effect a means by which to 'tame the wild' (Perkins, 2003) but one which also serves to reduce individual autonomy. Therefore, while only offering guidance, SENCos were seen to view the Code as a 'rule book', becoming overwhelmed by procedural processes. In this situation, it might be seen as justifiable for a newly appointed SENCo to adopt the behaviours expected by their colleagues particularly where, as Fullan (2003: 51) notes, 'relational trust atrophies when individuals perceive that others are not acting in ways that are consistent with their understanding of the others' role obligation'.

A second metaphor suggested by Kearns was that of the SENCo as 'rescue'. Here, there is an acknowledgement that at any one time in the complex narrative that accompanies the development of policy and practice in education, a number of competing agendas are likely to exist. The disparity within an agenda privileging attainment over achievement is one such example; a still more recent example might contrast the elitism that is seemingly inseparable from any increase in selective education with initiatives designed to reduce social inequality. Not all agendas might seem as polarised, of course; a perfectly well-intentioned practice introduced in a setting might be seen as failing to provide necessary support in meeting the learning needs of an individual child, creating a situation where 'rescue' might be required.

In these circumstances, the potential of a well-intentioned 'rescue' SENCo as a leader could create a situation where staff align themselves with an agenda that might be seen as oppositional to prevailing orthodoxies. Such demarcation lines have been termed 'Balkanisation' (Hargreaves, 1994) and serve to obscure the moral purpose of education which is grounded in equity, justice and the desire to enable all individuals to achieve their full potential. If SENCos, in response to beneficent, but vaguely articulated, guidance develop localised practices determined by particular policy initiatives, of which there are many, the result can often be seen as being what Lipsky (1980) termed 'street-level bureaucracy'. The notion of 'street-level bureaucracy' reflects a belief that policy implementation in the end comes down to the people who implement it, in managing complex demands, such as the need to negotiate targets and build relationships with a variety of 'clients', and pressures, such as working within limited resources. In terms of the SENCo role it is clear to see how such pressures, set within an environment allowing scope for the individual interpretation of policy, can produce an instrumental approach predicated on one, or more, policy initiatives. In the past, research on the role of the SENCo (Layton, 2005), mirrors Lipsky, describing practice in terms of powerlessness and a need to develop practice from conflicting, or unclear, policy guidance.

Kearns (op cit.) reported three further roles identified by the SENCos. The 'arbiter' SENCo prioritises 'negotiating, rationalising and monitoring the use of SEN resources in their schools', with a particular focus on the 'effective use and development of human resources'. This can certainly be configured as a management role, although the degree to which this incorporates the wider accountability and responsibility that stem from full knowledge of resources available within delegated budgets is debatable. At the same time, the configuration described seems to be limited; there seems to be little focus on extending the expertise of classroom practitioners to meet identified needs, as mention is made of using external expertise for this purpose, and this suggests a process conceptualisation of the role rather than a strategic one.

The 'collaborator' SENCo is perhaps the most readily identifiable metaphor, if not the most commonly found in respondents to Kearns' research. This approach involved groups of teachers engaging in collaborative processes to 'review, plan and evaluate activities' to meet the learning needs of identified pupils. This is seen as 'more democratic' than other metaphors and, interestingly, encompasses 'staff and curriculum development for diverse pupils in mainstream classes'. The 'expert' SENCo was the least identified metaphor; the main focus of work was with individual pupils where personal expertise, gained through both experience and further study, was seen to be of use in meeting the very specific or specialised requirements of 'high-need' pupils. This 'expert' role, which might be seen as consultative, suggests an externalisation of the role of the SENCo, rather than one that sits at the centre of school processes connected to meeting special needs.

In retrospect, and perhaps because of gathering data through reflection on critical incidents, the impression is given that these roles are largely separate and distinct, even though co-existence is mentioned. This is understandable; even in our recent conversations (see Chapters 4, 5 and 6) it was possible to identify respondents who closely fitted one of the metaphors. This was particularly the case with the arbiter and auditor roles, although there were also a number of occasions when a desire to 'rescue' was implicit in a desired response to the needs of an individual student.

It is undoubtedly the case that this demarcation of roles was more evident during the early development of the role of the SENCo, often as a response to role descriptions implemented within management structures offering centralised control; that is, where there was a reluctance to accord status to the role of the SENCo in a landscape that rarely placed marginalised children at the forefront of school development. It would seem that, in order to avoid SENCos identifying solely, or predominantly, with only one of these roles, there must be a recognition and development of an alternative view of teaching, learning and assessment that extends what is available for all learners, including those with special educational needs.

As argued earlier, the policy agenda has now shifted much more explicitly towards an expectation of the SENCo to 'lead, develop, and, where necessary, challenge' (NCTL, 2014) progress towards meeting the learning needs of pupils within their setting, and there is evidence to suggest that this agenda is being embraced by practitioners in the development of best practice. A number of examples from our conversations support this assessment. It could be that this is being shaped by the National Award for SEN Coordination, based on the most recent Learning Outcomes; it could also be that the principles contained within the most recent Code of Practice are having an effect.

This leads to the suggestion that the model proposed by Kearns can be extended. In a situation where whole-school developments are being designed to benefit the whole community of learners, and where the central vision that underpins these developments is shared by key staff, it can be argued that the role of the SENCo encompasses all of these metaphors. In this sense, it can be argued that the metaphors can be characterised as a nested hierarchy, rather than as a series of positions. The implementation of this hierarchy, and the positions occupied by an individual SENCo, would be determined by the permitting circumstances that obtain in the setting. These circumstances are likely to derive from the educational stance adopted within the setting, rather than through any particular skills or interests of the post holder.

The early development of the role for many was focussed on the desire to improve teaching and learning for pupils who stood on the outside of prevailing practice; the 'rescue' role would seem to fit this desire clearly. It seems very unlikely that there are any SENCos who now discharge their role wholly within this role type, if only because of the growth in numbers of support staff more likely to work directly with pupils. This does not mean that 'rescue' is no longer important; our conversations revealed SENCos who still wished that they could be more directly involved in everyday work with children and young people.

The increased adoption of the complex assessment, monitoring and reassessment bureaucratic procedures set out in the first and second Codes of Practice would seem to have shifted the focus of many SENCos away from the 'rescue' role to one more focussed on that of 'auditor'. This change seems to be in part predicated on an assumption in schools that work related to pupils who are special or different, rather than being something that was a necessary part of the work of all teachers, fell firmly within the remit of the SENCo; again, this view does not seem to have entirely disappeared, with termly reviews of pupils with EHCPs being seen, in one of our conversations, as the responsibility of the SENCo rather than a class teacher. It also seems to be the case that, where internal changes allowed, an increased focus on the management of resources for special educational needs further diversified the role. Here, the actions of the post holder might combine the obvious elements of auditor and arbiter without becoming overwhelmed by either. The discharge of the rescue role also sits comfortably within this model, if at second hand.

The next stage in this hierarchical argument would seem to be dependent on two particular permitting circumstances. The first is the degree to which key staff in a school or setting view special educational needs as additional to that which is normally available, or as integral to all teaching and learning that occur in the setting. The second follows from this; where there is alignment with the first position, it would seem likely that the role will be discharged in the style of 'arbiter' or 'auditor' or a combination of these. Where the alignment is with the second position, the possibility opens up that the SENCo as 'collaborator' can move forward in a much more collegiate and distributive way, with a focus on leadership for learning, embracing all pupils. Of course, in the absence of alignment, it is likely that role dissonance will occur, with either the SENCo, or the setting, becoming frustrated with progress.

Arguably, the systemic changes contained within the SEND Code of Practice (DfE/DoH, 2015), have served to reduce the bureaucracy involved in processes connected to special educational needs, and where collaborative working is possible, it seems quite possible for a 'collaborator' SENCo to be able to subsume the roles of rescue, auditor and arbiter within a key developmental role in the school or setting.

Given the requirement for a SENCo to attain a Post Graduate Certificate (PGC), equivalent to 60 level 7 (Master's level) credits, it is also likely that many SENCos will be increasingly seen as expert, particularly where this equates to a knowledge of the full field of SEND, without necessarily being expert in any one specific condition or special educational need; or at least, being able to use this knowledge to identify specific expertise in others, where needed. If the possession of a PGC leads an increasing number of SENCos to go on and complete a Master's degree, within the field, this expertise is likely to be further enhanced.

There is nothing in this configuration of the role that requires the SENCo to be a member of the senior leadership team (SLT) within a school or setting. However, this has been one of the long-term presumptions of the documentation that surrounds the role of the SENCo, including all of the Codes of Practice. While we recognise the value of this as a potential 'stepping stone' that could move practice forward, it could also result in surface-level change where 'what is being proposed sounds good and contains all the right concepts, where leaders can talk a good game and even mean it, but where ... ideas never get implemented with consistency or integrity' (Fullan, 2003: 31). However, it is possible to argue for an alternative model, which we have termed a 'distributive model for SEN coordination'. This nomenclature reflects a redrawing of the role of SEN coordination as one that harnesses the moral imperative of leadership for learning as a way of mobilising the knowledge, skills and commitment of all staff, in pursuit of the goal of transforming the learning experience of all students, to close the achievement gap that too frequently occurs for pupils at the margins.

The SENCo as a member of the senior leadership team: A flawed model?

By describing the SENCo being a member of the senior leadership team as a flawed model, we are aware that this runs contrary to the policy direction found in recent documentation. We argue this, despite the potential that might be offered for widening the narrow focus on resource limitation and targets described in the arbiter role above or to reduce the temptation to micro-manage the administration of SEN coordination as a rescuer, to a much more expansive view of teaching and learning across a setting. This stems from a need for caution; if schools are to avoid the limited role constructs highlighted in the first section of this chapter, it is argued that the purpose of the SENCo role, whether central to the SLT or not, requires thought.

First, as Gunter (2007), Stevenson (2007) and MacBeath (2010) have argued, new divisions of labour have served to create a divorce between those who plan and those who execute; for example, between teaching and pastoral care. Some consideration of why the SENCo should be a member of the senior leadership team is necessary if we are to address this concern. If the purpose of SLT membership for the SENCo is merely to plan necessary responses to policy initiatives and legislation, without also promoting a cohesive and collaborative acceptance of these changes, it would seem probable that teachers and support staff will adopt, at a class or individual level, the sort of street-level bureaucracy described above, as they attempt to navigate targets, negotiate the demands of 'clients' and compete for funding. Without considering how the interplay between leadership and learning can be examined and explored, increasing the likelihood of 'leadership for learning' (MacBeath, 2006, 2009), simply promoting the SENCo to the leadership team might do little to address the concern that 'most systems have enacted accountability policies in the absence of conceptualising and investing in policies that will increase the capacity of educators to perform in new ways' (Fullan, 2003: 25).

Alternatively, if the SENCo is appointed to the senior leadership team in order to influence teaching and learning across a school, the role of the deputy head teacher in many primary schools, or Curriculum Leaders in Secondary Schools, may need to be reviewed. This raises fundamental questions about responsibility for the planning and execution of strategies to meet the needs of all learners, including those with SEN and/or disabilities. If the SENCo, as a senior leader, moves away from a circumscribed role planning interventions and executing individualised learning programmes for learners with Special Educational Needs and moves towards a wider brief charged with planning and executing strategies that enable class communities to assume ownership of teaching and learning, it could be argued that the conflation of responsibilities shared with other senior leaders renders the need for a SENCo debatable.

Each of these alternatives highlights the importance, and potential impact, of role definition upon 'social capital' (the connections within and between social networks). Putnam (1999), Szreter (2000) and MacBeath (2009) discuss the difference between three forms of social capital: bonding social capital, bridging social capital and linking social capital. 'Bonding' social capital relates to relatively few strong connections between people creating a small number of strong groupings which can lead to insularity. In terms of educational settings, these groups might be the SLT, teaching staff or support staff. Bonding social capital of this nature would be evident in schools adopting hierarchical approaches to leadership where, for example, the SLT meet to decide policy, the teachers meet to discuss the curriculum and the support staff meet to discuss individual learners. If bonding social capital dominates an educational setting, simply relocating the SENCo to the senior leadership team may do nothing to break down existing structures or increase opportunities for the implementation of leadership for learning.

The example of provision mapping could illustrate this difficulty; a SENCo, appointed to the SLT could retain ownership of provision mapping across the setting in order to lead the creation of something akin to Group Education Plans (Frankl, 2005) for an identified body of learners. Whilst this might have the potential to reduce the bureaucratic workload of the SENCo and increase the likelihood of the devolution of planning responsibility to class teams, this is, once again, little more than a much needed response to a flawed system, where the danger is that such systems can often become a new form of bureaucracy in a situation with little bonding social capital. It is certainly the case that such initiatives are unlikely to be a driver for collaboration unless they can be embedded in a culture that embodies collective responsibility. As such, the narrowed SENCo role discussed both in our conversations and by those not appointed to senior leadership teams (Layton, 2005) could simply be reproduced within the leadership team, rather than outside of it. That this is likely to strengthen 'bonding' social capital rather than enabling a loosening to structures encouraging more collegial forms of leadership for learning to develop has to be acknowledged.

In contrast to 'bonding' social capital, 'linking' social capital operates vertically, making connections between people with differing degrees of power and authority. Such social links are evident in educational settings that seek to create connections between groups that possess bonding social capital, for example, between teachers and the senior leadership team or between subject coordinators and support staff, rather than to redistribute autonomy across a setting. While membership of the SLT might enable a SENCo to enact a deeply held desire to promote the extension of 'linking' social capital in a setting, it might be useful to question the moral purpose of such a move.

In this context, it is of interest that Layton (2005: 59) reported that 'the greatest barrier to achieving their moral purpose as SENCos was identified as not being a member of the senior leadership team'. While it is clear, from Layton's study, that SENCos believe membership of the senior leadership team to be an essential precursor to the discharge of a morally focussed role, we would caution against viewing such membership as a panacea. In fact, we would question any differentiation between the moral purpose of SENCos, articulated as a 'deeply held commitment to serve the best interests of all their pupils' (Layton, 2005: 58), and that of any member of the teaching profession. Indeed, we would argue that moral purpose can, and should, reside in the actions of all those involved in the education of children and young people; on the contrary, any assertion or feeling that is present only in those who have a declared affinity with pupils with special educational needs seems to be an example of an undesirable moral relativism that needs to be challenged.

Five major virtues central to the moral character of teaching professionalism were defined by Sockett (1993, 2006) as: honesty, courage, care, fairness, and practical wisdom. As these virtues are arguably no more, or less, central to the role of the SENCo than to any other teacher, to argue for membership of the senior leadership team for one member of staff on the basis of enabling them to achieve their moral purpose would seem to ignore both the collective moral purpose of the school and the moral responsibility of all staff for all learners.

Indeed, simply promoting the SENCo to the senior leadership team may do little more than redistribute accountability without embedding a philosophy that encourages what Eisner (1991) termed 'connoisseurship' which MacBeath (2009: 74) describes as knowing 'how to suspend preconception and judgement; to know what they see rather than seeing what they already know'. While connoisseurship may lend itself to the development of a collective moral purpose, the ability to suspend preconception requires a culture that moves beyond performativity in order to develop genuine dialogue around the intention, purpose and impact of education for all of our learners; in essence, a culture that embraces distributive and reciprocal practices that are driven by a core moral purpose.

A distributive model of SEN coordination: leadership for learning?

The third type of social capital cited by Putnam (1999), Szreter (2000) and MacBeath (2009) is described as 'bridging' social capital which occurs when social links are relatively weak but more numerous and are 'outward looking connecting people with others beyond their immediate reference group, opening up new ways of seeing, relating and learning' (Swaffield and MacBeath, 2009: 45).

Crucially, settings in which 'bridging' social capital is enabled move the conceptualisation of leadership away from process-led accountability towards 'leadership for learning'. This is concerned, above all, with keeping alive bridging social capital in the belief that 'it is the many and weak links that provide the scope and space for the exercise of agency in respect of both leadership and learning' (Swaffield and MacBeath, 2009: 46). The notion of agency (people being able to make choices and make a difference) is central to this approach. The degree to which learners, parents and educators can each express their agency will clearly inform the moral purpose of the school and the extent to which accountability for learning is shared and valued. That a collaborative approach such as this was included in the first and second SEN Code of Practice is unquestionable; it is also the case that the demonstration of agency features much more strongly in the SEND Code of Practice that frames current practice (DfE/DoH, 2015). It is a source of some disquiet, therefore, that the conversations with stakeholders already mentioned in this book do not always evidence any significant increase in the sort of collaborative activities that might mark a shared moral purpose, or that demonstrate the sort of bridging social capital suggested here.

By advocating a distributive model of SEN coordination, we are arguing that we should view an educational setting as a 'community of practice' (Lave and Wenger, 1991) focussing on the processes and activities of learning, rather than places containing hierarchical structures focussed on the products of learning and on the attendant but separate processes of SEN coordination. Central to the 'communities of practice' approach is an acceptance of what has been termed 'legitimate peripheral participation', where novices become experienced members of a community of practice or collaborative project (Lave and Wenger, 1991; Wenger, 1999; Wenger, McDermott and Snyder, 2002). In this way, novices are valued for their contribution, rather than viewed as individuals whose practice requires correction, recognising that participation is an 'encompassing process of being active participants in the *practices* of social communities and constructing *identities* in relation to these communities' (Wenger, 1999: 4). This notion operates on two levels. Firstly, in terms of staff participation, the approach does not validate harmful or neglectful practice; rather, the need to embrace legitimate peripheral participation recognises that practice varies in levels of expertise, and that expertise is not the only measure of value. In particular, this philosophy recognises the moral imperative of all practitioners above the particular expertise of some.

Secondly, this perspective persuades us to view learning as participation, enabling us to move beyond the 'competency traps' (Cousins, 1996: 79) of a standards-driven curriculum that necessarily marginalises and labels those deemed to be failing. By reconceptualising learning in terms of participation, rather than in attainment within a narrow curricular specification, the ethos shifts to one which encompasses a belief that 'teaching a child to read is an important contribution, but inspiring him or her to be an enthusiastic, life-long reader is another matter' (Fullan, 2003: 29). This encourages learning communities to unleash the potential contained within a moral imperative, and increase autonomy and agency in order to enable 'double loop learning' (Argyris and Schön, 1978). In contrast to 'single-loop learning', which adopts an approach where plans are created in response to targets that are rarely questioned, 'double-loop learning' requires a much deeper critique of the purpose of targets and the underlying assumptions of action. 'Double-loop learning' is intolerant of routine and simplistic answers to complex issues in the belief that 'the valuing of consistency leads to competency; the valuing of inconsistency leads to learning' (Argyris and Schön, 1996).

It is here that the National Award for SEN Coordination is seen to be influential. The way that the Award is structured requires participants to prepare a portfolio of evidence supportive of the Learning Outcomes, and this is generally seen to be reflective. Although reflection is not as clearly foregrounded in Initial Teacher Education as it used to be, it is clear that teaching is a reflective profession, one that should encourage practitioners to consider, in depth, how teaching and learning can be. It is therefore not surprising that some SENCos, having gained the National Award, are now seeking to position themselves at the centre of school developments promoting equity and equality.

We recognise that for many SENCos this will be a challenging approach to take. Nevertheless, until we recognise, and give permission for, legitimate peripheral participation, it is unlikely that the role of all SENCos will move beyond the seemingly limited, and limiting, metaphors of rescue, auditor or arbiter.

This recognition can move schools away from process management aimed at certain groups of learners towards leadership for learning and learning for leadership where any member of a school society can learn to effect change and the 'head teacher becomes the head learner' (MacGilchrist, Myers and Reed, 1997). Aside from the fact that the National College for School Leadership recognises that the potential 'influence from distributive leadership is up to three times higher than that reported for an individual leader' (NCSL, 2006: 12), this change in focus enables anyone to 'take on leadership as a right and responsibility rather than it being bestowed as a gift or burden' (Swaffield and MacBeath, 2009: 44). In this way learning becomes conceptualised as 'participation in social practice', something that can serve to challenge the prevailing staff and learner hierarchies, and encourage all members of a school community to explore the relationship between learning and the social situations in which it occurs (Lave and Wenger, 1991).

This ideal has real implications for transforming the role of the SENCo beyond that of a powerless negotiator of policy and practice; the street-level bureaucrat (Lipsky, 1980). It also demands some recognition of the fact that membership of the senior leadership team, in itself, might do little to empower all staff to take responsibility for diverse groups of learners. A distributive model of SEN coordination requires a radical re-think of practice.

Fullan (2003) discusses 'complexity theory' in this regard arguing that transformation cannot be effected in a top-down or linear fashion. In developing this argument he makes reference to the many disruptions that can occur within the most meticulously planned strategies when individuals within the system choose to exert their autonomy. This raises a crucial point; in a hierarchical system, individual autonomy or agency, whether in the form of street-level bureaucracy or in the individual expression of one's moral purpose, can be viewed as dissent or unprofessional practice. This can even be the case when the expression of individual autonomy, when viewed beyond the hierarchical system, exhibits those dispositions described by Sockett (2006), earlier in this chapter, as representative of teacher professionalism.

In essence, a distributive model of SEN coordination requires three conditions. Firstly, it requires a commitment to ensure that every member of the educational community is given the space to learn to lead and to lead to learn. This is not to argue that a school does not need a head teacher but it does require some consideration of additional roles in schools such as a deputy head teacher, SENCo and the myriad leadership roles that exist in many settings. Indeed, the desire to become an 'intelligent school' where 'change comes from within, from the staff and pupils, rather than imposed from above' (MacGilchrist, Myers and Reed, 1997: 108) requires school leaders to consider whether the ever increasing hierarchical layers of executive head teachers, CEOs, multi-academy trust chief executives serve any legitimate educational purpose or are created to merely sustain bureaucracy.

The second condition for a distributive model of SEN coordination relates to the balance between internal and external accountability (MacBeath, 2010), a review of which is necessary before an educational environment can begin to develop communities of mutually accountable practitioners. This is not to profess a naïve ignorance of external accountability; rather, we would suggest that a much needed reconsideration of the forms of accountability that drive practice is called for, recognising that 'what is worth fighting for is more of an internal battle than an external one' (Fullan, 2003: 19) and that moral accountability to all members of the school community may serve a higher purpose than presumed bureaucratic accountability to national directives.

The final condition that we feel to be central to a distributive model of SEN coordination is some recognition of the de-professionalisation that occurs, as evidenced in Kearns' (2005) study, when we create structures that serve to atomise the SENCo role. These structures can occur whether or not the SENCo is appointed to the senior leadership team. In fact, if we return to the dispositions that Sockett (2006) describes as the moral purpose of teaching, a distributive model of SEN coordination is likely to emerge from the sort of negotiation, collaboration and commitment to shared accountability that the continued development of these dispositions is likely to bring.

The demands and implications of the three conditions described here are considerable. However, for those settings with the drive and vision to review leadership structures, the role of the SENCo could be situated within an ethos where 'learning and leadership are conceived of "activities" linked by the centrality of human agency within a framework of moral purpose' (Swaffield and MacBeath, 2009: 42). The National Award for SEN Coordination has the power to support visionary SENCos to increasingly become the catalyst for a reinvigoration of the moral purpose of education and to review the potential for leadership for learning across settings. The resulting climate could be one which extols 'deliberately shared leadership of vision building, people development, organisational structuring and teaching and learning management' (Dempster, 2009: 29). The continued development of the SENCo role, supported by National Award for SEN Coordination, is seen increasingly as a vehicle for change, in those schools and for those SENCos with the imagination and foresight to maximise this unique opportunity.

References

Argyris, C., and Schön, D. (1978) *Organizational Learning: A Theory of Action Perspective.* Reading, MA: Addison-Wesley.

Argyris, C. and Schön, D. (1996) *Organizational Learning II: Theory, Method and Practice.* Reading, MA: Addison-Wesley.

Cousins, B. (1996) Understanding organised learning for leadership and school improvement, in K. Leithwood, J. Chapman, D. Corson, P. Hallinger and A. Hart (eds) *International Handbook of Educational Leadership and Administration.* Dordrecht: Methuen.

Dempster, N. (2009) What do we know about Leadership? in J. MacBeath and N. Dempster (eds) *Connecting Leadership and Learning: Principles for Practice.* London: Routledge.

DfE (1994) *Code of Practice on the Identification and Assessment of Special Educational Needs.* London: DfE.

DfE (2011) *Support and Aspiration: A New Approach to Special Educational Needs and Disability – A Consultation.* London: TSO.

DfE (2014) *Children and Families Act 2014.* London: TSO.

DfE/DoH (2015) *Special Educational Needs and Disability Code of Practice: 0 to 25 Years.* London: TSO.

DfES (2001) *SEN Code of Practice.* Nottingham: DfES.

Eisner, E. (1991) *The Enlightened Eye.* New York: Macmillan.

Fisher, H. (2012) Progressing towards a model of intrinsic Inclusion in a mainstream primary school: a SENCo's experience. *International Journal of Inclusive Education,* 16(2): 1273–1293.

Frankl, C. (2005) Managing individual educational plans: reducing the workload of the SEN coordinator. *Support for Learning,* 20(2): 77–82.

Fullan, M. (2003) *The Moral Imperative of School Leadership.* London: Sage.

Griffiths, D. and Dubsky, R. (2012) Evaluating the impact of the new National Award for SENCos: transforming landscapes or gardening in a gale? *British Journal of Special Education,* 39(4): 164–172.

Gunter, H. (2007) Remodelling the school workforce in England: a study in tyranny. *Journal for Critical Education Policy Studies,* 5(1): 1–11.

Hargreaves, A. (1994) *Changing Teachers, Changing Times: Teachers' Work and Culture in the Postmodern Age.* London: Continuum.

HMSO (2006) *House of Commons Education and Skills Select Committee Report on Special Educational Needs.* London: TSO.

Kearns, H. (2005) Exploring the experiential learning of special educational needs coordinators. *Journal of In-Service Education,* 31(1): 131–150.

Lave, J. and Wenger, E. (1991) *Situated Learning: Legitimate Peripheral Participation.* Cambridge: Cambridge University Press.

Layton, L (2005) Special educational needs coordinators and leadership: a role too far? *Support for Learning,* 20(2): 53–60.

Lipsky, M. (1980) *Street-level Bureaucracy: Dilemmas of the Individual in Public Services.* New York: Russell Sage Foundation.

MacBeath, J. (2006) *Leadership as a Subversive Activity.* Monograph, University of Melbourne: ACEL/ASPA.

MacBeath, J. (2009) A focus on learning, in J. MacBeath and N. Dempster (eds) *Connecting Leadership and Learning: Principles for Practice.* London: Routledge.

MacBeath. J. (2010) Stories of compliance and subversion in a prescriptive policy environment. *Educational Management Administration and Leadership,* 36(1): 123–148.

MacGilchrist, B., Myers, K. and Reed, J. (1997) *The Intelligent School.* London: Paul Chapman.

McKenzie, S. (2007) A review of recent developments in the role of the SENCo in the UK. *Support for Learning,* 34(4): 212–218.

National College for School Leadership [NCSL] (2006) *Impact and Evaluation Report 2004/05.* Nottingham: NCSL.

National College for Teaching and Leadership [NCTL] (2014) *National Award for SEN Coordination: Learning Outcomes.* London: DfE.

Pearson, S., Mitchell, R. and Rapti, M. (2015) 'I will be "fighting" even more for pupils with SEN': SENCOs' role predictions in the changing English policy context. *Journal of Research in Special Educational Needs,* 15(1): 48–56.

Perkins, D. (2003) *King Arthur's Round Table: How Collaboration Creates Smart Organisations.* Hoboken, NJ: John Wiley and Sons Inc.

Putnam, R. (1999) *Bowling Alone: The Collapse and Revival of American Community.* New York: Touchstone.

Robertson, C. (2012) Special educational needs and disability coordination in a changing policy landscape: making sense of policy from a SENCO's perspective. *Support for Learning,* 27(2): 77–83.

Sockett, H. (1993) *The Moral Base for Teacher Professionalism.* NY: Teachers College Press.

Sockett, H. (ed.) (2006) *Teacher Dispositions: Building a Teacher Education Framework of Moral Standards*. Washington, DC: American Association of Colleges for Teacher Education.

Stevenson, H. (2007) Restructuring teachers; work and trades union responses in England: bargaining for change? *American Educational Research Journal*, 44(2): 224–251.

Swaffield, S. and MacBeath, J. (2009) Leadership for learning, in J. MacBeath and N. Dempster (eds) *Connecting Leadership and Learning: Principles for Practice*. London: Routledge.

Szreter, S. (2000) Social capital, the economy and education in historical perspective, in S. Baron, J. Field, and T. Schuller (eds) *Social Capital: Critical Perspectives*. Oxford: Oxford University Press.

TDA (2009) *Standards for National Award for SEN Coordination*. London: TDA.

Wenger, E. (1999) *Communities of Practice: Learning, Meaning and Identity*. Cambridge: Cambridge University.

Wenger, E., McDermott, R. and Snyder, W. (2002) *Cultivating Communities of Practice: A Guide to Managing Knowledge*. Boston, MA: Harvard Business School Press.

4 Achieving the National Award for SEN Coordination (Part A): Professional knowledge and understanding

Fiona and Graham Hallett

It is tempting to think that the way to demonstrate the Learning Outcomes for the National Award is to take each outcome in turn, assemble evidence that shows that the outcome has been met, and place these in a sequentially organised folder. To demonstrate accountability, some SENCos may feel that several pieces of evidence should be provided for each outcome. There would need to be an examination of what constitutes evidence, how recent the evidence should be, and some consideration of whether the evidence should simply be descriptive, or whether it should contain a reflective element to demonstrate understanding as well as knowledge and skills. It is clear, from the preamble to the National Award Learning Outcomes, that the award must be equivalent to 60 credits at Master's level – a requirement that cannot be achieved in a folder of evidence. In this section, we hope to show that there might be a different way of completing the Award that has the further advantage of tackling the subtlety and nuance required in work at Master's level and beyond.

In writing about their work, in all of its variety, intensity, and range, SENCos can evidence a wealth of knowledge, experience, and skill; this will occur whether the starting point is the child, the family, the class, or the setting. By reflecting on this writing, whether developed as an assignment at Master's level, as a reflective portfolio or as a piece of school-based research, the SENCo can produce evidence that meets the Learning Outcomes in imaginative and thoughtful ways. If this writing is illustrative of the work done in a specific situation relating to a child experiencing barriers to learning, it is likely that many Learning Outcomes will be addressed, at least in part. It is probable that a series of reflections of this nature will extend this coverage, both in breadth and depth, without the need to produce disconnected and unrelated 'evidence' that does little to develop understanding, enhance practice, or initiate change. What follows is an exploration of what the Learning Outcomes actually look like in practice from the viewpoints of SENCos, Inclusion managers, parents, young people, people working in a local authority, and school governors. These conversations give an insight into the complexity of the role and the levels of reflective analysis required to do it justice.

Therefore, while we will deal with each section of Learning Outcomes, as described by the National College for Teaching and Leadership (2014), this will be done in a fluid and realistic manner drawing upon the richness of the conversations that have been conducted with the range of stakeholders outlined above.

These stakeholders are based in a variety of contexts and although all are subject to the same legislation, each voice offers a different perspectives on the role of a SENCo.

Part A: Professional Knowledge and Understanding

This section of the National Award deals with four themes:

1. The statutory and regulatory context for SEN and disability equality and the implications for practice.
2. The principles and practice of leadership in different contexts.
3. How SEN and disabilities affect pupils' participation and learning.
4. Strategies for improving outcomes for pupils with SEN and/or disabilities.

The first theme – the statutory and regulatory context for SEN and disability equality and the implications for practice – is covered in detail in the first chapter of this book but the day-to-day experiences of SENCos tell a more complex story.

For instance, on the one hand, we have Acts of Parliament such as the Disability Discrimination Act (2005), the Equality Act (2010) and the Children and Families Act (2014), endorsed by statutory guidance such as the *SEND Code of Practice 0 to 25 Years* (DfE/DoH, 2015), which are designed to protect rights. Yet, on the other hand, we have procedural structures, including Ofsted frameworks (see *Ofsted School Inspection Handbook 150066*, August 2016) and local authority systems that can make the execution of these rights difficult. Indeed, local authority interpretation of the *SEND Code of Practice 0 to 25 Years* (2015) was a major source of concern in many of the conversations that we had. Almost without exception, parents and school professionals expressed concerns about local authority capacity, and in some cases, a perceived unwillingness, to prioritise fundamental rights, even though attention is drawn to these in the Code of Practice.

For example, clear statements are made that:

> No-one should lose their statement and not have it replaced with an EHC plan simply because the system is changing.
> (Section 1.17, *SEND Code of Practice: 0 to 25 Years*, 2015)

and

> Local authorities may develop criteria as guidelines to help them decide when it is necessary to carry out an EHC needs assessment (and following assessment, to decide whether it is necessary to issue an EHC plan). However, local authorities must be prepared to depart from those criteria where there is a compelling reason to do so in any particular case and demonstrate their willingness to do so where individual circumstances warrant such a departure. Local authorities must not apply a 'blanket' policy to particular groups of children or certain types of need, as this would prevent the consideration of a child's or young person's needs individually and on their merits.
> (Section 9.16, *SEND Code of Practice: 0 to 25 Years*, 2015)

These rights were belied by the number of SENCos who typically said, '*I already know that she will lose her Statement as she won't meet the criteria for an Education, Health and Care Plan*' (primary school Inclusion manager). Whether or not this was the case, perceptions of practice based upon '*what is possible in a stripped down local authority*' (parent) appeared to be sending messages to all that children might very well lose a Statement solely because systems were changing. Concerns of this nature led to comments along the line of children '*needing to be on the ASD Pathway or the ADHD pathway*' (primary school SENCo) in order to be considered for an EHCP. This medicalisation of need was of concern to many, with one SENCo expressing real unease about '*a system that increasingly needs a label in order to respond*' (primary school SENCo).

Therefore, despite reference to disability equality in the first Learning Outcome, the presence of a legal requirement may not be enough to convince everyone of its importance. Consequently, although legislation and statutory requirements often serve to protect the rights of individuals – in this case, the rights of individuals with special educational needs and/or disabilities – the difference between legislation aimed at equality, and statutory and regulatory frameworks, can produce tensions around the types of strategic decision required to influence the alignment of policy to school practice.

Thus, while it goes without saying that knowledge of legislation is essential, the second, third and fourth themes focus more clearly on the 'understanding' element of professional knowledge and understanding.

For example, while the second theme in Part A – the principles and practice of leadership in different contexts – is dealt with more thoroughly in Part B of the Learning Outcomes, there is clear recognition, throughout the Learning Outcomes, that the SENCo role amounts to more than the administrative coordination of provision.

It was interesting that different local authorities were interpreting the Code of Practice in slightly different ways which impacted on the ways in which each SENCo was able to lead practice in their setting.

In some of the conversations, local authorities were described as focussing on accountability measures, for example, the need to ensure that:

> The whole process of EHC needs assessment and EHC plan development, from the point when an assessment is requested (or a child or young person is brought to the local authority's attention) until the final EHC plan is issued, must take no more than 20 weeks.
>
> (Section 9.40, *SEND Code of Practice: 0 to 25 Years*, 2015)

As a result, one Inclusion manager based in a primary school commented that:

> *Educational Psychologists haven't been Educational Psychologists – they have been doing assessments for transfer to EHC plans. We can't get one for other support unless we pay extra. Educational Psychologists are doing what they call 'statutory work' – we used to have a link meeting and then an additional allocation of hours – that has gone.*

Another frustration, articulated by more than half of the SENCos that we spoke to, related to a perceived lack of local authority preparedness with regard to the processes and paperwork involved in the development of an EHCP. A number of SENCos expressed their frustration at *'being sent outdated forms that they are trying to adapt for the new system'* (primary school SENCo) and *'having to transfer the information that you have already given on one form to another form, even though both forms were sent to me by different people in the same local authority'* (secondary school SENCo).

The small number of SENCos, Inclusion managers and governors that mentioned the Local Offer and Personal Budgets (major innovations in the 2015 *SEND Code of Practice*) were based in special schools and generally commented that *'it isn't really an issue here as the parents are happy with the facilities that we have'* (special school SENCo).

Without exception, the SENCos, Inclusion managers, governors and local authority representatives that we spoke to had a basic understanding of the 2015 *SEND Code of Practice* and were able to discuss how it was being implemented in their setting. In particular, many of the conversations focussed upon the fact that:

Effective participation happens when:

- it is recognised, valued, planned and resourced (for example, through appropriate remuneration and training)
- it is evident at all stages in the planning, delivery and monitoring of services
- there are clearly described roles for children, young people and parents
- there are strong feedback mechanisms to ensure that children, young people and parents understand the impact their participation is making.
(Section 1.12, *SEND Code of Practice: 0 to 25 Years*, 2015)

For example, one SENCo in a primary school setting discussed the need for a multi-agency approach to the effective participation of staff, young people and their families. In this instance, the school had commissioned two key-workers from a local children's centre to enable continuity of support and engagement throughout the year. While difficult to fund, this approach was seen as:

> . . . *vital in order to communicate with parents who are not in a formal process and therefore might not have as much contact with school. You get the chance to see what the parents worry about, what they want for their child.*

So, while very few SENCos or Inclusion managers talked about working more closely with Health and Social Care services (indeed, many expressed a lack of any real engagement across services), some did talk about the need for joined-up working that extends *'beyond the school gate'* (secondary school SENCo). It is worrying that, more than 12 months after the introduction of the new Code of Practice, very little was said about cohesive working across education, health and social care other than the fact that referrals, procedures and attendant paperwork were very different across the three sectors.

Where links between education, health and social care services were remarked upon, these related to social care. In one instance, a SENCo commented that *'Parents have liked being able to incorporate Social Care in the Education Health and Care Plan whereas they were separate processes in the old Statementing system'* and, in another, the SENCo in question demonstrated frustration over the fact that *'many of our pupils need access to short breaks, and are legally entitled to them, but cannot access these due to stripped back services'*. In the second instance, delays in the transfer process were not being addressed at Annual Review meetings.

The third theme – how SEN and disabilities affect pupils' participation and learning – demonstrated a move from *'being the only person who knows anything about SEN'* (secondary school SENCo) towards a desire to enable colleagues to understand that progress is non-linear and that other factors have an impact upon learning. In particular, SENCos and Inclusion managers talked about school leaders and teachers holding shifting expectations of success. With varying success rates, dependent upon school ethos, SENCos recognised a real need to encourage their colleagues to consider progress for pupils who experience a lack of a stimulating learning environment tailored to their needs.

This understandably proved to be a sensitive topic, but innovative approaches to *'challenging the status quo'* (primary school SENCo) will be of interest to SENCos new to the role and those in schools that fail to see the links between a lack of progress and Quality First teaching. In one example, an Inclusion manager talked about meetings with the class teacher and the head teacher *'so if a child isn't making progress, we agree that the teacher will do a, b, and c and the Head will follow up on that'*. In this case, the Inclusion manager asked for support from a like-minded head teacher in a way that encouraged other teachers to reflect upon, and adjust, their own practice. If these discussions are left to the SENCo alone, it may well be the case that the likelihood of tensions and disagreements is increased.

Another example was given by a SENCo working within a setting that *'couldn't see that what they were doing was only meeting the needs of the brightest children'* (secondary school SENCo). In this case, the SENCo felt somewhat isolated and unsupported by the head teacher, leaving her in a situation where she *'had to do what I can to change hearts and minds'*. A small, but powerful, change in practice was introduced in this setting that was simple to achieve without alienating colleagues. Given that a considerable number of children were on the SEN register, and therefore were monitored within a reviewed provision mapping system, the SENCo asked subject leaders to review provision in their subject area, including provision for children with SEND, prior to giving an overall report to her that would inform the report to governors. Given that schools are legally bound to advertise provision for children with SEND on their website, and that this would be reviewed by Ofsted, prospective parents, etc., it would be difficult for any subject leader to resist this process, enabling the SENCo to position herself as a central conduit for evidencing good practice, rather than the primary gatekeeper of information.

In a similar vein, the Annual Review meeting, for children with Statements, or EHCPs, was described as providing an ideal opportunity to review all aspects of provision rather than *'rolling over targets from the year before'* (primary school SENCo). Many of the SENCos cited the National Award as a motivating factor in reflecting upon what might be seen to be an administrative process, with one SENCo discussing the value of school-based research.

This SENCo had been concerned about the quality of Individual Education Plans (no longer required by the SEND Code of Practice). She felt that Statements of Special Educational Need did not '*feed into daily practice*' and decided to audit the number of children who had attended their Annual Review, and the degree to which teaching staff were aware of the content of the Statement.

This audit led to a school-based research project on pupil involvement in their Annual Review and staff training on linking daily practice to Statements of Special Educational Need. With regard to staff training, she explained that:

> *I wanted to protect the 'golden thread', so I said – here is the Statement (the legal document), targets set at Annual Reviews should link directly to the Statement and then IEPs should reflect smaller steps in order to attain Annual Review targets in order to attain targets on the Statement. I wanted colleagues to realise that we're all working towards the legal document that it has been decided that the child needs to have.*

(special school SENCo)

As a result of this small-scale research project, and subsequent staff training, the number of students meeting their Annual Review targets doubled. While acknowledging that IEPs were no longer mentioned in the new Code of Practice, this SENCo described a clear rationale for retaining IEPs saying that '*it's not all about the legislation*'.

On a less positive note, this SENCo, as with many of the others that we have spoken to, talked about the overwhelming nature of the bureaucracy of the role while refusing to allow paperwork to obscure the child and their family. In the words of a SENCo in a secondary school setting:

> *Parents very much welcome articulating their aspirations for their child as these sometimes have very little to do with formal education. They have been all about independence and accessing the community. It's good that they feel that their voice is being listened to.*

Similarly, one parent commented that she had found out about Social Services support to which she was entitled, but had not known about, prior to the meeting to transfer her child's Statement to an Educational Health and Care Plan (EHCP).

However, the very fact that the 2015 SEND Code of Practice emphasises parent and pupil voices can create challenges that all SENCos will have to face. For example, one SENCo described a difficult situation whereby parents struggled with the notion that their child might have been eligible for a Statement but would not now meet the criteria set by the local authority for an ECHP. This was a child who had been diagnosed as having ASD but was '*managing quite well in the classroom, working slightly below expected levels but working on the Key Stage 1 curriculum with support*'.

In this particular instance, the mother was unhappy that her son had not been assessed by an educational psychologist and was not willing to accept the fact that the school had been told that educational psychologists in that particular local authority were focussing on children who were likely to get an ECHP. This is a difficult situation for any SENCo, and perhaps particularly challenging for a SENCo new to the role. While the legislation specifies mediation structures with respect to decisions made once an EHCP had been requested, little is done to prepare SENCos for the mediation skills required for the role itself. As one SENCo described it *'we have to let parents know that we can't just jump on the CAMHS wagon'* (Child and Adult Mental Health Services now appear to be a primary route to an EHCP in many local authorities). Indeed, many SENCos expressed concern that *'Children who need support but don't meet the criteria for an EHCP can fall into "no man's land"'* (primary school Inclusion manager) and that we should not get to the point where, due to cuts in local authority resources, *'children need a label to get access to services'* (special school SENCo).

School governors also talked about concerns around the link between labels and funding. While fully acknowledging the need for schools to focus on Quality First teaching, and using devolved funding to support needs via the graduated approach, at least one governor felt that the only way to keep some children in the mainstream sector was via a label that would lead to an EHCP. For children with Social, Emotional and Mental Health (SEMH) needs, this can become a vicious cycle. One young person with needs that linked to SEMH described a situation where a lack of understanding of their needs led to what she felt were discriminatory behaviours. It would seem that, at times, schools can give the impression that *'if they cannot label it, they cannot deal with it'* (young person who left compulsory education last year).

Similar comments were made by SENCos in special schools who raised concerns that the *'CAMHS thresholds are not being met by many children in mainstream, resulting in children with Mental Health difficulties being overlooked'* and that *'there is a difference between educational needs and medicalised "assessed needs"'* (special school SENCo).

Equally, given that:

The School Admissions Code of Practice requires children and young people with SEN to be treated fairly.
(Section 1.28, *SEND Code of Practice: 0 to 25 Years*, 2015)

the experiences of one parent, who was attempting to find out why reasonable adjustments could not be made for her daughter who was transitioning from a secondary school to a sixth form college, make for depressing reading. The daughter had needs that are covered by the Code of Practice criteria of:

... a physical or mental impairment which has a long-term and substantial adverse effect on their ability to carry out day-to-day activities.
(Section xviii, *SEND Code of Practice: 0 to 25 Years*, 2015)

Using this definition, reasonable adjustments would have to take the nature of the need into account in a more person-centred manner; unfortunately this was not the case. The college had protocols for reasonable adjustment that were limited to a fairly narrow student profile and did not seem willing to adapt these. The parent had approached the SENCo of the college three times, asking for a written explanation as to why reasonable adjustments were only being interpreted with regard to physical and resource-led adjustment, while suggesting that both the Disability Discrimination Act (2005) and the Equality Act (2010) invite more person-centred interpretations. She received no reply. As the date of enrolment drew near, the parent 'gave up' under the impression that the college did not want her child and might, therefore, treat her unfairly.

In relation to this, a number of questions have been raised by SENCos and governors about the impact of academisation, with one SENCo asserting that *'academies can set their own admissions codes – results will drive these choices'* (primary school SENCo). It will be interesting to see whether these concerns will materialise over the next few years.

The fourth theme – strategies for improving outcomes for pupils with SEN and/or disabilities – could be viewed in terms of individual interventions, designed by a SENCo and, at times, delivered by a teaching assistant with very little input from the teacher. Yet, some of the SENCos demonstrated a desire to go beyond deficit-focussed withdrawal sessions.

An example of this was given around another piece of small-scale research which was conducted by a school governing body in relation to home-school communication. In this instance, the research did not stem from a concern about something that was fundamentally flawed; home-school communication was seen to be a strength of the school and, therefore, something that was worthy of deeper analysis. This case was unique for two reasons, firstly, it is uncommon for a governing body to engage in school-based research projects; this is the first example that we have heard of. Secondly, the fact that governors were able to discuss a piece of research that they had decided to conduct had the potential to revolutionise the school culture and encourage reflection on the ways in which each teacher could support children and their families. In this school, discussions around the progress of all children was recognised as the responsibility of each class teacher.

Therefore, while many SENCos, including those new to the post, might be tempted to focus on areas of concern, the professionals approached for this book were clear about the conditions within which this could be successful. For one newly appointed SENCo, *'the fact that I can do mixed ability teaching with a challenging year group, and not just talk about it, makes a difference'* (primary school SENCo). This SENCo went on to contrast her position with *'someone telling you what to do when they are the people who walk the corridors rather than doing the job themselves'*.

In contrast, a very experienced Inclusion manager recognised the value of the respect that she had built up with her colleagues over a number of years, reflecting that *'it must be quite daunting for new SENCos to have to ask people to do something that they don't want to do'* (primary school Inclusion manager). Interestingly, the support of a like-minded head teacher was, once again, seen to be crucial.

Head teacher support, and willingness to assume ultimate accountability, were also commented upon in several conversations as reducing pressure with regard to Ofsted inspections. Given the section in the *Ofsted School Inspection Handbook* on pupils who have special educational needs and/or disabilities (2016: 55), a lack of support from the head teacher would make the role of the SENCo very challenging. Three items specified in the handbook require thoughtful consideration by senior leaders, governors, SENCos and Inclusion managers:

1. Inspectors will consider the progress of pupils who have special educational needs and/or disabilities in relation to the progress of all pupils nationally with similar starting points. Inspectors will examine the impact of funded

support for them on removing any differences in progress and attainment. The expectation is that the identification of special educational needs leads to additional or different arrangements being made and a consequent improvement in progress.

2. Inspectors will consider whether any differences exist between the progress and attainment of pupils in resource-based provision and those with similar starting points who have special educational needs and/or disabilities in the main school. Inspectors will report on any differences and the reasons for these. When considering any whole-school published data on progress and attainment, inspectors will take into account the impact that a large number of pupils in resource-based provision might have on these figures.

3. For groups of pupils whose cognitive ability is such that their attainment is unlikely ever to rise above 'low', the judgement on outcomes will be based on an evaluation of the pupils' learning and progress relative to their starting points at particular ages and any assessment measures the school holds. Evaluations should not take account of their attainment compared with that of all other pupils.

(*Ofsted School Inspection Handbook 150066*, August 2016: 55)

All of the SENCos that we spoke to had additional provision for children with SEND for one-to-one interventions beyond the classroom and teaching assistant support within the classroom. In addition, all SENCos and Inclusion managers had detailed provision maps for each child in receipt of additional support, including those with SEND. In most cases, the provision maps were created by the class teacher and monitored by the SENCo / Inclusion manager with a typical rationale being that *'teachers have got to own it'* (primary school Inclusion manager).

However, systems and processes of this nature can often become meaningless: bureaucratic pieces of paper filed on a shelf to prove to external bodies that pupil progress is being considered. There is a need to reconsider the effect and impact of such processes within the busy school setting: to re-evaluate the purpose and values of the education that we are providing to the pupils within our schools, and how those processes are currently contributing to the development and evaluation of practices and experiences which are enhancing the lives of children with SEND and enabling them to make progress and achieve in the broadest, most holistic, sense of the term.

As mentioned earlier, if we are not careful, the SENCo role, and issues relating to provision for children with SEND more generally, are seen as very separate to other whole-school practices and systems. The SENCo, therefore, can end up working separately, reacting to situations as they arise, while trying to understand and meet the needs of pupils with SEND more fully. In the words of one SENCo, *'the systems are crucial, of course they are, but the big challenge is to make them work'* (special school SENCo).

Resource-based provision in the secondary school context was seen to be a little more complex. In general, SENCos, Inclusion managers and governors of secondary school provision accepted the need for 'SEN Departments' due to streaming for English, Mathematics and Science. These departments tended to run funded 'catch-up' group-work but some SENCos expressed discomfort about a system that encourages teachers to *'see students with SEND as somebody else's problem*' (secondary school SENCo). However, most of these professionals saw '*no other way in a system driven by attainment rather than achievement*' (secondary school Inclusion manager).

In a climate such as this, one has to question whether the SENCo is seen to be wholly responsible for the outcomes of pupils with SEND; as one SENCo put it '*Instead of being the person who coordinates the provision, I am having to be the provision*' (secondary school SENCo).

A consequence of such realities is that the SENCo cannot be the sole champion of Quality First teaching. While it should go without saying that:

> The quality of teaching for pupils with SEN, and the progress made by pupils, should be a core part of the school's performance management arrangements and its approach to professional development for all teaching and support staff.
>
> (Section 6.4, *SEND Code of Practice: 0 to 25 Years*, 2015)

it could be argued that, if this were the case, SENCos would not have to be the provision or '*battle with staff about doing their one-page profiles*' (primary school SENCo).

One Inclusion manager in a primary school setting recognised the importance of specialist input for specialist interventions but maintained that '*the sessions that I run on Quality First teaching are the most crucial for all staff*'. Whether this reflects concerns about Initial Teacher Education (as discussed in the *Carter Review of Initial Teacher Training*, DfE, 2015), performance cultures or other factors will be explored further in the final chapters of this book.

One route to evolving a less instrumental culture is via the remodelling of the school workforce; in particular, rethinking the role of the teaching assistant. One SENCo described an innovative project that she undertook with a large group of teaching assistants in her setting. Prior to the project, the SENCo was aware of growing tensions across, and between, the teaching assistants around role demarcation and the degree to which each staff member felt valued. She was aware that challenges of this nature are unlikely to be resolved quickly and started with regular meetings with the teaching assistants to discuss, fairly informally, their views about their role within school. The SENCo described these conversations as '*informal yet professional*', covering a wide range of topics from job specifications to pay. She described the difficulties of some of these discussions as 'wrinkles' that needed to be overcome rather than insurmountable barriers.

Surprisingly, one of the tangible outcomes of this process involved the reintroduction of an appraisal system; rather than seeing appraisal as a judgement of capability, the teaching assistants expressed the view that appraisals of performance required a time commitment to which they did not feel entitled. The first stage towards this involved a review of job specifications with the whole team. Three meetings were spent on this and the TAs appeared to enjoy thinking about what was required by their contract, including what they did do and anything that they did not currently do. From this, some difficult conversations ensued about pay differentials with the SENCo acknowledging the importance of the National Award (with respect to thinking about coaching strategies and management styles) in helping her to get through these meetings.

The final stage of this project involved the class teacher setting targets for the TA in their classroom, one of which was related to personal development. A concern here, for the SENCo, was that she had spent a considerable amount of time and energy on improving self-esteem across the group of teaching assistants, over which she now had little control. Fortunately, as a set of Professional Standards for Teaching Assistants were introduced in June 2016, a framework for target setting was available. Although non-mandatory and non-statutory, these standards:

> sit alongside the statutory standards for teachers and headteachers and help to define the role and purpose of teaching assistants to ensure that schools can maximise the educational value and contribution of employees working directly with pupils.
>
> (UNISON et al., 2016: 3)

For example, a teaching assistant may perceive themselves as having a different role in creating an inclusive classroom than a classroom teacher. Therefore, differing views from all those involved in a setting need to be actively sought, rather than focussing on the most vocal or powerful. In all, this project was a huge undertaking, and certainly not for the faint-hearted, but the SENCo had a vision for her school and was developing coaching and leadership skills along the way.

Other Inclusion managers and SENCos expressed similarly long-held visions. In some cases these related to *'setting up systems that might not be required officially but that benefit the child'* (primary school Inclusion manager) and in others, simply to *'be willing to have those difficult conversations with colleagues who are not working in the best interests of the student'* (secondary school SENCo). Most, however, emphasised the fact that they were *'a teacher first and a SENCo second'* (primary school SENCo).

Indeed, it was clear, from the conversations with all stakeholders, that a major attribute of a good SENCo is the ability to continually ask questions and to take a lead in areas where they are passionate about the outcomes. One SENCo described this as creating a role that enables her to meet the needs of the pupils *'without having to be ruled solely by school policies and bureaucracy – I don't want to sit at the round table"* (primary school SENCo) and another described the value of being on the senior leadership team *'as it allows me to steer policy for the benefit of the pupils'* (primary school SENCo). These differing views demonstrate there is no single way to enact the types of leadership that impacts upon all learners, including those with SEND. When the first version of the National Award was conceived, much was said about the need to ensure that the SENCo was a member of the senior leadership team. It would now appear, given the content of these conversations, that this may not make a difference to the influence that a SENCo has on school practice; this issue is discussed in greater detail in the chapter on leadership in this book.

In essence, the points of view expressed here demonstrate a need to be reflective, to question practice and to keep the child at the centre of the process. We have heard about a move away from recommending what you should do with children (strategies, programmes or interventions based on theory X or theories X, Y and Z) towards the importance of maintaining a questioning attitude which can help guide decisions on how all members of a school community respond to children or young people at a more fundamental level. In the words of one SENCo,

> *I like to write about what has happened during the day, it helps me to map out my trains of thought, of what I am going to do with information or how I'm going to sit down with a colleague to talk about things or to resolve conflicts. Everything ends with a question mark – it is what informs how I digest what has happened in the day – helps me to frame what I will do tomorrow.*
>
> (primary school SENCo)

Although this SENCo was new to the post, working through questions in an open-minded way is likely to be a highly beneficial for any professional at all stages of their career. The ultimate aim of this endeavour is to help forge a considered response by professionals towards all children, including those with SEND: one where you have 'thought through' your actions, decisions and reasoning.

Clearly, in the examples discussed above, each SENCo sought to find a way to meet the needs of the children in their school within the structures and strictures of their particular setting. Allied to this, it is worth remembering that, if challenged, few teachers would disagree that:

> Teachers are responsible and accountable for the progress and development of the pupils in their class, including where pupils access support from teaching assistants or specialist staff.
>
> (Section 6.36, *SEND Code of Practice: 0 to 25 Years*, 2015)

Or that:

> High quality teaching, differentiated for individual pupils, is the first step in responding to pupils who have or may have SEN. Additional intervention and support cannot compensate for a lack of good quality teaching.
>
> (Section 6.37, *SEND Code of Practice: 0 to 25 Years*, 2015)

In this sense the classroom not only operates as a space for learning; the role of the teacher also includes being an agent of socialisation and promoting values, aspirations, and behaviours that prepare students for the adult world. As such, it cannot be ignored that the teacher is also a significant agent of social welfare, safeguarding vulnerable students, and promoting ideas of equality and diversity.

Yet many of the conversations, particularly those with parents, disavowed this viewpoint. In response, it is worth considering an interesting project designed by a SENCo in a special school that has relevance for SENCos struggling to get teachers to take greater responsibility for all of the learners in their class.

In general, children who are taken out of their class for extra support have a one-page profile. So while all of the SENCos and Inclusion managers talked about ensuring that the one-page pupil profiles were child-centred 'living' documents rather than forms that were *'kept in a folder on the shelf and never looked at from one term to the next'* (primary school SENCo), this SENCo outlined an experiment in which the staff in her school took this one stage further.

She described a training event that involved all staff members completing a one-page profile for themselves. The benefits of this activity were twofold: firstly, the teaching teams were able to see the value of the one-page profile, as she explained *'this is not in the standards, it isn't necessary but it made a real difference to class teams'* (special school SENCo). However, a powerful, and unanticipated, benefit of the exercise only came to light once the activity was completed. From what was a short and relatively simple task, she realised that:

> *I now know the people who want to have one-to-one conversations, the people who prefer emails, those that are happy to come in early but want to leave on time due to child care commitments. We learned that this has a direct impact on the children because if we have got a happy team who are working to their strengths and the best of their abilities, they are going to get the best out of the pupils.*

If this activity were to be replicated in a mainstream setting, it might be a useful way to encourage teaching staff to see all of the pupils in a more holistic manner, rather than viewing some of them as having 'difficulties' that require intervention beyond the classroom.

Projects of this nature enable SENCos to explore possibilities, and a truly reflective SENCo will look beyond their initial expectations in order to see the potential of the unexpected. Where this can be achieved, meeting the needs of children with SEND can become fully embedded within a whole-school approach that seeks to meet the needs of all pupils and identify and address progress and underachievement strategically and systematically through a unified whole-school approach.

In an era where schools are required to work more closely with Health and Social Services (which may highlight differences in priorities with respect to organisational structures, professional practice and financial arrangements), a lack of clear structure to determine responsibilities in inter-agency working can create tensions when resources are under pressure. These concerns are more relevant than ever in the current climate and are indicative of the pivotal position of the SENCo.

In summary, Part A of the Learning Outcomes demonstrates that in fulfilling their responsibilities, a SENCo needs to have a strong knowledge base, operational skills, leadership qualities and an understanding of the controversies that continue to be part of any discussion regarding teaching and learning. The days of the SENCo being *'the person with the keys to the resources cupboard'* (primary school SENCo) are well and truly over.

References

DfE (2015) *Carter Review of Initial Teacher Training.* London: TSO.
DfE/DoH (2015) *Special Educational Needs and Disability Code of Practice: 0 to 25 Years.* London: DfE and DoH.
HMSO (2005) *Disability Discrimination Act.* Retrieved August 2016 from: www.legislation.gov.uk.
HMSO (2010) *The Equality Act.* Retrieved August 2016 from: www.legislation,gov.uk.

HMSO (2014) *Children and Families Act*. Retrieved August 2016 from: www.legislation.gov.uk.
National College for Teaching and Leadership (2014) *National Award for SEN Coordination: Learning Outcomes*. Retrieved August 2016 from: https://www.gov.uk/government/publications/national-award-for-sen-coordination-learning-outcomes.
Ofsted (2016) *School Inspection Handbook 150066*. London: Ofsted.
UNISON, NAHT, NET, MPTA, RTSA (2016) *Professional Standards for Teaching Assistants: Advice for Headteachers, Teachers, Teaching Assistants, Governing Boards and Employers*. London: UNISON.

5 Achieving the National Award for SEN Coordination (Part B): Leading and coordinating provision

Fiona and Graham Hallett

This section of the National Award covers five areas related to leading and coordinating provision.

1. Working strategically with senior colleagues and governors.
2. Leading, developing and, where necessary, challenging senior leaders, colleagues and governors.
3. Critically evaluating evidence about learning, teaching and assessment in relation to pupils with SEND to inform practice and enable senior leaders and teachers to develop their own practice.
4. Drawing upon external sources of support and expertise.
5. Developing, implementing, monitoring and evaluating systems.

These areas represent a significant increase in the focus on strategic leadership than was evident in the first version of the National Award, indicating a vision for SENCos beyond simply coordinating provision across their setting.

The first theme – working strategically with senior colleagues and governors – highlights the need for systems to support, and develop, all members of the school community. Often, despite a succession of initiatives, policies, and legislative frameworks to ensure that practice does meet the needs of all learners, there are children who, in the words of one SENCo, *'fall through the cracks in the system'* (secondary school SENCo). Concerns of this nature highlight the need for SENCos to focus upon strategic leadership without getting bound up in process management in order to ensure that they do not simply perpetuate existing systems.

This Learning Outcome has the potential to empower SENCos who would rather focus on broader issues around teaching and learning as a means to meeting the needs of all pupils. A number of SENCos were not particularly keen on one-to-one interventions as the primary response to children who were not making progress. This was exemplified by a primary school SENCo who reflected that:

> *I can see the perceived benefits of small group work and one-to-one sessions but I have yet to be convinced that over the time that a child is in primary school this feeds back into closing the gap between them and their peers – I see much more worth from a child being immersed in it with everyone else, and having that feeling of 'that is what I am, this is what I do, this is where I am at, and that is OK.'*

While virtually all of the SENCos and Inclusion managers expressed similar views, historic practice was certainly seen as '*a barrier to change. Some people say "This has worked before, why are you trying to change things?"* (secondary school SENCo). In this regard, one Inclusion manager commented that '*once they get it in their minds that this child has Dyslexia or this child has ADHD, they see them as someone I should be looking after rather than a member of their own class*'. This observation resonated with other SENCos who reported that '*teachers, and even parents, want an assessment if a child is not keeping up with the rest of the class*' (primary school SENCo) or that '*I know that the mantra is that every teacher is a teacher of children with special needs but it doesn't always work like that*' (secondary school SENCo).

As mentioned before, despite clear guidance that:

> The purpose of identification is to work out what action the school needs to take, not to fit a pupil into a category.
> (Section 6.27, *SEND Code of Practice: 0 to 25 Years*, 2015)

It can be difficult to change a school culture that is seen to have worked in the past, whether or not that practice was equitable.

When analysing resistance to change, in order to work more strategically with senior managers, one SENCo expressed concern that '*teachers often do not have the confidence, or belief, that they can meet the needs of all children in their classroom*' (secondary school SENCo). This raises important questions about Initial Teacher Education (as noted in the *Carter Review*, DfE, 2015) or around forms of learned helplessness that can be created by teachers who already feel pressurised by a need to '*get the grades rather than worrying about a child who is never going to show up on the 5 GCSEs list*' (secondary school SENCo).

This may leave SENCos, and Inclusion manager's in an invidious position; whatever benchmarking instruments a school uses to set targets, national expectations of attainment data are, according to Ofsted, 2016, there to inform rather than to dictate the process of personalised target setting. Thus any analysis of progress for a pupil with SEND has to be informed by teacher knowledge of overall ability. If this analysis is left to the SENCo, it is inevitable that partial information, in limited contexts, will be used to set targets that may not inform classroom practice.

As argued by an Inclusion manager in a primary school setting: '*If you really wanted to be inclusive, you would have to have the staff all on-board and fully trained.*'

Another SENCo, constrained by a prevailing performativity culture, was concerned about having to run a SEN department that focussed on a small number of staff taking responsibility for all of the students on the SEN Register. When reflecting on what would happen if the SEN department was disbanded, she expressed concern that '*Some teachers would try very hard to meet the needs of children with SEN and others would just write those children off*' (secondary school SENCo).

A further interesting point was raised by a school governor, when talking about a part-time SENCo who was not based at the school. In an era where multi-academy trusts might elect to have a 'Trust' SENCo, one has to wonder whether it is possible to be a strategic leader in any setting where the SENCo might be viewed as a visitor rather than a core member of staff. While the Code of Practice specifies that:

> The SENCO must be a qualified teacher working at the school.
>
>   (Section 6.85, *SEND Code of Practice: 0 to 25 Years*, 2015)

the term 'working at the school' is clearly open to interpretation. In an example which involved a child with Social, Emotional and Mental Health difficulties who was seen to be disrupting the learning of other children in his class, a school governor described the frustration of the head teacher and part-time peripatetic SENCo in having to '*respond to immediate difficulties rather than being more strategic overall*'. This governor expressed sympathy for the SENCo who:

> *. . . views her primary role as working more closely with individual teachers. She wants teachers to develop the skills and abilities to be able to deal with immediate issues rather than passing them on to her.*

This raises an interesting point, if we move to multi-academy trusts that share a SENCo (this may not be the case but, for the purpose of this chapter, it is worth thinking through a range of possibilities), the ways in which funding mechanisms, and strategic priorities are set will dictate the remit of the SENCo. As such, no matter how strongly strategic leadership is advocated in the National Award Learning Outcomes, a SENCo might find themselves reacting to situations as necessary rather than impacting upon provision across settings.

With regard to this, those SENCos who had completed the National Award talked about how difficult it was '*to know how much funding there is or how it is being distributed*' (primary school SENCo). This is less than surprising given that:

> Schools have an amount identified within their overall budget, called the notional SEN budget. This is not a ring-fenced amount, and it is for the school to provide high quality appropriate support from the whole of its budget.
>
>   (Section 6.96, *SEND Code of Practice: 0 to 25 Years*, 2015)

Where SENCos were members of the senior leadership team, a greater understanding of how the budget was being distributed was clear, nevertheless, a number of the SENCos commented upon the value of '*having to find out about the budget as part of the Award*' (primary school SENCo).

For those less involved in decision making, there was a sense of trepidation around '*having to anticipate what we will need to resource each year*' (primary school SENCo) or '*having little to spare if a child comes on appeal with significant needs but without a Statement or EHCP*' (secondary school SENCo).

In one setting, the school governor talked about being able to fund targeted interventions due to a surplus budget which was the result of '*prudent management over previous years*'. This governor pointed out that schools are encouraged to future-proof spending decisions but that the consequences of being able to fund additional teaching assistants or resources could act as an incentive for the school to be identified as one that could provide emergency placements for children with Social, Emotional and Behavioural Difficulties which, as she pointed out, resulted in *a school that went from a successful inclusive school due to intelligent use of funding to a school teetering on the edge of being able to keep all of the children safe.*

Another SENCO highlighted the tensions that can be created by funding formulae that might not be responsive to the individual needs of a child. For this SENCo, the need to be able to place a child within a recognisable 'category' – typically ASD or ADHD – was leading to having to find the money for external educational psychology reports.

Both of these examples raise fundamental questions around whether control over funding allows you to barter for provision and whether individual needs will become subsumed within a model of category needs. A typical example of the latter was given by the parent of a child who had mental health difficulties that prevented him from entering the school during test or exam periods. These difficulties were clearly covered by the Equality Act definition, as cited in the Code of Practice, as:

> . . . a physical or mental impairment which has a long-term and substantial adverse effect on their ability to carry out normal day-to-day activities.
>
> (Section xviii, *SEND Code of Practice: 0 to 25 Years*, 2015)

In conversation with the class teacher, SENCo and head teacher, the parent expressed frustration that '*it's as though they think he's putting it on*'. A major concern here, is that schools will begin to return to a medical model of wanting a recognisable label for a child. This parent researched the behaviours that her child was exhibiting and decided to return to the school to inform them of the links between what they were seeing and the condition that she had researched. Although the parent reported that she '*was taken seriously after that*', it is difficult to imagine a less confident parent challenging funding and provision arrangements in the same way.

A secondary school SENCo described the use of pupil premium funding as:

> . . . *making a big difference when targeted to specific children and preventing some of them falling back to the degree that the teachers will start to ask for an assessment.*

For some SENCos or Inclusion managers, the intelligent use of funding was firmly embedded in the process of provision mapping where it is recognised that:

> Provision management can be used strategically to develop special educational provision to match the assessed needs of pupils across the school, and to evaluate the impact of that provision on pupil progress. Used in this way provision management can also contribute to school improvement by identifying particular patterns of need and potential areas of development for teaching staff.
>
> (Section 6.77, *SEND Code of Practice: 0 to 25 Years*, 2015)

In the words of one Inclusion manager, '*provision mapping is central to everything. You've got to get that right if you want to support the children properly.*' In this case, provision maps were written by each teacher and then given to the

Inclusion manager and head teacher so that '*I no longer have to chase people for them*' (primary school Inclusion manager). While it could be argued that practice of this type can only be created by the head teacher, a SENCo very new to role argued that:

> *If it helps the children, I will make sure that everyone knows that it has to happen. Everyone knows that I don't ask for anything for the sake of a piece of paperwork.*

> (primary school SENCo)

The second theme – leading, developing and, where necessary, challenging senior leaders, colleagues and governors – highlights the often fragmentary nature of provision for learners with SEN and/or disabilities, with some acknowledgement of the fact that the opportunity to lead provision depends upon the existence of a collaborative ethos. In this regard, the term 'challenge' offers a real opportunity to raise fundamental questions about practice. As articulated in the *SEND Code of Practice*:

> The SENCo has an important role to play with the head teacher and governing body, in determining the strategic development of SEN policy and provision in the school.

> (Section 6.87, *SEND Code of Practice: 0 to 25 Years*, 2015)

A number of SENCos mentioned the value of the National Award in this regard, with one talking about using the Learning Outcomes as levers for change. This SENCo had a vision for provision in her school that was not necessarily shared by more established colleagues. By citing the Learning Outcomes, she was able to point out that parents have a right to hold the school to account and that, as a consequence of this, it was her role to analyse Quality First teaching as a basis for discussions with the senior leader and governors. As a result, she found that '*difficult conversations with colleagues were less contentious than they might otherwise have been*' (special school SENCO).

Another area for strategic debate related to pupil voice and the degree to which each SENCo or Inclusion manager felt that they were in a position to be a change agent in order to overcome the types of inertia that prevent the adoption of good practice.

One primary school SENCo described a situation where she was able to use the Learning Outcomes as a basis for discussion around pupil voice across the school commenting that '*I pointed out that the school council wasn't representing the voice of all children in the school. All children should be able to believe that they have something to contribute.*' She went on to tell us that she was able to talk to all staff '*on a one-to-one basis*' before presenting her ideas to the senior management team. In this example, genuine consultation acted as a first step towards addressing tokenistic practice and this SENCo had the courage to challenge inertia across systems and day-to-day practice.

Staff meetings were another area that came up in several conversations, with particular emphasis on difficulties around the structure of meetings. Several of the SENCos talked about their role in staff meetings tending to take two forms. Firstly, most talked about leading training on different aspects of SEND with one talking about leading discussions around Quality First teaching. This was an experienced Inclusion manager who recognised that *'this would probably be quite daunting for a new SENCO, I just take it for granted and the staff know that I will follow it up'* (primary school Inclusion manager). In stark contrast, a SENCo in a secondary school talked about the difficulties of negotiating practice with subject leaders as *'they are more interested in getting the grades than in making sure that each student has the support to achieve as well as they can'.*

It is easy to assume that this type of difficulty relates only to secondary schools and sixth form colleges, however, some primary school SENCos described the challenges associated with convincing colleagues that grouping children by ability can make many children feel excluded, including those with SEND. An example of this was given by a SENCo who also happened to be the Year 6 class teacher. She described the benefits of modelling inclusive mixed ability grouping with a year group preparing for national exams. On reflection, she realised that:

> *This enabled other teachers to see that I don't just talk the talk which helped me to encourage everyone else to accept new ideas and interventions that are based around the needs of the children.*

When discussing this process, which she had not really examined before talking to us, this particular SENCo explored what was happening in greater detail reflecting upon the potential for role conflict. In her case, being an inclusive teacher was, in her own words *'who I am'* but this does raise questions for SENCos who may feel the need to conform to 'grade expectations'. Taking on the SENCo role can prove to be a daunting responsibility but by living her convictions, this SENCo realised that *'those that lead by example have greater credence than those who lead by status or position'.* This is an important message for those SENCos who may feel unable to challenge school priorities in a meeting; leading by example can convince people more easily than giving direction.

In turn, this signifies important opportunities when undertaking the National Award; we often take our successes for granted while focussing on areas of difficulty but by taking the opportunity to reflect in the depth required for a Master's level award, successes can be built upon in order to begin to address the more challenging aspects of the role.

As mentioned earlier, critical reflection also gives an insight into the overlapping and interactive nature of the Award Learning Outcomes. While these sections are dealing with particular Learning Outcomes that are the focus for each part of the Award, this is not to ignore the potential each section has to enable critical reflection of the overall role of the SENCo and the complex interplay between coordination and strategic leadership. Alongside any benefits in terms of achieving the Award, this approach more naturally reflects the role itself; the most effective leaders do not atomise responsibilities; rather, they look for areas of cohesion in order to create a coherent culture. Whether this comes naturally, or has to be learnt, is irrelevant, the important thing is to realise that a successful leader maintains a vision of what they want to create.

The third theme of this section of the Award – critically evaluating evidence about learning, teaching and assessment in relation to pupils with SEN to inform practice and enable senior leaders and teachers to develop their own practice – enables the SENCo to evidence their vision (or adapt it where necessary). It is one thing to move from writing a provision map to getting teachers to write their own provision map, but going beyond reviewing what has been written by each teacher requires deeper levels of analysis. Indeed, to simply move from a system where teachers file the provision map written by the SENCo, to a system where the SENCo files what has been written by the teacher, is of little value in the long term. One opportunity afforded by completing the Award relates to the Master's level requirement to analyse evidence. Obviously, this will include evidence gathered in the school, but the need to read about models of leadership or inclusive practice (to take just two examples) will hopefully become a working habit. One SENCo discussed this in terms of thinking about collaboration by reflecting that:

> *Before I did the Award, I thought of collaboration as something you do with other agencies but I realised that I should be thinking about all types of collaboration. Maybe with just one teacher and a TA or between children.*
>
> (primary school SENCo)

Other SENCos who had recently completed the work talked about *'the value of focussing on one child in order to complete an assignment'* (special school SENCo) or *'looking at target setting across the school'* (secondary school SENCo).

Helpfully, for this SENCo, the Code of Practice makes specific reference to the fact that:

> The National Curriculum Inclusion Statement states that teachers should set high expectations for every pupil, whatever their prior attainment. Teachers should use appropriate assessment to set targets which are deliberately ambitious.
>
> (Section 6.12, *SEND Code of Practice: 0 to 25 Years*, 2015)

which enabled her to point out that she was not simply talking about separate provision. Nonetheless, as every SENCo will realise, the need to challenge colleagues to have high expectations for children with SEND can be daunting.

For example, many schools make the strategic decision to assign a teaching assistant to a particular class to ensure consistency and continuity between teacher and teaching assistant. However, in some cases, support from a teaching assistant was described as becoming disjointed due to several classes 'sharing' support, resulting in effective communication often being hindered due to time constraints. An example of this was given by one SENCo who described the common practice in secondary schools of assigning teaching assistants to subject areas. In this case, the difference between subjects posed the most significant pressures as:

> *In English, Maths and Science, where the students are set by ability, the teaching assistants run interventions with the catch up set, but in Design Technology or ICT, which are mixed ability, they can work with individual students in the classroom.*
>
> (secondary school SENCo)

While accepting the situation, this SENCo expressed frustration that '*it's difficult to support students equitably within a setting environment*'.

Similarly, a SENCo based in a primary school explained that teaching assistants had been moved '*back into classrooms*' in order to reduce the amount of one-to-one withdrawal work. In this example, many of the teaching assistants had originally been employed to work one-to-one with Statemented children who had since left the school. In order to retain high quality support staff, each TA had completed different specialist qualifications (for example, around Dyslexia or speech and language difficulties) with their skills being used more generally across the school. In some cases, the teaching assistant worked in a classroom that included children with specific needs that aligned to their qualification and in others, the teaching assistant acted as a conduit between external experts and class teachers.

Both of these SENCos highlighted the benefits of having teaching assistants in the classroom rather than '*in the SEN room*' while showing caution about '*risking the teacher handing responsibility for the children with SEN to the TA*' (primary school SENCo). The challenge here, as mentioned previously, is to ensure that all teachers realise that they:

> Are responsible and accountable for the progress and development of the pupils in their class, including where pupils access support from teaching assistants or specialist staff.
>
> (Section 6.36, *SEND Code of Practice: 0 to 25 Years*, 2015)

This can become even more problematic when teaching assistants have developed very specialist areas of expertise.

One SENCo discussed the importance of whole staff training in this regard. The school ran extensive training around adopting a person-centred approach to developing high quality one-page profiles. One of the strategic benefits of this project was that the school leaders decided to create booklets of one-page profiles for each year group rather than limiting these to students in the SEN register. In some ways, this approach could be seen to be the reverse of the need to:

> establish and maintain a culture of high expectations that expects those working with children and young people with SEN, or disabilities to include them in all the opportunities available to other children and young people so they can achieve well.
>
> (Section 1.31, *SEND Code of Practice: 0 to 25 Years*, 2015)

In this instance, the whole-school population benefitted from provision that might have been limited to children with SEND, demonstrating the importance of recognising that including children in the activities available to others can take many forms.

The fourth theme – drawing upon external sources of support and expertise – was both a source of tension and of innovative practice. At one level, concerns were raised about the slimming down of local authority support services yet, at another, some SENCos decided to create different forums that value the knowledge of a wide range of people enabling the school to learn about itself and its practices. One SENCo in a special school talked about a recent situation which involved the senior leaders in her school thinking about the benefits of joining a multi-academy trust. Having met with the CEO of an existing trust, she formed the opinion that the trust was interested in incorporating a special school in order to draw upon expertise rather than in developing inclusive and collaborative working practices. As a result, her school made the decision to offer outreach services – including training, observations, practical advice and parent/carer workshops – thus increasing links with mainstream settings on their own terms.

As a leader, this SENCo was able to influence these changes by creating opportunities that demonstrated, persuasively, the need for change and the wider benefits of any change. This innovation has the potential to reduce competition between schools that can evolve from a lack of clear vision for inclusion; building productive networks with other SENCos can be one way forward in an increasingly performative educational culture.

From the mainstream point of view, unless collaborative practices of this type already exist, the temptation to '*buy in expensive services*' (primary school SENCo) may prevail. From '*spending more than £500 for a single educational psychologist assessment*' (primary school Inclusion manager) to '*having to find the money for some training from a speech and language therapist*' (primary school SENCo), drawing upon external sources of expertise appeared to cause financial concerns.

The fifth theme – developing, implementing, monitoring and evaluating systems – covers everything from individual interventions to strategic engagement with the school governing body. It is understandable that some SENCos, particularly those new to the role, will focus upon pupil-level systems rather than stepping back to see how these are framed by whole-school ethos. However, the whole tenor of the Learning Outcomes encourages much more.

Where SENCos talked about working with school governors, they predominantly described regular updates, often used to ensure that governors meet their responsibilities, such as:

> The governing bodies of maintained schools and maintained nursery schools and the proprietors of academy schools must publish information on their websites about the implementation of the governing body's or the proprietor's policy for pupils with SEN.
>
> (Section 6.79, *SEND Code of Practice: 0 to 25 Years*, 2015)

Yet it was heartening to hear that some governors were keen to explore the opportunities that they had to engage with the school beyond requirements of this nature. For example, one SENCo discussed the fact that the governing body had recently approved funding for an educational psychologist in order to set up school protocols. Given the previously described concerns that educational psychologists were '*increasingly thin on the ground*' (primary school SENCo) and that '*we can't get hold of a psychologist to see individual children*' (secondary school SENCO), it was refreshing to see a SENCo working closely with the school governing body in this way. Redefining how we use external expertise is central to the ways in which we move practice forward and this SENCo (and her school) were turning a potentially challenging circumstance into an opportunity for improved practice.

So, while aspirations were, quite rightly, expressed by governors with respect to wanting to '*Oversee that all that was required by the new changes has been completed and that the school was compliant with new legislation*' (primary school governor), it could be argued that the SENCo is well placed to challenge the governing body to see beyond what *should* be done in order to consider what *could* be done. This can be difficult in times of legislative change where governors are overwhelmed by '*long-winded processes that appear to have been set up to reduce the number of students on Statements*' (primary school governor). As governors are, in general, volunteers who take on a role for altruistic reasons, it is important that the school makes full use of this human resource. One governor, who was particularly interested in becoming the governor with responsibility for SEND, described a particularly frustrating experience with regard to professional development. Having attempted to join a professional development course on legislative change, he was disappointed to find that the local authority had cancelled the training in order to ensure that they had the most up-to-date information. The governor accepted that this was understandable but was less than impressed when the subsequent course was cancelled due to confusion over the number of attendees. Similarly, a SENCo in a secondary school had offered governor training and was disappointed that only one governor attended (who subsequently became the SEN governor for the school). These experiences may be pointing to a missed opportunity for SENCos to engage more fully with the governing body who, after all, are giving their own time to support school development. Indeed, there are dual motives for developing a constructive relationship between the SENCo and the SEN governor/governing body. Firstly, strong links enable both to fulfil their duties as outlined above and, secondly, potential benefits can only be fully realised when the SENCo and governing body share the same vision.

At the whole-school level, all of the conversations emphasised the relationship between head teacher interest in inclusion, and the school climate. In addition, some SENCos recognised the value of being treated as a leader and being respected as such. One example of this involved the head teacher being attuned to potential difficulties and '*heading them off at the pass so that I don't become the big bad wolf*' (primary school SENCo). This is not to say that inclusive climates are only going to develop if the head teacher has a particular commitment to inclusion, but in a world of competing agendas, the SENCo is duty bound to explore ways in which equality prevails. An Inclusion manager in a primary school setting described a manageable demarcation of responsibility where the head teacher and school governors developed the accessibility plan '*as it would be difficult – and beyond my role – to do that*'. Some SENCos in the same position might feel obliged to take responsibility for such tasks themselves, if asked, which might produce a completed form rather than a leadership team effort.

In terms of middle management, many SENCos talked about an intersection of roles with one focussing upon '*joint planning with year and subject leaders*' (secondary school SENCo) and another on '*the importance of middle tier management in changing the culture*' (primary school SENCo). This SENCo reflected upon the fact that '*not everyone has to be on the senior leadership team*' which might, arguably, be a better recipe for progress than the move to ensure that all SENCos are members of the SLT. She was clearly of the opinion that SLT membership can shackle a SENCo to a performativity culture stating that:

> *Thinking about areas of management and leadership has allowed me to have an insight into how to manage change. Working with the middle tier I'm better able to pre-empt potential conflict. Knowing staff members allows me to predict friction points.*

Nonetheless, for some, being on the senior leadership team *'gives me a say'* (special school SENCo); it is important to recognise that there is no 'one-size-fits-all' scenario.

At the class/pupil level, mention is made, throughout the Code of Practice, of Quality First teaching, and high expectations of all pupils, being the key to ensuring that:

> Schools . . . regularly and carefully review the quality of teaching for all pupils, including those at risk of underachievement. This includes reviewing and, where necessary, improving, teachers' understanding of strategies to identify and support vulnerable pupils and their knowledge of the SEN most frequently encountered.
>
> (Section 6.37, *SEND Code of Practice: 0 to 25 Years*, 2015)

Those SENCos who conceptualised this target from the 'Assess, Plan, Do, Review' perspective, mentioned throughout the Code of Practice, appeared to be able to break the *'they're not my responsibility'* mantra. As familiar concepts, it is easy to overlook the degree to which we engage with these elements of teaching and learning in a way that promotes inclusive practice.

The first step – 'Assess' – is familiar to all SENCos, the differences articulated in the conversations that we had with SENCos and Inclusion managers demonstrated a range of approaches, such as:

- assessment by external expert
- assessment by trained teaching assistant
- assessment by SENCO
- assessment by class teacher with the support of a SENCo.

The first of these – assessment by external expert – tended to be triggered when the school were concerned that a child was *'falling behind their classmates to a degree that we felt that we needed expert help'* (secondary school SENCo). In these cases, the SENCo described *'receiving a plan of work for the TA to carry out, usually on a one-to-one basis'* (primary school SENCo). There were similarities, here, with the second approach – assessment by trained teaching assistant. Many of the SENCos and Inclusion managers talked about the benefits of having *'in-house expertise to assess things like Dyslexia'* (primary school Inclusion manager) with more than one school having employed an 'SEN TA'. In some instances this was described as a necessary response to reduced local authority support and in others, as a form of professional development for teaching assistants.

The third approach, assessment by SENCO – tended to be highlighted by SENCos who felt that they were *'too busy dealing with the paperwork to be able to work with the children any more*' (primary school SENCO) or by SENCos who were worried that '*teachers don't see that the assessment strategies that they already use can be adapted for children with SEN*' (secondary school SENCo). In this sense, some SENCos raised concerns about assessment being an exclusionary process, underpinned by a medical model of disability, and with an underlying aim of identifying deficits within individual children as a means of rationing resources for support. For some, unease about the underlying purposes and values of assessment were evidenced by comments such as '*we need to think about inclusive approaches to assessment across the school*' (primary school SENCo).

From 'Assessment', we move to 'Plan'. Only one Inclusion manager talked about class teachers taking responsibility for planning teaching activities for all children, including those with SEND. At the other end of the continuum, two SENCos, working in schools that appeared to have deeply embedded structures privileging attainment (rather than achievement), described '*having to do all the planning for the children on the SEN register*' (secondary school SENCo). As secondary settings tend to be organised by subject, one of these SENCos was resigned to the fact that '*it is difficult for me to put in subject-specific plans which means that whatever I write might be ignored as irrelevant*'.

These concerns were very closely linked to the third step – 'Do'. Most of the SENCos and Inclusion managers, regardless of the particular personalised target setting approach being used, talked about the expectation that pupils will make some level of progress as a direct result of being actively engaged in an intervention activity, rather than whole class teaching.

In some cases, this seemed to be a reflection of concern that the teacher's judgement about the level of progress each pupil makes was often problematic or that:

> *the systems in our school have always been designed around children being taken out of class to work with a teaching assistant if they have a target relating to a special need, even if that need could easily be met in class.*
>
> (primary school SENCo)

This raises an interesting issue; while some class teachers clearly argue that they do not have 'need-specific' knowledge, it has to be assumed that all would claim a high level of pedagogical understanding. While inclusive pedagogy is discussed in more depth later in this book, arguably pedagogical knowledge is, at the very least, the art of teaching that encompasses the development of relationships that promote learning, curiosity and intrinsic motivation. Ultimately, teaching and learning practices that create experiences that are effective in engaging a diverse range of learners, and schools that support such approaches, will clearly be well placed to develop more inclusive practices. The involvement of all stakeholders is vital in order to achieve an inclusive, accessible learning environment, where learners are equally aware of how they learn and what they are learning. If children with SEND are removed from class in order to receive an 'intervention', it could be argued that the class teacher loses an opportunity to further develop their pedagogical skills and the school loses the opportunity to make all members of the school community feel valued and respected.

The implications of this for the fourth aspect of the cycle – 'Review' – are somewhat obvious. In schools much emphasis is placed on the analysis of numerical data, for example, improvements in reading scores, yet such data can tell you very little about why a pupil makes progress. For one SENCo, this *'absolute focus on scores'* (primary School SENCo) was a source of tension while for another, *'the opportunity to get class teachers to review results'* (special school SENCo) afforded the chance for genuine collaboration. In this case, the SENCo recognised the value of using test outcomes as a starting point for more in-depth discussions about the processes and experiences that had led to these outcomes. In this way, he was able to introduce a broader range of information that had emerged from people's accounts of 'what happened' and 'why it happened'. The importance of this was captured by a primary school SENCo who argued that *'we need to reflect upon particular events or observations that have challenged or informed our thinking'*.

Inevitably, SENCos and Inclusion managers will need to consider how to work strategically with colleagues in order to develop an approach to working which ensures the involvement of all in the discussion and agreement of shared inclusive values and principles. As such, contradictions between what a SENCo is attempting to achieve and what is possible in a particular setting – which might be conceptualised as role dissonance – could lead to the development of collaborative and creative communication strategies that might enable role clarification from the ground up. One Inclusion manager described this process as *'gaining the trust and respect of other teachers in order to be able to challenge poor practice without being seen as a manager'* (primary school SENCo). In this sense, each example discussed in this section offers an insight into ways in which SENCos can develop, use, monitor and evaluate systems in order to move their role from that of coordinating provision towards one which involves leading, developing and supporting colleagues to recognise the value of exploring more inclusive practices. As one SENCo suggests: *'no one can be an expert in everything and perhaps that's a good thing, expertise should be pedagogical NOT diagnostic'* (primary school SENCo). Given that more than one SENCo commented on the fact that the SENCo is the only member of staff that (currently) has to be a qualified teacher, this reflection seems particularly important:

> This gives us the opportunity to focus upon inclusive rather than specialist ways of being. If I'm the only person who has to be a qualified teacher, my expertise as a teacher should be at the forefront.
>
> (special school SENCo)

This SENCO raised concerns about mainstream school referral, stating that:

> Evidencing the use of funds in mainstream is weak. At times, lack of knowledge, engagement and responsibility in the mainstream sector is staggering. Quality First teaching is a useful concept, mainstream teachers need to focus upon that before trying to define a child as having SEN.

As other SENCos and Inclusion managers appeared to see special schools as *'somewhere that the children might end up in order to go to get access to specialist resources'* (primary school Inclusion manager), the focus upon Quality First teaching, from one of the SENCos currently working in a special school setting, lays down an important gauntlet. If teachers view the Assess, Plan, Do, Review as something that enhances their own pedagogical practices, the SENCo has the space to lead discussions around Quality First teaching rather than '*what resources do we have for a child with X?*' (primary school SENCo).

In all, this part of the Learning Outcomes enables SENCos and Inclusion managers (even in the more restrictive environments) to bring a particular aspect of the role to the attention of senior leaders and school governors; to *challenge* practices that are based upon deficit models of teaching children with SEND and to exemplify inclusive practice in their own teaching and learning interactions. Whether these opportunities come from '*the need to publish what we do on the website*' (secondary school SENCo) or the fact that '*the SEN governor is on board*' (primary school SENCo) is less important than the fact that all SENCos have a remit for strategic leadership.

In the words of one SENCo:

> *When I talk to other SENCos, those that have been in the role for a long time, I realise how lucky I am to be able to say that I need to do something in order to achieve the Award. Once I had done that, it kind of became an accepted part of what I do.*

> (primary school SENCo)

Part B of the Learning Outcomes offers this opportunity. For those SENCos who work in settings that make this aspect of the role fairly straightforward, the challenge is to extend the degree to which they can make a pedagogic difference. For those working in more restrictive environments, the challenge is to begin to make in-roads wherever possible; the desire to make a difference being the common aim.

References

DfE (2015) *Carter Review of Initial Teacher Training*. London: TSO.
DFe/DoH (2015) *Special Educational Needs and Disability Code of Practice: 0 to 25 Years*. London: DfE and DoH.

6 Achieving the National Award for SEN Coordination (Part C): Personal and professional qualities

Fiona and Graham Hallett

This section of the National Award brings elements of Part A and Part B together with a particular focus on:

- high expectations for all children and young people with SEN and/or disabilities;
- person-centred approaches that build upon and extend the experiences, interests, skills and knowledge of children and young people with SEN and/or disabilities;
- *the need to ensure that* the voice of children and young people with SEN and/or disabilities is heard and influences the decisions that are made about their learning and well-being;
- family leadership where parents and carers are equal partners in securing their child's achievement, progress and well-being.

In effect, in line with the 2015 *SEND Code of Practice*, these Learning Outcomes seek to put the child, and family, at the centre of decision making.

While it is somewhat obvious to say that teachers should have high expectations for all children and young people with SEN and/or disabilities, one SENCo based in a special school setting, as mentioned in Part B, argued that *'Quality First teaching is a useful concept, mainstream teachers need to focus on that before trying to define a child as having SEN'*. This is an interesting comment worthy of further reflection in this section. If, as a result of reduced local authority services, children need a label in order to access specialist support, it could be argued that teachers are pre-empting the kind of intervention processes that lead to labelling. As such, SENCos based in mainstream settings may face unforeseen challenges. This was exemplified in one conversation where the SENCo described *'having to set up withdrawal interventions even when I don't believe in them or don't think that they are needed'* (secondary school SENCo). In most cases, provision mapping was seen as one way in which practices of this nature could be challenged. One SENCo, based in a large primary school, described provision maps as being based upon Pupil Profile targets but, increasingly, being owned by the class teacher. While acknowledging that *'teachers sometimes struggle with the management of Pupil Profiles'*, she was able to argue that:

> . . . when targets are set by the teacher, with the intention of feeding into main classwork, staying away from separate targets, literacy targets, for example, the overall needs of each child can be met across all activities.

In her school, the move to 'teacher owned' provision maps had been a two-year project but, over time, had incorporated *'pupil voice and input from the Teaching assistant or anyone else working with the child'*; they are also reviewed weekly. As this development had proved successful, with children being able to *'reflect on how they have done'*, there were plans to extend the system across the whole school with the ultimate aim being:

> ...*for children to be much more articulate about how they are feeling about their learning – how do we label it? How do I feel about what I have just produced? How would I describe it?*

Initiatives of this nature, wherein good practice for children with SEND amounts to good pedagogic practice for all, place the SENCo at the centre of whole-school development.

Another approach, that may be of interest to those new to the role, involved a SENCo working with a 'SEND teaching assistant' to monitor the progress of children who they felt *'may just be getting lost in everything that is happening in the classroom'*. This approach involved the teaching assistant working with children on an individual basis for a whole range of activities *'but not just the children with a Statement or Education, Health and Care Plan'*. (primary school SENCo). The SEND teaching assistant produced reports on progress at the end of each term which were reviewed by the SENCo and class teacher in order to *'see what needed doing in the classroom – what could be learnt from the report'* with the class teacher then resuming full responsibility for the child.

Each of these approaches aimed to achieve the same outcome, that is, to empower teachers to take responsibility for all of the children in their class, and to hold to account those who absolved themselves of responsibility for children with SEND. In the words of one primary school Inclusion manager, when reflecting upon the support given to a particular child:

> *One-to-one support all the time is not Inclusion – nor is it moving him towards being included in a mainstream High School – it only serves to manage his anxiety.*

This Inclusion manager expressed concerns that *'external advice that focusses on one-to-one support only serves to marginalise him'*, thus highlighting the double-edged sword of labels.

Alongside these philosophical concerns, some SENCos and Inclusion managers also pointed out the impracticalities of targeted support that *'becomes difficult to actually do when the support is student-specific and clashes with timetabling'* (secondary school SENCo). This SENCo gave the example of a child with high functioning ASD who was in the *'higher stream for maths and science but in the lower stream for subjects like Design Technology'*. While children with an Education, Health and Care Plan might have specified one-to-one support, it may be the case that *'more creative ways of using the funding can do more for the child than simply taking them out for Maths or English'* (primary school SENCo). This raises an interesting point about parents now having more control over how funding is spent; extensive conversations with the pupil, and their parent(s), might result in more inclusive and innovative approaches to teaching and learning.

A small-scale research project that had been conducted by a SENCo in a special school has been referred to in other sections of this book. When reviewing Annual Review processes, this SENCo analysed pupil participation in their Annual Review meeting. Pertinent to this section of Learning Outcomes, one thing that she discovered was that class teachers had been asked to write a general report on the child but that this was not reflecting their Statement of Special Educational Need. On further examination, she realised that many of the teachers had never seen a copy of the Statement. There is very little difference, here, between teachers in a special school being unaware of the details in a Statement of Special Educational Need (or EHCP) and teachers in a mainstream setting being unaware of individual pupil profiles. Clearly, this lack of awareness can lead to lowered expectations of children with SEND.

Pertinent to this, a secondary school Inclusion manager described class teachers as *'setting very low targets for the pupils, as though they aren't capable of anything beyond the basics'*. Her concern, here, was that some of the children with special educational needs in relation to cognition and learning were developing challenging behaviours *'because they were bored'* and were then being identified as having Social, Emotional and Mental Health difficulties. Whether this situation had arisen from a *'lack of knowledge, engagement or responsibility'* (special school SENCo) is unknown, however, these conversations certainly point to the need to accept that attitudes will exist that might inhibit high expectations for all children. One young person with a Social, Emotional and Mental Health condition described the reality of not wanting to become *'the weird kid in the corner'* remarking that:

> *I never told anyone so I was never given support but equally so, I never asked for it. When I was really bad, it was quite obvious that something was wrong and yet I was never approached in any way. I know it's not easy for teachers but more education on basic signs would be really useful. If the teachers, including the SENCo, knew more about signs of mental health difficulties, they would deal with it with a lot more confidence rather than just going with what they think or what they've heard.*

One reaction to such concerns is for the SENCo to explore the attitudes of colleagues – perhaps in particular those colleagues who seem unable, or unwilling, to set high expectations for students with SEND – and challenge school leaders and governors to develop a school ethos that demonstrates a belief that:

> High quality teaching, differentiated for individual pupils, is the first step in responding to pupils who have or may have SEN. Additional intervention and support cannot compensate for a lack of good quality teaching.
>
> (Section 6.37, *SEND Code of Practice: 0 to 25 Years*, 2015)

In line with this, one SENCo remarked that *'you don't want children to feel insignificant'* (primary school SENCo), and another that *'I don't like that we have a ceiling on expectations'* (secondary school SENCo). Contrary to attitudes that serve to limit ambition for children with SEND, these SENCos were advocating a climate that recognises, and extends, the skills, aptitudes and talents of all. Furthermore, another secondary school SENCo discussed the need to reflect upon *'how the children with SEN can get involved in activities that are available for children in the school who do not have SEN'*, noting the need to change attitudes as a necessary pre-condition to changing practice strategically.

A sense of the SENCo as change 'champion', acting as an advocate, rather than a provider, of high expectations and Quality First teaching came across in almost all of the conversations. For one SENCo, this involved challenging a dual-level assessment system and *'removing the situation where some children have learning evidenced in their pupil profile whilst others have that evidence in their books'* (primary school SENCo), describing this battle as being as much about *'equality and identity'* as it was about high quality teaching for all.

A starting point must be for teachers to maintain high expectations for all children and discuss these with both the child and his/her parents; a consequence of this being that some settings may need to develop new conceptualisations of leadership and management. When the first edition of this book was published, in 2010, few SENCos talked about challenging senior managers around standards of teaching and learning; it is encouraging to now see that the National Award is focussing more clearly on the potential for SENCos to provoke positive change for all children.

Nonetheless, as pointed out by a school governor, change may have unintended consequences and constant evaluation is required to prevent these *'creating bigger problems than before'*. Significantly, this governor was keen to establish accountability procedures when initiating change. In her own words, *'my job is to enable the people in school to do their job and to support them'*. She talked about observing lessons and having an input into staff appointments describing the impact of change on a governing body as leading to *'increased professionalisation as opportunities, and challenges, demand'* (primary school governor). A clear assumption, in the Code of Practice, is that all members of the school community need to think about the opportunities and challenges that can become the impetus for changes that benefit all children. The examples given, from our conversations with a wide range of stakeholders, signify a real appetite to embrace positive change across the whole-school community.

This leads to the second theme – person-centred approaches that build upon and extend the experiences, interests, skills and knowledge of children and young people with SEN and/or disabilities. In most conversations, person-centred approaches were exemplified by the ways in which SENCos were developing the one-page profile. These developments ranged from *'using websites so that the child can choose their own format, for example,* SpongeBob SquarePants' (primary school SENCo) to *'Starting from "What does a good day look like and what does a bad day look like?"'* (secondary school SENCo). In these conversations, drawing upon the interests of the child was seen as being *'key to making it truly person-centred'* (special school SENCo). One person who had been through the education system, commented that:

> *It really depends upon the person, the options should be there but it really should be the child's choice. I would not have wanted the teachers to know, I would have worried that it would make people treat me differently and you just wouldn't want it. Especially when you are young, you don't want to be the*

odd one out and you just want to fit in and make friends. You don't want to be the one left on their own and I was worried that if the teachers knew, then they might make you that person.

It is all too easy for the teacher to propose an intervention without exploring whether the child would actively want that kind of support. Aligned to this, one SENCo linked child-centred approaches to being a reflective practitioner:

The job has become so difficult now if you can't take whatever has happened and be analytical about it and put it into some form of perspective, you lose sight of the child.

In a similar comment, an Inclusion manager argued that:

I do not think you can survive as a teacher if you do not have an ability to reflect on yourself, on the experiences you create, the experiences you have, I don't think it is possible to do the job properly if you don't do this.

(primary school SENCo)

It is encouraging that all of the SENCos who had completed the National Award talked about the importance of having to reflect at Master's level, in order to *'think about the bigger questions'* (primary school SENCo) and to *'explore what we mean by terms like person-centred'* (special school SENCo). However, in some cases, SENCos appeared to feel thwarted by *'systems that pay lip service to what the child wants'* (secondary school SENCo) or by the attitudes of colleagues *'who don't really care, I'm worried that they would write the children off if I wasn't here'* (secondary school SENCo).

It may be the case that the term 'person-centred approach' has become meaningless, the use of terms of this nature becoming so commonplace that we no longer stop to think about the degree to which our practice mirrors our language. The same might also be said for the terms 'Inclusion', 'equality' or 'discrimination'; unless we constantly reflect upon these – very complex – concepts, we run the risk of other agendas driving our practice.

For example, discrimination by stereotyping is commonplace with respect to individuals with SEND but may not be seen as particularly problematic by all teachers. In this sense, we can learn much from the young people and parents themselves, who often expressed frustration that *'to say that all autistic children need routine is an oversimplification that needs to be challenged'* (parent) or that *'some teachers generalise when they hear a label, they assume that they understand what it is like because they have heard about it'* (young person).

Likewise, the possibility that interpretations of Inclusion or equality depend upon personal situated-ness must be explored by the truly reflective SENCo – including those that are *'overwhelmed by the bureaucracy'* (primary school SENCo).

If we acknowledge that teachers bring their own experiences and views to the classroom, and will interpret the same practice in a range of ways, we must also recognise that what is person-centred for one child might not be the same for another – even if both children have the same 'label'. One parent illustrated this point when expressing concern that *'teachers don't always notice that my child is an individual, she is funny, kind and likes the same things as other children'*. Indeed, whether particular spaces or practices are inclusive or not, very much depends on who is experiencing them, who is witnessing them and who has the power to do anything about them. One young person described teachers as *'the most important witness'* arguing that:

> They see things whereas the SENCo, for example, doesn't necessarily know all of the children that well, doesn't know everyone but teachers see the same class every day, or every couple of days and can see changes that are really important.

This is a sobering thought for those SENCos working within a culture that *'refuses to acknowledge that all teachers are teachers of all children'* (primary school SENCo). Perhaps it could be argued that, for some teachers, other agendas take precedence over this quite fundamental belief.

As mentioned above, one SENCo conducted a piece of small-scale research on pupil involvement in their Annual Review with the intention of making the Annual Review process *'more child-centred'*. From a starting point of children not attending their Annual Review, this SENCo decided that she *'wanted to make the one-page profile about them and not just about what other people think about them'*. While many SENCos, quite understandably, identify a spectrum of barriers to gaining the views of the pupils, this SENCo used a wide variety of communication aids creatively. One outcome of this process was that the children wanted to pick the drinks to be served at Annual Reviews and attend at least part of the meeting. While this might not sound like a hugely significant change, it was important for this child and, therefore, was important for the SENCo. This approach extended to the meeting, itself, where instead of *'just going through the paperwork, we listened to each other in order to formulate ideas around the table'*.

Another aspect of person-centred planning worthy of consideration, here, relates to how we define SEND and whether we need a specific label in order to plan additional support. Given that:

> Many children and young people who have SEN may have a disability under the Equality Act 2010 – that is '. . . a physical or mental impairment which has a long-term and substantial adverse effect on their ability to carry out normal day-to-day activities'. This definition provides a relatively low threshold and includes more children than many realise: 'long-term' is defined as 'a year or more' and 'substantial' is defined as 'more than minor or trivial'.
>
> (Section xviii, *SEND Code of Practice: 0 to 25 Years*, 2015)

Person-centred approaches must involve some consideration of how we understand 'long-term and substantial adverse effects' and the degree to which these indicate a special educational need. For example, some children and young people with Social, Emotional and/or Mental Health Difficulties may find it difficult to carry out day-to-day activities. In the words of one young man:

> Teachers should be active in terms of notifying the right people but they shouldn't assume that what they think they know is actually right, that they know what this person is going through. It's not really their job. They see the

children every day so they should see when something is wrong but that doesn't mean that they have to know what is wrong, they just have to know that something is wrong. It's less important that they understand the whole scenario than that they observe it and do something about it.

Responses in these circumstances, whether decisions, actions or behaviours, can often be inequitable. While this is understandable in a climate where the focus is upon *'whether they meet the criteria for an EHCP assessment'* (primary school SENCo), the need for senior leaders to challenge inequitable responses to some forms of SEND is a moral, and legal, imperative.

This concern may be most problematic in schools that stream by ability – most commonly in secondary education. For instance, descriptions of a 'top stream' student may be based on characteristics such as 'hard working', 'accepting of authority', and 'academically successful', while the descriptions used for the 'catch-up stream' student might include terms such as 'struggling', 'disinterested' or 'not coping'. These perceptions have the potential to influence the way that teachers engage with students and may, in the worst cases, lead to interactions that exacerbate needs. Some young people talked about *'not wanting to drink water as I was terrified of using the school toilet'* or *'becoming exhausted by the end of the day'* commenting upon the fact that some teachers might be less than tolerant of these behaviours.

In such cases, it is difficult to see how practice can be described as person-centred, building upon and extending the experiences, interests, skills and knowledge of all children and young people, including those with SEN and/or disabilities. In the words of one SENCo, *'it does not take an adult to label them'*.

It may well be that legislative changes and developments introduced to extend diversity and equality have acted to reduce the potential effects of labelling described in these examples. However, the suggested re-introduction of selective schooling, as part of the raising standards agenda, might prompt us to return to research findings that discuss the unintended consequences of similar systems (for example, grammar schools).

In an era of competing political agendas, it might be difficult for some school leaders to remember that:

> Public bodies, including further education institutions, local authorities, maintained schools, maintained nursery schools, academies and free schools are covered by the public sector equality duty and, when carrying out their functions, must have regard to the need to eliminate discrimination, promote equality of opportunity and foster good relations between disabled and non-disabled children and young people.
>
> (Section xix, *SEND Code of Practice: 0 to 25 Years*, 2015)

Those SENCos working in local authorities that still use the 11+ testing system, in order to allocate grammar school places, expressed real concerns about increased levels of discrimination and reduced levels of equality of opportunity. While we continue to have school climates where *'Some people kind of push you away as they think you're a bit weird'* (young person), we should, in the words of one Inclusion manager *'be very wary of the future, of what it means for kids if we become even more focussed on performance'* (primary school Inclusion manager). Given that current political mantras link the proposed return of selective schooling to a desire for all children to excel in terms of academic attainment, one has to wonder what the outcome will be for those children who do not fit this mould.

This brings us to the third theme, the need to ensure that the voice of children and young people with SEN and/or disabilities is heard and influences the decisions that are made about their learning and well-being. Voice, as it is used in this statement, is more than simply allowing children and young people to share their feelings; crucially, the Learning Outcome specifies that the voice of students should *influence* the decisions made about their learning and well-being. One young person described this, very clearly:

> *It should always be what the child wants. Sometimes decisions are taken out the child's hands which is really a bit stupid because, at the end of the day, it's their needs and most of the time they know what's best for them more than most other people.*

Many of the SENCos and Inclusion managers talked in detail about systems that had been set up to enable children and students to express their opinions. In some cases these systems had become a central part of current practice in their school, and in others, inherent complications in the case of pupils with additional needs were raised as a concern. An example of this was given in relation to a child with very limited verbal communication skills where '*the tendency is to let her teaching assistant talk for her*' (primary school SENCo). In contrast, another SENCo talked about '*challenging systems that are simply disrespectful*' echoing comments made by many with regard to the expectations that we have of '*someone like Stephen Hawking*' and those that we have for children that require alternative avenues for communication. It might be argued, therefore, that the rights of the child, even when clearly and aspirationally defined, can be difficult to enact. As exemplified in these comments, we cannot accept the marginalisation of pupils where the voice of the child is lost, either because it cannot be elicited or because it is misunderstood or where a proxy voice, for example, that of the teaching assistant, is heard in preference.

In this way, the National Award challenges us to consider the value given to the voices that surround the pupil. In the busy school or classroom, practice develops in unforeseen and sometimes chaotic ways without staff realising that this is the case. This has the potential to produce missed opportunities, difficult relationships, and competing perspectives, where the desire to reach out and help a young person is overshadowed by other agendas. It is certainly true that many SENCos talked about '*competing agendas*' (secondary school SENCo) and '*the need to listen to the child over the noise of everyday life*' (primary school Inclusion manager) illustrating the fact that the urgent often overtakes the important.

One SENCo described using Pupil Passports as a means to '*encourage children to take more ownership and responsibility for managing their learning journey and needs*' (primary school SENCo). In an attempt to encourage staff to use the Pupil Passports more effectively, targets were set more frequently '*to move away from the IEP system where the children were stuck with a target for a whole term*'. This SENCo pointed out the need to be '*a bit more savvy with tightly focussed targets for a week or fortnight, then move on if they are not working and revisit things with a different focus*'.

A particular area of difficulty, raised by a number of the SENCos and Inclusion managers, related to transition points, either between school settings or moving from one age phase to another. In all cases, the need to access pupil views were paramount and three cases, in particular, demonstrate a range of challenges, responses and points for reflection.

The first case involved a child being withdrawn for one-to-one intervention sessions. On the one hand, the child talked very positively about having enjoyed the intervention but, on the other, the SENCo talked about:

> *That moment when they have to leave the room to go out for their interven-tion, you can see it on their face, they feel embarrassed about having to leave the room even if they get a lot out of the one-to-one session.*
>
> (primary school SENCo)

This scenario will be familiar to many teachers; the degree to which the interven-tion outweighs excluding the child for any part of the lesson is always question-able. In this instance, the SENCo talked about *'building up a child to feel bold enough to say "I can be a part of this, I don't need to be left out", I want our children to get to this point'*.

Another example of creating systems that enable children and young people to gain confidence is the willingness of staff to hear their voice related to the experiences of children on their first day at a new school. The SENCo of this school explained that, as part of the pastoral care system, the first day of each academic year was given to new students. She reflected on the fact that this allowed all of the students, including those with SEND, to feel properly welcomed into the school and to talk to staff about their hopes or concerns prior to the return of the rest of the school. As this activity had been designed for all stu-dents, the school were able to avoid the situation where they were forced to contrive specific support days for a group of children who already feel 'differ-ent'. In this case, the SENCo was instrumental in identifying and eliminating common forms of marginalisation while working in a system which can so easily be compromised by pragmatic solutions. While recognising that her school was committed to a number of practices that could be described as exclusionary, this SENCo was able to see ways in which an environment could be adjusted towards one in which pupil voice is seen as central to the life of the school.

Like many of the conversations described in this section of the book, this SENCo talked about being hampered by a school climate that, intentionally or not, suppressed the voices of some students while privileging others. In some cases, SENCos and Inclusion managers related this to the language used with, and about, children or to more subtle messages conveyed to them about what really counts in a school context. At times these behaviours were described as ignorant and at others as *'well-meaning but not really helpful'* (special school SENCo). For those new to the role, it is worth remembering that:

> *It's not trying to understand someone, but just trying to understand that they're different from you and that everyone requires different treatment in order to succeed.*
>
> (young person)

It was heartening to hear SENCos talk passionately about wanting to be advocates for children and young people, to *'make people listen'* (primary school SENCo) and to *'just get everyone to stop and think about how the children see things'* (secondary school SENCo). In terms of this section of the National Award, these Learning Outcomes can be seen to afford SENCos a range of opportunities to improve practice by inviting participants to reflect upon their own practice and on systems within their experience that rely on collaboration, communication and teamwork.

The third example of the challenges inherent in transition involved a child being moved to a setting following exclusion from another school. This was a particularly fraught experience for all involved; the school was under the impression that this would be a temporary measure, the local authority appeared to see this as a fixed solution and neither the child, nor his parents, appeared to have a voice in the process. Unfortunately, the transition was not successful and it transpired that the school were unable to meet the child's needs within their current resources. In order to safeguard the needs of all of the children on roll, the school decided that the new pupil required two-to-one support due to his behaviour but the local authority were unable to fund this. Eventually, the school and local authority agreed that the child had to be permanently excluded and the child was moved to provision that his parents were unhappy with. The final outcome was the child was removed from this provision and schooled at home. In situations like this, where short-term solutions disintegrate with speed, it can be impossible to 'hear' the voice of the child at the centre of what was clearly a difficult situation for all. Indeed, it could be argued that systems for capturing the voice of children with challenging behaviours might be the least developed of all.

In each of these cases, the interplay between culture, attitudes and practices served to amplify, or silence, the voices of the children involved. As such, each of these incidents could serve as a starting point for SENCos wishing to question claims to collaboration, inclusivity and negotiation within their own practice.

This brings us to the final theme in this section of the Learning Outcomes – family leadership – where parents and carers are equal partners in securing their child's achievement, progress and well-being. If it is difficult to see the world through the eyes of the children that we teach, it can be even more challenging to attempt to see the world from the viewpoint of the parents of children with SEND. One parent talked of the sense of isolation when you have a child with SEND reflecting that:

> *You no longer socialise with the same set of people. They often talk about their child meeting this milestone or that milestone and you know that your child might never be able to do that.*

Many teachers, or indeed SENCos, may never think about this, about the very real obstacles facing the parents of children with SEND. For those that do, parental voice will be seen as crucial but parental leadership may be a new concept altogether. At the most basic level, this involves genuine recognition that:

> *Parents know their children best and it is important that all professionals listen and understand when parents express concerns about their child's development.*

> (Section 6.20, *SEND Code of Practice: 0 to 25 Years*, 2015)

Another parent pointed out that SENCos in a mainstream setting could act as a parental advocate – both educationally and socially – in order to:

> *Signpost groups that other parents might not be aware of. When your child is in a special school, you get to hear about support groups but I know that the parents of children with special educational needs in mainstream schools don't always know about them.*

In this regard, the SENCo could be an agent for information-sharing, which was evident when talking to SENCos working in schools that had strong links with other schools in their locality. In one example, a cluster of SENCos had been meeting once a term to discuss areas of interest, and expertise, with one Inclusion manager commenting that:

> *I can't believe that . . . school is just around the corner and I'd never really spoken to their SENCo. They know so much about autism that they have been able to support us in practical ways which means that one little girl will be staying with us now rather than moving to a special school and we now have much better conversations with Mum and Dad.*

This move towards family leadership and more equitable home/school partnerships is long overdue, as evidenced in a conversation with one parent who talked about having to home-school her child in response to a perceived lack of teacher understanding. This parent, on finding out that her child had autism, had attended a specialist course in order to find out more about how her child's needs could be met. Following an extensive training course, she visited some local schools in order to make a decision about which setting would best meet his needs. Unfortunately, both schools, although specialist, fell short in terms of staff knowledge of autism, resulting in her deciding that her only option was to home-school. At a time where '*more children are coming through with a diagnosis of autism*' (primary school SENCo), one would hope that the first recourse for specialist input would be to approach the parents/carers and, where possible, the child or young person themselves with an open, enquiring mind.

Integral to this is the expectation that:

> Schools should meet parents [of children with SEND] at least three times each year.
>
> (Section 6.65, *SEND Code of Practice: 0 to 25 Years*, 2015)

And that

> These discussions should be led by a teacher with good knowledge and understanding of the pupil who is aware of their needs and attainment. This will usually be the class teacher or form tutor, supported by the SENCO.
>
> (Section 6.67, *SEND Code of Practice: 0 to 25 Years*, 2015)

In all but one interview, the latter point was described as '*difficult*' (primary school SENCo) and '*nigh on impossible*' (secondary school SENCo).

Nonetheless, where schools effectively communicate their vision and take the time to listen to parents:

> These discussions can build confidence in the actions being taken by the school, but they can also strengthen the impact of SEN support by increasing parental engagement in the approaches and teaching strategies that are being used.
>
> (Section 6.66, *SEND Code of Practice: 0 to 25 Years*, 2015)

The National Award can be useful in this regard. By engaging with modules that explore the *'importance of collaboration and reflection'* (secondary school SENCo), SENCos have the opportunity to *'stop and think more clearly about Inclusion – to think about what this actually means'* (primary school SENCo). The National Award was also talked about in terms of *'not letting the time pressures get in the way of thinking'* (primary school SENCo). A number of SENCos worried that *'if I'm not careful, I would spend all of my time on paperwork, phone calls, meetings, tracking and monitoring'* (special school SENCo), citing the Award as *'an opportunity to remember why I am doing the job in the first place'* (secondary school SENCo).

A further benefit of the Award was identified as *'getting to know the new legislation inside out'* (special school SENCo), however, for some this became a source of discomfort. An example given by a SENCo based in a secondary school setting explained that the Code of Practice specified that meetings between the school and parents with Education, Health and Care Plans should be conducted by the class teacher. The SENCo had asked all form tutors, who should, in theory, have the most rounded understanding of the pupil, to hold these meetings, in order to provide an opportunity for the parent to share their concerns and, together with the teacher, agree their aspirations for the pupil. She was met with such strong opposition and resistance to this request that she eventually held all of the meetings herself, a situation that did not bring any reaction from the senior management of the setting. When reflecting upon this, she commented that *'they* [the teachers] *think they don't have enough knowledge of SEN to talk to the parents'*.

This SENCo was in an unenviable position recognising that:

> At times, parents, teachers and others may have differing expectations of how a child's needs are best met. Sometimes these discussions can be challenging but it is in the child's best interests for a positive dialogue between parents, teachers and others to be maintained, to work through points of difference and establish what action is to be taken.
>
> (Section 1.7, *SEND Code of Practice: 0 to 25 Years*, 2015)

Yet, even knowing this, the SENCo was struggling within a system that failed to see the links between practice, dialogue and achievement.

At first glance, SENCos new to the role may feel that the Code of Practice includes too many recommendations. However, another way of thinking about this is to view the Code of Practice from a parent's perspective. If all of the recommended actions are addressed, and the system increases parental confidence, the benefits for SENCos will outweigh the '*everyday tussles with colleagues about what is important*' that seem to be all too frequent (primary school SENCo). As new models of parent partnership begin to emerge, it can only be hoped that the strategic role of the SENCo will encourage school leaders to rethink how they engage with all parents, including the parents of children with SEND. For some SENCos, the greatest challenge will be to encourage the whole-school community to work more respectfully with parents; for others, the greatest challenge may be to ensure that teachers see the potential of children with a range of special educational needs. Some of the conversations with parents highlighted concerns that although the Code of Practice asserts that:

> Families need to know that the great majority of children and young people with SEN or disabilities, with the right support, can find work, be supported to live independently, and participate in their community. Health workers, social workers, early years providers and schools should encourage these ambitions right from the start. They should seek to understand the interests, strengths and motivations of children
>
> (Section 8.5, *SEND Code of Practice: 0 to 25 Years*, 2015)

some teachers only appeared to uphold these aspirations '*for those children who will be able to achieve exam results*' (parent).

One SENCo utilised support from key-workers with a view that '*we don't want parents to get hung up on the label*' (primary school SENCo) and another emphasised the importance of the school leading Annual Review meetings in order to avoid medicalised conversations, acknowledging that, rather than asking experts to run meetings:

> Reviews led by the educational institution will engender the greatest confidence amongst the child, young person and their family.
>
> (Section 9.175, *SEND Code of Practice: 0 to 25 Years*, 2015)

Allied to this are progress meetings between staff and parents that are not related to Annual Reviews. While these can often be fraught, for example, one Inclusion manager talking about '*a parent wanting an EHCP in preparation for a move to High School . . . just in case*' (Inclusion manager in a primary school), the value of these conversations cannot be underestimated. This was a tricky situation, balancing parental leadership with what might be perceived as unrealistic demands, which can lead to difficult conversations. Nonetheless, trust can only be gained when supportive home/school conversations become '*part of the fabric of what we do*' (primary school SENCo).

One SENCo described the flip-side of this conundrum – where the school felt that a child required additional outside support and the parent disagreed. He dealt with this via '*graduated conversations, not just springing things on parents but listening to what they want*' (primary school SENCo).

Alongside these challenges, it is important to recognise that the views that the teacher brings to the classroom about pupils, their families and the communities from which each student hails, can easily influence the ways in which they approach conversations with parents. For example, all teachers have their own personal history and heritage that may, or may not, coincide with the backgrounds of the parents of their pupils. Examples of divergence in perspectives, including those that proved to be extremely challenging for a number of SENCos, related to two areas of need – autism and behavioural difficulties. With regard to autism, comments varied from '*Mum wants a label but he is doing fine*' (primary school Inclusion manager) to '*It can be difficult for some teachers to accept that you might know more than they do*' (parent).

With regard to behaviour, SENCos and Inclusion managers described the difficulties of '*differing expectations of behaviour – they don't all have ADHD*' (primary school SENCo) and:

> *Some of our parents have challenging behaviour, you can end up in very confrontational circumstances when they don't want to accept our advice.*
>
> (secondary school Inclusion manager)

Again, the need to have a balanced overview, strong home/school links and an openness to the views of all is paramount when working with parents who may be finding it difficult to communicate with some members of school staff.

In all, this section of the Learning Outcomes evidences a changed perspective around SEND, with the emergence of ways of thinking that challenge the power of professionals in making decisions on provision, placing that power much more firmly in the hands of young people and their parents. For those SENCos open to reflection, this will come naturally; in the words of one SENCo:

> *Reflections are quite easy for me as I write a lot as I go, so even now I will go home and write about this conversation as it helps me to map what I am going to do with information or for when I sit down with a colleague to talk about things or to resolve conflicts. Everything ends with a question mark – it is what informs how I digest what has happened in the day and helps me to frame what I will do tomorrow.*
>
> (primary school SENCo)

For SENCos who find critical reflection more challenging, the National Award opens a door to a way of being that is more equitable, more thoughtful and, ultimately, more inclusive of the views of all.

Reference

DfE/DoH (2015) *Special Educational Needs and Disability Code of Practice: 0 to 25 Years.* London: DfE and DoH.

PART II

7 Perspectives on Inclusion, disability and 'special educational needs'

Artemi Sakellariadis

'Do you always write your chapters while doing the housework?' Sophia, my trusted writing partner, has arrived to help.

'It helps me think', I say with a smile, putting a duster in her hands. *'Would you mind making a start on these bookshelves?'* I kneel back down and continue brushing the ash out of the wood burner. I intend to give it a thorough clean, ready for when we come to light a new fire. I try to capture some loose fragments of thought, suggesting some sort of significance in clearing away the dust of the past, but Sophia's words return me to the here and now.

'"Voices of inclusion . . . " What is this?' Has she really forgotten the first time we wrote together or is she teasing again?

'Oh, you don't need worry about that.' That is for me to worry about, I silently reprimand myself. It is my doctoral thesis, which has been gathering dust for years. I silently promise myself, once again, to try to have it published.

'Yes, I thought I heard that people aren't bothering with Inclusion any more. Reversing the bias, or something.' The brush falls out of my hand onto the pile of ash under my nose, which prompts a spectacular coughing fit. Sophia brings me a glass of water and waits until I am able to speak again.

'That wasn't what I meant at all!' When someone hands you such a hot potato, it is hard to know where to pick it up from. Should I remind her that the offensive phrase about reversing the bias towards Inclusion (DfE, 2011a) quietly disappeared without a trace after responses to the Green Paper consultation were published (DfE, 2011b) and it became apparent that 'a number of respondents' (ibid.: p. 24), I think the only place in this document where a percentage was not mentioned, said that there never had been such a bias in the first place? Or should I steer our conversation towards exploring the multiple ways in which people understand the word Inclusion in education? This seems a more constructive way forward.

'But surely those who believe Inclusion has had its day are only thinking about the word in its narrower sense; about including disabled children in ordinary schools?'

'Do you mean children who have special educational needs?' I wince but let this go; we can talk about terminology later.

'Well, sort of. But that was only its original meaning, when the word Inclusion replaced the word integration in the 1990s.' Thomas and Vaughan trace the change in terminology, from 'integration' to 'Inclusion', to a meeting in July 1988 when

> 'a group of 14 people from North America who were concerned about the slow progress of integration in education brainstormed around a table at Frontier College, Toronto, Canada, and came up with the concept of Inclusion to formally describe better the process of placing children and adults with disabilities or learning difficulties in the mainstream. This group included educators, writers, parents and disabled adults who had first-hand experience of segregated education. Switching their thinking from "integration" to "Inclusion" at this legendary meeting was indeed a radical gesture and the use of the word Inclusion caught on quickly across Canada and the US. It took a few years for Inclusion to be accepted more readily in the UK and elsewhere'.
>
> (Thomas and Vaughan, 2004: 89)

'Oh, and doesn't it still mean that?'

'Well, for many people it still does. But for others, the word has acquired a much wider meaning over the years, to imply processes that make everyone feel welcome, visible and respected in schools; not only children with impairments.' I consider quoting to her from the *Index for Inclusion*: 'Inclusion is about increasing participation for all children and adults. It is about supporting schools to become more responsive to the diversity of children's backgrounds, interests, experience, knowledge and skills' (Booth and Ainscow, 2011: 9).

'So are you saying that inclusive education is about other minorities too? I thought education had eliminated racism years ago.'

'Schools certainly take racist incidents very seriously but that doesn't mean it has gone completely; and there are others at risk of discrimination or exclusion too. Think of lesbian, gay, bisexual and trans children and young people, for example.' A couple of years ago an Ofsted report showed that disabled and LGBT pupils bear the brunt of bullying in schools, but this is often dismissed by staff as banter even in schools where other forms of prejudice-based bullying are dealt with effectively (Ofsted, 2012).

'Yes, I can understand that. So, for some people Inclusion is about the education of disabled children and for others it is about all equality issues in education. How confusing!'

'You took the words right out of my mouth', I say with a grin, and think I would have added that, in its widest sense, inclusive education is concerned with adults as well as children. There is the added complication that, when the term is used in the context of disabled children's education, it can still be understood in contrasting

ways. For some, inclusive education implies children being in their local school as full participants and active learners. For others, it implies a good education tailored to children's perceived needs and can take place anywhere, even in a separate school away from the child's local community. There is no time to discuss this today, however, and I choose to focus on another common misconception.

'But please don't imagine a number of different minority groups, all distinct from one another.'

'I thought that was what you were just saying.'

'Inclusion is about dealing with a range of equality issues, yes. But that doesn't mean these are embodied in discreet groups. We all have multi-faceted identities. In other words we all have an ethnic or cultural background, a gender identity, a sexual orientation, a religion or belief (or no belief) and may be (or may one day become) disabled.' There is also the cumulative effect to be considered. A recent report suggests that the current system of school exclusions is in breach of the UN Convention on the Rights of the Child and of UK legislation. It identifies disturbing variations in exclusion rates between children with different characteristics and flags up the compounding effect of this: Black boys with labels of SEN who are eligible for free school meals were shown to be 168 times more likely to be permanently excluded than white girls from middle-class families and no labels of SEN (Office of the Children's Commissioner, 2012).

'So who is responsible for all of these issues in schools?'

'It varies. In some schools the SENCo role has evolved to that of an Inclusion manager, who takes on this brief.' I wish I could give every Inclusion manager a copy of CSIE's 'seductively practical' award-winning equality guide that helps schools address prejudice, reduce bullying and promote equality holistically (CSIE staff and associates, 2016).

'Wow, that really is transforming the role of the SENCo!'

'Isn't it just! The trouble is that, with such a wider remit, some aspects of disability equality may slip off the radar. Schools do not always see it as a priority to build capacity to provide for the full diversity of learners.'

'Surely they shouldn't have to! Isn't that what special schools are for?' I bite my lip. Yes, that might be how the idea of special schools originally emerged: to offer what was not available in ordinary schools. But that was at a time when disabled people were thought to have no place in mainstream society.

'That is what many people assume, without necessarily stopping to explore the reasons why things are the way that they are.'

'And you think there is a good reason to avoid sending children to the tailor-made provision that already exists?' I resist the temptation to challenge assumptions about tailor-made provision or to clarify that this is about redistributing, not losing, experience or expertise. At a time when schools are increasingly expected to provide personalised learning, there is no reason why tailor-made provision has to be offered in separate institutions. The issue of mainstream or segregated school placement is often seen as a polarised argument that has yet to be resolved. I see it differently and seize the opportunity to discuss this.

'But, Sophia, don't you see that this is not about what children learn in school?'

'How do you mean? What else could it be about?' I ignore her second question; she might switch off if I were to mention children's rights now.

'I mean that there is nothing that goes on in a special school that cannot take place in an ordinary school.' Perhaps I should add that this is about who you go to school with and the message this gives you about yourself.

'Don't be silly. What about all the specialist facilities that special schools have?'

'Do you mean things like hydrotherapy pools and Snoezelen rooms that some special schools have?'

'Precisely.'

I wonder if I should remind her about the Warnock Report's recommendation that special education should be seen as 'additional or supplementary' as opposed to 'separate or alternative' (DES, 1978). Would Sophia know that this is the thinking that underpinned the Education Act 1981 and the start of the process which was then called integration and later Inclusion (in its original sense)? Or maybe I should mention the alarm bells that the Audit Commission sounded more than a decade ago, effectively saying that the education system was evolving in a direction that had not been intended and does not serve disabled children and young people.

> The existence of separate structures and processes for children with SEN may have allowed their needs to be seen as somehow different – even peripheral – to the core concerns of our system of education. This needs to change . . . 'SEN' must truly become a mainstream issue.
>
> (Audit Commission, 2002)

I decide to say neither but, rather, stay focussed on gently introducing the argument for non-discrimination.

'I'd say if a child needs them, they can still be accessed even if they are not on site. Children have timetabled sessions out of school all the time, for example, to go swimming or play sports.'

'I guess so. But why are you so committed to an idea which deprives children of specialist facilities and staff?'

Now is as good a time as any. I approach this slowly and carefully.

'I don't want to deprive anyone of anything, Sophia. But if some children need specialist facilities – or teachers, or therapists, for that matter – the idea is that this is offered in addition to an ordinary school experience, not instead of it. Otherwise it would be like sending children to hospital and not allowing family and friends to visit, on the grounds that they are getting the professional expertise they need. By sending children to separate special schools we are depriving them of the ordinary school experience itself! They don't get to go to school with their brothers and sisters, friends and potential friends from their local community. They don't learn and develop alongside them, forming friendships that can last a lifetime.' The practice is so widespread that people do not bat an eyelid, but

routinely excluding disabled children from schools, and the widely held belief that this is acceptable, seem to be better suited to last century's social values.

'But what sort of education would they be getting? And how would this be a positive experience? You said yourself that disabled children get bullied.' I postpone talking about the need to transform schools for this to work.

'I did, but in the same breath I said that LGBT pupils get bullied as well. Are you suggesting we withdraw anyone who is at risk of bullying and set up separate schools for LGBT children as well? I don't think so. Personally I'd rather educate people away from prejudice.'

'OK, I'll give you that; you've got a point there. But I still find your suggestion of educating everyone under one roof quite unrealistic.'

'Please don't imagine schools as you know them, educating such a wider range of pupils. Schools would have to transform how they organise teaching and learning, to make sure all pupils receive a good education. But it can be done. Indeed, it has.' I guess it must be very difficult for her to imagine a system so very different to what she has always known. It is true, though, that in other parts of the world education has transformed and all children go to their local school. I remember my 2011 trip to the Hamilton-Wentworth Catholic District School Board in Canada, which closed down all special schools in 1969 and has been successfully educating all children in ordinary schools for more than 40 years (Hansen et al., 2006). I wish there was time to share with Sophia some of the wonderful stories from the schools I had visited!

'But why do you want to change a system that works so well?'

I choose not to challenge her assumption that the system works well. With the exception of the call for separate, signing, schools for Deaf children and young people (Ladd 2003; West 2012), disabled people have, for years, been saying that segregated education does not serve disabled people (Oliver, 1995; Rieser, 2000a; Chib, 2011).

'For a start, let me clarify that it's not just me who says this. The UN Convention on the Rights of the Child, the UN Convention on the Rights of Persons with Disabilities and, closer to home, the Equality Act 2010 all emphasise disabled children's right to inclusive education.' There is so much more I could tell her if we had time! The Committee on the Rights of the Child periodically reviews how the Convention is applied in each country. The UK was last examined in 2016 and, in its concluding observations, the Committee expressed concern that '[m]any children with disabilities are still placed in special schools or special units in mainstream schools' and recommended that the UK should 'set up comprehensive measures to further develop inclusive education' (Committee on the Rights of the Child, 2016: 13–14). In its explanatory General Comment No. 9, on the rights of disabled children, the Committee had stated that disabled children are still 'facing barriers to the full enjoyment of the rights enshrined in the Convention' and that 'the barrier is not the disability itself but rather a combination of social, cultural, attitudinal and physical obstacles which children with disabilities encounter in their daily lives' (Committee on the Rights of the Child, 2007: 2). It also clearly states: 'Inclusive education should be the goal of educating children with disabilities' (ibid.: 18).

With regard to the Convention on the Rights of Persons with Disabilities, Article 24 (Education) state signatories are required to ensure that all disabled children and young people can fully participate in the state education system and that this should be 'an inclusive education system at all levels'. When ratifying the convention in June 2009, the then government issued a declaration which said, among other things: 'The United Kingdom Government is committed to continuing to develop an inclusive system where parents of disabled children have increasing access to mainstream schools and staff, which have the capacity to meet the needs of disabled children' (UK Government, 2009).

'Well, I never!' Sophia seems genuinely surprised.

'And that is not all,' I tentatively add. *'The Equality and Human Rights Commission has recently revealed that hundreds of thousands of disabled people regularly experience harassment or abuse but a culture of disbelief, or "collective denial", is preventing it from being tackled effectively. The EHRC suggested that the government should explore whether segregated education, or inadequately supported integrated education, affects people's perceptions of disability or disabled children's chances of being included within mainstream society (EHRC, 2011).'*

'That sounds like a good suggestion. And has this happened?' I raise my eyebrows in a 'what-do-you-expect?' manner.

'The government said that this would not be necessary because it is the quality of provision that matters, not the type of setting (Office for Disability Issues, 2012). This probably came from an earlier Ofsted report that put forward this finding (Ofsted, 2006). I cannot understand how the Department for Education can be perpetuating a system without knowing – and without being prepared to find out – whether this has an adverse impact on disabled people's lives. Anyway, the EHRC's follow-up report picked up on the contradiction between the positive reporting on disability surrounding the 2012 Paralympics, and the day-to-day reality for many disabled people who are often labelled as scroungers, benefit cheats or "not trying hard enough". It reiterated the original suggestion that the Department for Education should undertake research into the long-term impact of segregated schooling. It also suggested that "schools and colleges should develop material for helping students understand disabled people and the social model of disability, and the prejudice that disabled people face within society" (EHRC, 2012: 27).' I wonder if she has come across the social model of disability. A conventional way of thinking (the belief that some people become disabled by their physical, sensory or mental impairments) has become known as the medical model of disability; a proposed alternative (the belief that some people become disabled by the way our society is organised) is known as the social model of disability (Rieser, 2000b).

'Hmm, it sounds as though the current system is too deeply rooted to be able to change.'

'I am not sure I agree with you. No big social change, be it the abolition of slavery or of child labour, ever happened overnight or took place without resistance. Education has been slowly shifting for many years in this country and abroad.' I wonder if some changes were introduced too soon, so that people have become accustomed to resisting or ignoring them. In the UK, the legal shift

of replacing the 11 categories of 'handicap' with the concept of 'special educational needs' and the suggestion that all children should attend an ordinary local school came just over a decade after the Education (Handicapped Children) Act 1970 established, for the first time ever, that children previously labelled Educationally Subnormal (Severe) should be considered 'educable' and become part of the education system (CSIE and University of Nottingham, 2013).

'So where does all this leave us?'

'Well, I'd say that the question of mainstream or special schools for disabled children is often seen as a polarised argument, but it needn't be. Supporters of a mainstream education for all advocate this in the name of disability equality and the understanding that, if some children are excluded from ordinary schools, prejudice and discrimination will persist. Supporters of special schools, on the other hand, argue that these are needed because they offer provision that is not regularly available in mainstream schools. The two positions do not contradict one another. The first represents a human rights position, the second a partial reflection on existing practice.'

'Now hang on a minute, isn't this taking it a step too far?' She turns so sharply that she accidentally knocks a framed photograph to the floor. I am relieved it did not break; the photo is from a recent outing with a group of old school friends to whom, more than 30 years on, we remain very close.

'Oops, sorry, didn't mean to do that.' She picks it up and puts it back on the mantelpiece. *'But if you claim the moral high ground, it's as if you are saying that to value special schools is a flawed position, unethical even. I cannot agree to sweeping statements about what is right or wrong. My commitment as a teacher is to look at every case separately and do what is best for each child.'* I feel uncomfortable at her use of the word 'case' but let that go. There are far more important issues to pick up here.

'Sophia, of course everyone wants to do what is best for each child. Who wouldn't? The trouble is, we understand children's needs so differently that we end up having very different ideas about what is best for a child.'

'How do you mean? We have had multi-disciplinary assessments for years!' Should I bring up the medical and social model of disability now? No, we are still pushed for time.

'What I mean is that some professionals focus on the differences between children and may foreground a child's perceived need for physiotherapy or speech and language therapy. Others consider similarities as well and may foreground needs shared by all children, for example, to make friends or to learn about collaboration and negotiation.' A voice in my head is screaming for me to add having a sense of belonging to your local community, which most of us take for granted.

Sophia heads for the door and for a fleeting moment I worry she might storm off. Far from it, as it turns out. She tells me she was going to get the vacuum cleaner so we can finish off here but stays rooted in the spot for a good few seconds. Neither of us speaks. She seems to be mulling all this over in her head. She takes a sharp intake of breath, as though she is about to say something, then falls silent again. She lets out a soft, slow sigh before looking up at me again.

'I think you've just put your finger on something very important there. I hadn't thought about this and I agree you've got a point. But then, how do you begin to make these decisions?'

'How would you begin to?'

'By discussing it . . . with . . . the parents? Trying to establish what they consider most important for their child's future?'

'And then what?'

'Organising the right support for the child in the type of setting the parents have chosen? Isn't that what the government means by promising parental choice of type of school?'

It is now my turn to sigh. How can I help my friend understand? A thought suddenly comes to me and I glance at my watch, then look up at her with a smile.

'Sophia, it's late and we haven't eaten, are you hungry?'

'Yeah, starving actually; haven't eaten since breakfast.' We exchange an understanding, if not a bit mischievous, smile.

'Well, let me think. I can make you a ham sandwich or a ham sandwich.'

'Well, that is not much of a choice!' she exclaims, sounding a bit annoyed.

I give her a kind, yet prolonged, 'do-you-get-it-now?' stare and leave the room. The fact remains that special schools are remnants of a different era, when disabled people were thought to have no place in mainstream society (CSIE and University of Nottingham, 2013). Now that our social values have shifted and disability equality is far better understood and accepted in society, isn't it time for education to catch up? The Department for Education insists that it is offering a genuine choice to all parents. For some disabled young people, however, an ordinary school place is still considered unrealistic by some education professionals. What is more, many schools do not feel able to meet the needs of disabled children and seem to see no reason why this should change. This generates a vicious circle of not developing provision because such provision has not been developed before. I have written elsewhere that promising choice without developing provision is like issuing a ticket and keeping the door locked (Sakellariadis, 2014). I take a few minutes to calm myself down, then return with Sophia's ham sandwich.

'Thank you but I can't eat this; I am a vegetarian, remember?'

'I am so sorry Sophia, I don't know what I was thinking, this is quite unforgivable.' I mean this; I really do find it indefensible to offer her something that is totally inconsistent with her wishes and her needs. I wonder if she sees the similarity with what we have been discussing. I leave the plate on the coffee table and take a look around to see what else needs doing. I walk over to the window and start cleaning it. We are almost done here.

'So have we said enough for one day about children with special educational needs?' I grab the opportunity to touch upon terminology.

'Sophia, could I encourage you to avoid saying that children <u>have</u> special needs? I avoid using the term altogether or, if needs be, talk about children who have labels of special needs.'

'Are you pulling my leg? What's the point of saying the same thing in a more cumbersome way?'

'It's not the same thing at all, I find the second version much kinder to children.'

'I'm sorry but I don't get you.'

'Let me try to explain. I find this hugely problematic for two reasons: the term itself is dreadfully ill-defined, making it impossible to establish exactly which children we are talking about. But aside from that, I don't think it should be used as though it describes children or their abilities.' Sophia looks baffled and maybe a little irritated.

'Look, you're entitled to your opinion but I'm not sure I want to play word games. People up and down the country, throughout the world even, have been using this term for decades. Why is there suddenly a problem?'

I have to tread very carefully, I don't want her to switch off. I stop cleaning the window and turn to look at her, giving her my full attention.

'I can understand your frustration. There are lots of people who find the term unproblematic and use it without giving it a second thought. We can leave it at that if you like.'

'No, no, I'm intrigued now. Happy to hear you out.'

I thank her, perch on the coffee table and give her the calmest and most succinct overview I can manage. I tell her about the Warnock Report, which the term 'special educational needs' is widely believed to originate from, and how it recommended that children's educational difficulties should be seen as a combination of within-child factors and aspects of the child's educational context (DES, 1978). I say that the same message has been repeated over and over again for decades and mention a couple of examples I can quote word for word: 'Educational difficulties result from an interaction between what the child brings to the situation and the programme provided by the school' (Ainscow and Muncey, 1989: 11). 'Special educational needs are needs that arise within the educational system rather than the individual, and indicate a need for the system to change further in order to accommodate individual differences' (Dyson, 1990: 59). We joke that the bookshelves she has just been dusting contain numerous iterations of a similar message (Clough and Barton, 1995; Ainscow, 1999; Allan, 1999; Farrell, 2001; Armstrong, 2003; Slee, 2011). Sophia says nothing for a while. Then she walks over to the bookshelves and, running her finger along a row of books, says:

'I hear what you're saying, but I don't want to be splitting hairs. It's just a form of words and it's simple to use.'

'If you are trying to understand barriers to learning, why choose to use language which overlooks institutional barriers? If you are concerned about the progress of a child, is it appropriate to turn all attention on assessing the child, looking for flaws in the way they learn? If a plant wasn't growing, wouldn't you want to look at the soil and if a cake wasn't rising, wouldn't you be checking the oven?'

'I guess so. This is bringing back memories. Wasn't there a big fuss with an Ofsted report a few years ago?'

'Yes, it certainly attracted a lot of media attention. "A statement is not enough" (Ofsted, 2010) showed that vast numbers of children were being inappropriately identified as "having" special educational needs, when the issue was understood to be the way teaching and learning were organised in the school. Applying a label which assumes within-child deficit certainly seemed inappropriate there.'

'OK, so let's say I agree with you. In an ideal world we would all be using impeccable language, perfectly suited to each occasion. But it's not an ideal world and we've got a shorthand that works. What harm could it do to carry on using it?'

'To the young people for whom we are talking about, this could make the world of difference.' I remember something I wrote a few years ago:

> Labels of 'special educational need' draw attention to perceived differences, in ways that allow for similarities with peers to be overlooked. This, in turn, encourages children to be seen, and to see themselves, as significantly different (often inferior) from their peers. No matter how constructive the learning support that comes as a result of labelling, the stigma of difference can be harmful.
>
> (CSIE staff and associates, 2009)

'Meaning?'

'Meaning that the difference between whether a child "has" or "experiences" difficulties is similar to whether a child "brings" or "finds" difficulties at school. You might consider this a futile word game; but such words can have a powerful impact on young people's sense of identity.' I am reminded of the words of Wayne Veck: 'Labelling learners in terms of what has been deemed deficient within them, can form a barrier to listening to them as speakers with distinct voices. This barrier can deny learners the opportunity to contribute to the culture, organisation and character of educational institutions and, as a result, can ensure they are excluded *within* them' (Veck, 2009, emphasis original). Sophia yawns and I sense we have probably exhausted this topic.

'You said you found this problematic for two reasons. What was the other one?' Good, that makes two of us wanting to move on.

'Oh, that would be the pitifully weak definition. It's just a circular description which says that you have special educational needs if you need special educational provision. The term was first-'

'Hang on a second, I can't hear you.'

Sophia begins hoovering the floor and I carry on cleaning the window, thinking how extraordinary it is that such an ill-defined concept has enjoyed such a long shelf-life. For decades educators seem to have been collectively content with a nebulous term which loosely refers to anybody who does not fit a perceived norm. The term 'special educational need' has been traced back to the 1960s and the writing of a Headteacher of an infant school (Gulliford and Upton, 1992) and is also the title of a book by Ronald Gulliford, published long before the Warnock Committee was formed (Gulliford, 1971). Professor Gulliford was later co-opted on the Warnock Committee (DES, 1978), which proposed the single category of special educational need as an alternative to the 11 categories of handicap defined in the Education Act 1944. This proposal was taken up by the Education Act 1981, which stated that children should be identified as having special educational needs if they have 'a learning difficulty which calls for special educational provision to be made for them'. It is staggering to see how enduring such a poor definition can be. The term has formed part of education law for more than 30 years and the definition still applies today, appearing in the new Code of Practice as: 'A child or young person has SEN if they have a learning difficulty or disability which calls for special educational provision to be made for him or her' (DfE, 2015: 285).

'Sorry, what were you saying?' Sophia unplugs the vacuum cleaner and heads out of the room to put it away.

'Nothing, don't worry. Just that the definition has been repeatedly criticised as inadequate.' Baroness Warnock herself called it 'the purest vicious circle you will ever know' and added 'Well, that is not much of a definition but is the only definition there is' (Warnock, 2005).

'Ha ha, look at that woman's hat!' Sophia calls out from the doorway and gestures to me to look at the house across the street. I follow the direction of her gaze and can see someone at the window of the house opposite, but have no idea what my friend finds so amusing. I look back at her, baffled.

'Sophia, what on earth is so funny? That's Mary, but she is not wearing a hat.'

'No, no, you can't see it from where you are, come and look from over here!'
I walk over to the door and look again; this time I see it and stifle a little giggle of my own.

'You are right, that <u>does</u> *look funny!'* Looking from this spot, the reflection of a lamppost with a large bird perched on top appears exactly on the part of the window where Mary is standing. With the two images superimposed in this way, it looks as though the bird is standing on Mary's head. As we are watching, Mary's son appears at the front door, closes it behind him and walks away, looking up and waving to his mother as he leaves. She waves back and, at this precise moment, the bird chooses to fly away. Sophia and I keel over with laughter.

When we have recomposed ourselves, I return to finish off cleaning the window and Sophia picks up the duster and folds it away.

'You know, that's a really good note to end our conversation on!'

'What, the pointlessness of the definition?'
'No, no, you calling me over to show me what you could see from where you were standing.' Can she really not see the significance? This whole conversation has been about how the way people understand disability shapes their perception of children's needs, which in turn has a bearing on how education is organised.

'Oh it was, was it? Pleased to hear this. So we're done for today, are we?'
'M-hm! I think this will do for now.'
We look around us and admire the fruit of our labours. The whole room is glistening, the wood burner sparkling clean, inviting a new fire to be lit.

'It's been great to see you again, I've really enjoyed today's conversation.'

'So have I, *thanks again for coming,*' I reach out to take the duster she is handing me back, as I finish off my sentence *'let's meet again soon.'*

'Yes, that would be great.' Sophia doesn't let go and we stand awkwardly close, each holding one end of the duster. I let my end drop, leaving the duster in her hands, and take a step back. She looks at me and smiles expectantly, saying nothing.

'What?' I say with a smile, feigning incomprehension.

'When are you going to tell them?' She reaches over to the wood burner and gives the brass handle a gentle rub.

I know what she means. She wants me to reveal to readers that she is a figment of my imagination, conjured up when I was a doctoral student (Sakellariadis, 2007) and appearing in more examples of my writing since then (Sakellariadis 2012, 2016). She would probably want me to explain that scripting this chapter as a fictional dialogue with an imaginary friend is my response to the self-imposed challenge of creating a text which is both scholarly and engaging. She might even want me to comment on some of the added benefits of writing in this way, or to mention the term 'dialogic inquiry' for it. Perhaps I should.

'Well . . . ?' Sophia interrupts my thoughts. I give her a mischievous smile, which is the closest I can get to conveying my thoughts without voicing them. She was probably expecting me to articulate my proposal for education practitioners, especially SENCos, to make time to engage in an internal reflective process, calling into question conventional practices widely accepted by virtue of their longevity.

'You know, *I don't think I'm going to say anything this time'*, I tease, and we leave it at that. She leads the way and we both exit the room, closing the door behind us.

References

Ainscow, M. (1999) *Understanding the Development of Inclusive Schools*. London: Falmer.

Ainscow, M. and Muncey, J. (1989) *Meeting Individual Needs in the Primary School*. London: David Fulton.

Allan, J. (1999) *Actively Seeking Inclusion: Pupils with Special Needs in Mainstream Schools*. London: Falmer.

Armstrong, D. (2003) *Experiences of Special Education: Re-evaluating Policy and Practice Through Life Stories*. London: RoutledgeFalmer.

Audit Commission (2002) *Special Educational Needs: A Mainstream Issue*. London: Audit Commission.

Booth, T. and Ainscow, M. (2011) *Index for Inclusion: Developing Learning and Participation in Schools* (Third edn). Bristol: CSIE.

Chib, M. (2011) *One Little Finger*. London: Sage.

Clough, P. and Barton, L. (1995) *Making Difficulties: Research and the Construction of Special Educational Needs*. London: Paul Chapman.

Committee on the Rights of the Child (2007) *CRC/C/GC/9/Corr.1 General Comment No. 9 (2006); The Rights of Children with Disabilities*. Available at: http://www2.ohchr.org/english/bodies/crc/docs/GC9_en.doc (accessed August 2016).

Committee on the Rights of the Child (2016) *CRC/C/GBR/CO/5 Concluding Observations on the fifth Periodic Report of the United Kingdom of Great Britain and Northern Ireland.* Available at: https://documents-dds-ny.un.org/doc/UNDOC/GEN/G16/149/88/PDF/G1614988.pdf?OpenElement (accessed August 2016).

CSIE and the University of Nottingham (2013) *'Special' Education Revisited.* Available from: https://www.youtube.com/watch?v=XO0sJEbNo-sandfeature=youtu.be (accessed August 2016).

CSIE staff and associates (2009) *The Welcome Workbook: A Self-Review Framework for Expanding Inclusive Provision in Your Local Authority.* Bristol: CSIE.

CSIE staff and associates (2016) *Equality: Making It Happen – A Guide to Help Schools Ensure everyone Is Safe, Included and Learning.* Bristol: CSIE.

DES (1978) *Special Educational Needs: Report of the Committee of Enquiry into the Education of Handicapped Children and Young Persons (The Warnock Report).* London: HMSO.

DfE (2011a) *Support and Aspiration: New Approaches to Special Educational Needs and Disability.* Available at: http://webarchive.nationalarchives.gov.uk/20130401151715/https://www.education.gov.uk/publications/eorderingdownload/green-paper-sen.pdf (accessed August 2016).

DfE (2011b) *Summary of Results to Green Paper Consultation.* Available at: https://www.education.gov.uk/consultations/index.cfm?action=conResultsandconsultationId=1748andexternal=noandmenu=3.

DfE (2015) *Special Educational Needs and Disability Code of Practice: 0 to 25 Years.* Available at: https://www.gov.uk/government/publications/send-code-of-practice-0-to-25 (accessed August 2016).

Dyson, A. (1990) Special educational needs and the concept of change. *Oxford Review of Education,* 16(1): 55–66.

EHRC (2011) *Hidden in Plain Sight: Inquiry into Disability-Related Harassment.* Available at: http://www.equalityhumanrights.com/sites/default/files/documents/disabilityfi/ehrc_hidden_in_plain_sight_3.pdf (accessed August 2016).

EHRC (2012) *Out in the Open: Tackling Disability-Related Harassment; A Manifesto for Change.* Available at: https://www.equalityhumanrights.com/en/publication-download/out-open-tackling-disability-related-harassment-manifesto-change (accessed August 2016).

Farrell, P. (2001) Special education in the last twenty years: have things really got better? *British Journal of Special Education,* 28(1): 3–9.

Gulliford, R. (1971) *Special Educational Needs.* London: Routledge and Kegan Paul.

Gulliford, R. and Upton, G. (1992) *Special Educational Needs.* London: Routledge.

Hansen, J., Leyden, G., Bunch, G., and Pearpoint, J. (2006) *Each Belongs: The Remarkable Story of the First School System to Move to Inclusion.* Toronto: Inclusion Press.

Ladd, P. (2003) *Understanding Deaf Culture: In Search of Deafhood.* Clevedon: Multilingual Matters.

Office for Disability Issues (2012) *Government Response to Hidden in Plain Sight, the Equality and Human Rights Commission Report on Disability Related Harassment.* Available at: https://www.gov.uk/government/uploads/system/uploads/attachment_data/file/258945/HM_Government_Progress_on_EHRC_Recommendations_Nov_2013.pdf (accessed August 2016).

Office of the Children's Commissioner (2012) *They Never Give Up On You.* Available at: http://www.childrenscommissioner.gov.uk/sites/default/files/publications/They%20never%20give%20up%20on%20you%20final%20report.pdf (accessed August 2916).

Ofsted (2006) *Inclusion: Does it Matter Where Pupils are Taught?* London: Office for Standards in Education.

Ofsted (2010) *The Special Educational Needs and Disability Review: A Statement Is Not Enough.* London: Office for Standards in Education.

Ofsted (2012) *No Place for Bullying: How Schools Create a Positive Culture and Prevent and Tackle Bullying.* London: Office for Standards in Education.

Oliver, M. (1995) Does special education have a role to play in the twenty-first century? *Journal of Special Needs Education in Ireland*, 8(2): 65–76.

Rieser, R. (2000a) Special educational needs or inclusive education; the challenge of disability discrimination in schooling, in M. Cole (ed.), *Education, Equality and Human Rights: Issues of Gender, 'Race', Sexuality, Special Needs and Social Class*. London: RoutledgeFalmer.

Rieser, R. (2000b) Disability discrimination, the final frontier: disablement, history and liberation, in M. Cole (ed.), *Education, Equality and Human Rights: Issues of Gender, 'Race', Sexuality, Special Needs and Social Class*. London: RoutledgeFalmer.

Sakellariadis, A. (2007) Voices of inclusion: perspectives of mainstream primary staff on working with disabled children. Unpublished PhD thesis, University of Bristol.

Sakellariadis, A. (2012) Inclusion and SEN: A dialogic inquiry into controversial issues, in L. Peer and G. Reid (eds) *Special Educational Needs: A Guide for Inclusive Practice*. London: Sage.

Sakellariadis, A. (2014) Issuing a ticket but keeping the door locked: The need for real change on disability equality. *Race Equality Teaching* special issue on public sector equality duty, 32(2): 13–17.

Sakellariadis, A. (2016) Inclusion and SEN: A dialogic inquiry into controversial issues, in L. Peer and G. Reid (eds) *Special Educational Needs: A Guide for Inclusive Practice* (Second ed.) London: Sage.

Slee, R. (2011) *The Irregular School: Exclusion, Schooling and Inclusive Education*. London: Routledge.

Thomas, G. and Vaughan, M. (2004) *Inclusive Education: Readings and Reflections*. Maidenhead: Open University Press.

UK Government (2009) *Interpretative Declaration upon Ratifying the UN Convention on the Rights of Persons with Disabilities*. Available at: https://treaties.un.org/pages/ViewDetails. aspx?src=TREATYandmtdsg_no=IV-15andchapter=4andclang=_en#EndDec (accessed August 2016).

Veck, W. (2009) Listening to include. *International Journal of Inclusive Education*, 13(2): 141–155.

Warnock, M. (2005) Select Committee on Education and Skills: Minutes of oral evidence taken on 31 October 2005. Retrieved August 2016 from http://www.publications.parliament.uk/pa/cm200506/cmselect/cmeduski/478/5103101.htm.

West, D. (2012) *Signs of Hope: Deafhearing Family Life*. Newcastle-upon-Tyne: Cambridge Scholars Publishing.

8 What implications do changing practices and concepts have for the role of SEN coordinator?

Brahm Norwich

Introduction

This chapter takes an overview of the historical origins and position of the SEN coordinator role and uses this to identify some of the key dimensions and tensions associated with this role. There have been many studies and discussions about the role of the coordinator since its formal inception in the 1990s. Some of these will be drawn on to illustrate the dimensions under discussion. This then leads onto a brief examination of current debates and of recent developments in the field and what these might mean for the SEN coordinator role. The role of the SEN coordinator was described as 'pivotal' for policy and practice in the Government's Inclusion strategy Removing Barriers to Achievement (DfES, 2004: 116). This is not surprising as there are such high, if not unrealistic, policy expectations about what teachers in this role can do for the education of pupils with special educational needs and disabilities. From another perspective, it could be argued that this role was likely to be constructed following the landmark Education Act 1981 with its increased commitment to educating pupils with special educational needs in ordinary schools. However, uncertainties about the role are evident from the fact that one commentator was wrong, if not premature, in predicting some years ago that SEN coordinators were a 'dying breed' (Dyson, 1990: 116), while another more recent author considers that the role is still 'under construction' (Cole, 2005: 303). Part of this uncertainty is over what to call the role, whether SEN, Inclusion or SEN and Disability (SEND) coordinator. The labelling reflects the rise and fall of different terms and conjunctions of terms that represent different orientations to the field. In the current context with the new Children and Families legislation (DfE, 2014a) Inclusion coordinator is less favoured and SEN coordinator is written into regulations, although with the new SEN Code integrating aspects of disability legislation, it might better be called SEND coordinator.

The origins of the role arise from practical moves to enable the development of whole-school provision for pupils identified as having SEN. These moves reflect the commitment of specialist teachers in the 1970s to widen their remit to supporting pupils with SEN beyond the confines of special classes. The key point in the official development of the role can be seen as the interaction of two key school policy developments, the Education Act (DfES, 1981) and the Education Reform Act (DfES, 1988). As mentioned above, the 1981 Act introduced the first explicit commitment to what we would nowadays call inclusive education. The onus was to educate as many pupils in ordinary schools as possible, subject to various conditions. This implied that ordinary schools had to consider how to develop and support whole-school policies for special educational needs (Thomas and Feiler, 1988). However, seven years later, the Conservative Government introduced radical changes to the school system with the Education Reform Act (DfES, 1988), which introduced the National Curriculum and a national testing system alongside the introduction of a quasi-market system of funding schools and more local management of schools. These measures were designed to raise standards in schools through increasing competition between schools.

At the introduction of the 1988 legislation there were mixed feelings among those interested in special educational needs about these significant and complex changes to the school system. On one hand, the principle of a common curriculum for all including pupils with SEN was welcomed, but on the other hand, the central direction of the curriculum design for national assessment purposes was seen to have none of the flexibilities required for those with SEN or disabilities. It is notable that the introduction of the National Curriculum adaptations for pupils with learning difficulties and the P levels came a decade later (QCA, 2001). This assessment-driven curriculum was part of the central establishment of more competition between schools for pupils as a way of driving up academic standards. School performance was to be judged by parents as users of schools in terms of average school attainment levels. With school funding becoming linked to pupil numbers, the introduction of a quasi-market system became a dominant feature of the school system. It was anticipated at the end of the 1980s that schools would became less tolerant of those presenting behaviour difficulties. This was what happened, as shown by the growth in permanent exclusions into the 1990s. Schools also tended to focus more on increasing attainment levels in the school league tables and sought further funding to support pupils with SEN. This was indicated by the increase in the level of Statements of SEN through the 1990s, which only flattened out at about 3 per cent in the early 2000s.

The tension between the push for externally visible standards and providing inclusively and flexibly for pupils with SEN had been recognised since the implementation of the 1988 Act (Wedell, 1988). The concerns aroused by the 1988 legislative changes and the resulting turbulence led to moves to focus more on the needs of those pupils who had SEN without Statements. The 1981 legislation had focussed predominantly on those with more significant SENs (2–3 per cent with more significant SENs) and not the larger group in ordinary schools (12–13 per cent). The introduction of the Code of Practice in 1994 (DfE, 1994) was the Government's response to these problems. Among other guidance, a graduated model of identification and individual planning for pupils with SEN was to be introduced and all schools were required to have a SEN coordinator. Seven areas of responsibility were set out for this role in the 1994 Code:

1. daily operation of SEN policy
2. liaising with and advising fellow teachers
3. coordinating provision for pupils with SEN
4. maintaining the school's register of SEN; overseeing records on pupils with SEN

5. liaising with parents
6. contributing to in-service training
7. liaising with external agencies

There have been a series of research reports and publications about the SENCo role since 1994, by the government, teacher unions and researchers. It is not the aim of this chapter to review these findings and conclusions (for this, see McKenzie, 2007). However, it is relevant to this chapter to note the recurrent concerns about the role from surveys, for example, about time available for the role, the unmanageability of the role, the support of the head teacher/senior management, the issues about understanding SEN funding in their schools, whether or not teaching assistants could act as SENCos, and SENCo training opportunities. However, McKenzie concludes her review in terms of the difficulty of generalising about the SENCo's work which varies according to local circumstances, e.g. phase, membership of senior management team, extent of direct class teaching responsibilities and the same person having the SENCo role alongside other responsibilities.

Another point relevant to this chapter is the consensus that the SENCo's role has widened since the 1994 Code of Practice (Cheminais, 2005; McKenzie, 2007). This widening involved the SENCo in more strategic work in schools concerned with management and leadership. This conception of the SENCo role was first formally set out in the Teacher Training Agency's attempt to capture the core purpose of the role in its SENCo National Standards (TTA, 1998). Not only was the SENCo to be responsible for the day-to-day provision for pupils with SEN but also the guidance and leadership of other staff. The four identified areas were about:

1. strategic direction and development of SEN provision
2. teaching and learning
3. leading and managing staff
4. efficient and effective deployment of staff and resources

Although the revised Code of Practice (DfES, 2001) did not change the main conception of the role set out originally in the 1994 Code, the widening of the role was also underlined by the Government Inclusion strategy – 'Removing Barriers to Achievement' (DfES, 2004). Not only were SENCos expected to be members of senior management teams, but they were supposed to be central to managing change even though there was no clear specification of what this involved. The most recent learning outcomes for the National Award for SEN Coordination (NCTL, 2014a) specifies these outcomes in terms of three areas which clearly show a dual focus on the operational and strategic aspects of the role:

A. Professional knowledge and understanding

- The statutory and regulatory context for SEN and disability equality and the implications for practice in a school or work setting
- The principles and practice of leadership in different contexts
- How SEN and disabilities affect pupils' participation and learning
- Strategies for improving outcomes for pupils with SEN and/or disabilities

B. Leading and coordinating provision

- Work strategically with senior colleagues and governors
- Lead, develop and, where necessary, challenge senior leaders, colleagues and governors
- Critically evaluate evidence about learning, teaching and assessment in relation to pupils with SEN to inform practice and enable senior leaders and teachers to develop their own practice
- Draw on external sources of support and expertise
- Develop, implement, monitor and evaluate systems

C. Personal and professional qualities

The Award should enable SENCOs to develop and demonstrate the personal and professional qualities and leadership they need to shape an ethos and culture based upon person-centred, inclusive practice in which the interests and needs of children and young people with SEN and/or disabilities are at the heart of all that takes place. This is evident when:

- There are high expectations for all children and young people with SEN and/or disabilities
- Person-centred approaches build upon and extend the experiences, interests, skills and knowledge of children and young people with SEN and/or disabilities
- The voice of children and young people with SEN and/or disabilities is heard and influences the decisions that are made about their learning and well-being
- Family leadership is encouraged and parents and carers are equal partners in securing their child's achievement, progress and well-being.

Important dimensions of the SENCo role

The main aim of this chapter is to identify and discuss some of the key dimensions and tensions associated with the SENCo role that have arisen since the 1990s and continue to the present. The following four interrelated aspects will be discussed:

1. functions versus roles
2. justification and boundary of specialism
3. coverage of the coordination functions/role
4. focus of the coordination activities

In analysing these aspects, I assume that central government guidance and strategies are applied to the school system with the aim of promoting particular practices in the name of special educational provision. I will also assume that some of the basic issues confronted in carrying out the SENCo role arise from differences in how special educational provisions are understood, while other issues arise from the way that a general model of the coordination role does not exactly fit the particularities of schools. This lack of fit can be understood in terms of differences associated with:

i.   school phase (primary-secondary)
ii. school size (number of staff, distribution of roles)
iii. school priorities (inclusive and learner-centred commitment-in-action)
iv. school governance (maintained school, sponsored academy, converter academy, free school)
v.   local authority setting (special needs and Inclusion policies and practices)

These five dimensions and others will emerge as having a bearing on the discussion of the above aspects of the SENCo role in what follows.

1. Functions versus roles

Not only have there been practical questions over the years about time avail-ability to undertake the SEN coordinator role, but, as discussed above, the role has operational and strategic functions. The role of the SENCo as set out in the Codes of Practice since 1994 has been focussed around a cycle of individualisa-tion of teaching; that is, the assessment of pupils with SEN, the development of individual educational plans (IEP), the implementation/teaching to these plans, their review and further adaptive planning. Much of the criticism in the 1990s of the overload of the role was attributed to the bureaucratic nature of the IEP process, especially in larger schools with more pupils identified as having SEN. The 2001 Code reduced the workload for SENCos by reducing the need to have IEPs by introducing group educational plans (GEP) where pupils had similar needs. Frankl (2005) showed that using GEPs reduced the number of IEPs in some primary schools and released SENCos from paperwork, enabling them to work with teachers, and supported class teachers in taking more responsibility for pupils with SEN.

That GEPs were seen to reduce the workload of the SENCo and at the same time enable class teachers to be more responsible for planning for pupils with SEN raised questions about how the SENCo role and its associated responsibilities related to other roles and responsibilities in schools. The more recent emphasis on 'provision mapping' (section 6.70–6.71; *SEND Code of Practice*) (DfE, 2104b), sees this approach being used strategically to develop special education provision and contribute to school improvement. This is part of the SENCo's role as regards 'leading and coordinating provision' as the second of the three broad areas set out in the latest National Award for SEN Coordination (NCTL, 2014a). As with the GEP model, provision mapping so used raises questions about the SENCO's roles and responsibilities in relation to other roles and responsibilities in schools.

In analysing the range of responsibilities set out in the 2009 and 2014 outcomes for SENCo training, it can be asked if this range of responsibilities is best located in a single role (see Figure 8.1). Would strategic development, coordinating provi-sion, leading, developing and supporting colleagues and partnership working with pupils, families and professionals be better distributed across various school staff roles? In Figure 8.1 the arrows going from SEN coordination to various func-tions represent how SEN coordination contributes to these generic functions. What is important to understand is that there is little evidence that these generic

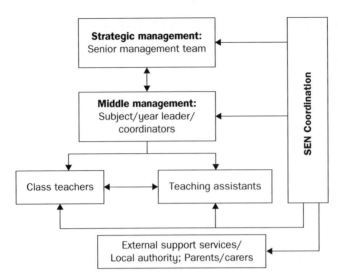

Figure 8.1 Levels of activity relevant to SEN coordination

functions have been expected officially to interrelate with and share these specialist functions. This lack of shared responsibility in the official government position was first pointed out by Garner (2001), when he identified that though the first SENCo standards (TTA, 1998) were meant to be allied to subject coordinator standards, these middle management standards made no reference to their role in relation to pupils with SEN. As Garner argued, the implication was that it is for SENCos 'to develop and sustain collaborative practice' (2001: 123) and that middle management responsibility for pupils with SEN was not formally and specifically recognised. The same point also applied to senior management standards. In only 2 of the 6 areas set out in the TDA (2004) standards for head teachers was there reference to Inclusion and diversity, with no references specifically to disability/SEN. Under the 'Shaping the Future' area in these standards, heads were expected to be committed to 'Inclusion and the ability and right of all to be the best they can be' and under the 'Leading Learning and Teaching' area, they were expected to have knowledge of 'the development of a personalised learning culture within the school' and 'strategies for ensuring Inclusion, diversity and access'.

With the Coalition government closing the Training and Development Agency (TDA) which set these teacher standards, there is even less detail under the new National College for Teaching and Leadership (NCTL). There are now no teacher standards for these generic teaching roles, but there are qualifications for these roles that set out what is to be learned, from which standards can be inferred. For the National Professional Qualification for Middle Leadership (NPQML), there are two essential modules which cover 'Leading teaching' and 'Managing systems and processes', neither of which refer specifically to pupils with SEN and/or disability (NCTL, 2014b). However, there is a further module in which there is a choice of one of four options, one of which is about 'Effective leadership of special educational needs provision'. Though an option, the SEN further module is not an essential part of the implied standards. The same is evident for the National Professional Qualification for Senior Leadership (NPQSL) (NCTL, 2014c), where there is no reference to SEN/disability in either the two essential or the further modules. In the National Professional Qualification for Headship (NPQH) (NCTL, 2014d), there are three essential modules, covering 'Leading and improving teaching', 'Leading an effective school' and 'Succeeding in headship', none of which refer specifically to SEND. Of the nine further modules from which two need to be selected, one refers to 'Leading Inclusion' and is about the Achievement for All approach (Humphrey and Squires, 2011). So, prospective head teachers need not even do this one optional module.

This analysis indicates a significant and persistent imbalance in the official guidance about the interconnections between and respective responsibilities of senior/middle management and SEN coordination. It is evident that this imbalance might not be reflected in the particular practices of schools, where there might be a sharing of responsibilities and a collaborative approach to providing for pupils with SEN. However, it is reasonable to assume that the continuing official imbalance does reflect a dominant trend in school practices, where school priorities and practices are not as inclusive and whole-learner centred as they could be (see the conclusion of the Lamb Inquiry report (DCSF, 2009)).

Some of this trend may reflect internal school factors, but schools also operate within a national policy context with strong pressures to meet national priorities, such as raising attainments in a way that is in tension with and undermines inclusive priorities (MacBeath et al., 2006; Ellis et al., 2012). This discussion leads on to the second key aspect of the SENCo role to be addressed in this chapter.

2. Justification and boundary of specialism

In this section I discuss whether there can be a justification for distinct SEN coordination as a function. There are two parts to this question: one about whether there is a need for specialist coordination, whatever it is called, apart from middle and senior management general coordination of school provision: the other, whether this kind of coordination should be labelled as and confined to SEN. These issues parallel the on-going debates about whether the term 'special educational needs' continues to be useful and justified in addressing these questions (SEN Policy Options Group, 2009).

One way to consider the question about specialist coordination as apart from middle and senior management coordination is to weigh up the arguments in favour of and against a specialist function. A specialist function can be justified if there is something distinctive and useful about the knowledge and skills that others cannot easily acquire or do not have the time to acquire. But, it is not just a matter of capability, it is also whether or not others have an interest and willingness to acquire the knowledge and skills and use them. For example, a curriculum subject coordinator could be trained and so develop the capabilities to lead, develop and support colleagues, one of the SENCo's functions, in her/his subject area as regards pupils with SEN. But, perhaps the curriculum subject coordinator does not identify this as an important part of their role and so comes to depend on the SEN coordinator to carry out this function. The key point is that whether

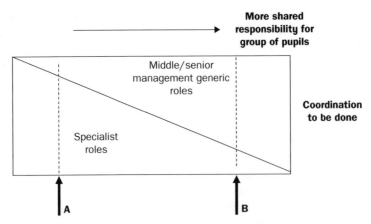

Figure 8.2 The balance between specialist and generic roles as responsibility for group of pupils is increasingly shared

this happens or not, the subject coordinator will collaborate with the SEN coordinator in a more inclusive and collaborative school context and in so doing take on some of the SEN coordination functions. From the SEN coordinator's perspective, this would be seen as distributing the coordination function.

This kind of middle management collaboration could be seen as good practice in terms of promoting shared responsibility for inclusive provision. But, how far could this sharing or 'handing over' go? Could it go so far that specialist coordination is no longer seen to be required, a 'doing away with itself'? Would middle and senior management be willing to take over what is to be done for a specific group of pupils, however defined, so that there would be no further requirement to have specialist coordination and a role to cover these functions?

Figure 8.2 shows schematically one way of understanding the balance between specialist and generic coordination in an area such as SEN. The vertical axis in the rectangle represents the amount of coordination to be done. How this is shared between specialist and generic roles depends on the extent to which responsibility for this group is shared across roles. At position A on the left of the figure, where there is less shared responsibility; the balance is towards much more specialist coordination in a specialist role and rather little in a generic role. However, at point B, which is in the direction of more shared responsibility, there is more coordination in generic than specialist roles, but with some specialist role retained.

It seems that, even if much of the specialist capability/expertise can become generic, it is likely that there will be some residual specialist functions. There has been a strong reaction against the idea that there is some specialist expertise in the teaching of pupils with SEN/disability as part of the movement for inclusive education (Thomas and Loxley, 2007). However, Lewis and Norwich (2004) in their review and analysis about whether or not there is a specialist SEN pedagogy, concluded that there is no simple position about specialisation because of (1) the range of areas of difficulties and disabilities and their levels of severity, and (2) that pedagogy can be specific or specialist in terms of curriculum, knowledge relevant to teaching and learning and/or teaching strategies. Where generic teaching strategies may be relevant to those with some kinds of difficulties (e.g. moderate learning difficulties and specific learning difficulties) and there are no specific set of teaching strategies, there are grounds and evidence for believing that generic approaches require being applied in a more intensified way. Lewis and Norwich (2004) concluded that the principle of intensification of generic teaching strategies is an important principle of teaching in the above-mentioned areas of SEN. In other areas of SEN/disability, there were also arguments that the area of difficulty (e.g. autism) was relevant to informing, but not determining, teaching strategies in combination with other principles and factors. For these reasons it is argued that some specialist or specific knowledge will continue to be required in the field; not a kind of specific knowledge that is esoteric and detached from general teaching principles and practices, but one that is connected to general teaching. This position expresses the concept of 'special' as a 'connective specialisation' not as a detached separate specialisation (Norwich, 1996).

But, as important as the specialist function argument above is the degree of commitment and interest to the specific or specialist field. If there is some requirement for something additional to generic coordination in schools and those doing generic roles feel low levels of responsibility for this additional aspect, then their interest will be in separating the functions and finding others to undertake them. However, not only is there a tendency in these circumstances to externalise the coordination outside generic responsibilities, but there are those within schools who identify with and are committed to particular groups, e.g. SEN and disabilities, who wish to champion their interests and advocate for them. In this way there can be a settlement between those willing to take on responsibilities for specific aspects of coordination and those with generic coordination responsibilities wishing to externalise them. It may be that the interest of the champions for this group of pupils arises in response to the externalising of responsibility by those in generic roles. But it is also possible that those who come to champion this group of pupils developed these interests from experiences outside schools, for instance, in their families.

3. Coverage of coordination function

The third of the four aspects under discussion relates to the question raised in the previous section: whether the specific coordination should be labelled as and confined to SEN? In this section I discuss and analyse some of the issues about whether it is justified that coordination in schools is identified with a group, such as those with SEN.

Figure 8.3 represents some of the different areas where there can be specialist coordination and their relationships to each other. At the top of Figure 8.3 is the overarching learning support consultancy function. Dyson (1990) argued 20 years ago that the SEN coordinator role would be better framed as learning support consultancy. The reasons for this are to have a broader role that is not confined to pupils with SEN, a role that focusses on teaching and teachers and avoids the negative labelling of support functions. Though learning support has a more generic connotation as all pupils might require such support at some time, not just a minority, this label has not become as established as Dyson anticipated. There are

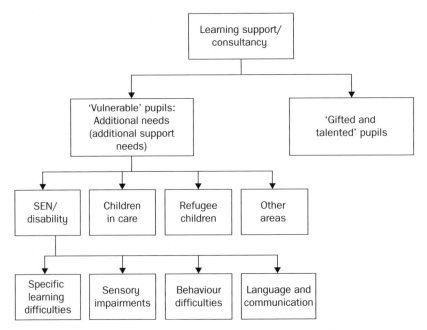

Figure 8.3 Levels and areas for specialist coordination (not all sub-areas are represented)

probably two key reasons for this; first, that the coordination functions become labelled in accordance with government policy initiative and guidance, and second, that the potential breadth of the function cannot be managed by a single role.

There are two interpretations of 'learning support' as a specialist function, one that recognises additional needs and another associated with a radical Inclusion commitment that rejects any concept associated with 'needs'. By opting for a broader concept of 'additional needs' coordination, we do not avoid issues about the nature, scope and origins of these needs. 'Additional needs' might appear to offer a way of adopting an approach to inclusive schooling, which can be justified in terms of removing barriers to participation and learning and the social model (Inclusion Index: Booth and Ainscow, 2011). However, although 'additional needs' is broader than SEN/disability, this is not a justifiable position. Many current advocates of the social model criticise and reject the concept of 'needs', whether it is 'special' or 'additional needs' (Runswick-Cole and Hodges, 2009). This is because of the assumed negativity and specialisation of 'needs' and its association with the medical model rather than with a social model of disability and educational rights. So, there is no place within a concept of Inclusion that rejects SEN (e.g. the Inclusion Index model) for specialist coordination whether under the title of SEND or additional needs coordination.

There is a tension over the labelling of specialist coordination for a subgroup, whether a smaller one, such as SEN/disability, or a larger one, such as additional educational needs. The labelling restricts the coordination to a 'vulnerable' minority, with stigmatising and devaluing risks; but on the other hand, to leave learning support coordination open to all learners risks not focussing the coordination on those who require it. This tension is an example of the dilemmas of difference found in other aspects of specialist provision (Norwich, 2008). There are different ways of resolving this dilemma about coordination which involve weighing up the respective risks and opting for the option with the lesser risks. I favour a resolution which recognises that SEN, which is about learning difficulties and disabilities, has outlived its usefulness (Norwich, 2008), but that retains a concept of need (taken as implying a requirement that takes account of individual strengths and difficulties) as useful and necessary (Warnock and Norwich, 2010). Rights are critically important and in practice rights and needs are compatible and complementary (Norwich, 2013). But what rights have traditionally not done is take account of individual functioning, as rights have been predicated on group membership (as in the phrase 'the rights of the disabled'). A commitment to what is required for an individual pupil means that we use a concept beyond rights that protects the additional resourcing for that pupil. Perhaps the term 'needs' should be replaced by another, perhaps it could be 'capabilities' (Terzi, 2007) or 'needs' could be used with a more positive meaning. This can be achieved through recognising and using a more elaborate model of needs in which all pupils have common needs and through using it for pupils who are not identified as 'vulnerable', such as those identified as gifted and talented.

In arguing for learning support coordination based on additional needs, it is still important to note that the SENCo function is probably the best and longest established of the coordination functions established for 'vulnerable children'. It is notable that when other coordination functions have been subsequently established, e.g. for children in care, the 'designated teacher' (DCSF, 2008) and the 'coordinators' for gifted and talented pupils, these have not been formally linked to the SENCo functions and role. These functions share common pedagogic and administrative aspects concerned with promoting appropriate provision relevant to minority groups of 'exceptional' pupils. They can be integrated into an overarching function in which there are still specialisms, as set out in Figure 8.3. The fact that coordination for pupils identified as 'gifted and talented' and 'vulnerable' has not been integrated in national guidance might be due to the historic separation of these kinds of provision. However, some schools have additional needs departments that integrate functions as regards 'vulnerable' and gifted/talented pupils.

The lack of national guidance about the integration of provision in the 'vulnerable' pupil area at school level, during the period of the Labour government's Every Child Matters integration at local authority level, reflects a significant and regrettable aspect of recent English policy. Though some schools established 'Inclusion managers' and 'Inclusion coordinators' and despite the Common Assessment Framework (CAF) for assessing and planning for the needs of 'vulnerable' children, including those with SEN/disabilities, the 2009 SENCo standards did not cover the wider group of those with 'additional needs' as defined in the CAF (TDA, 2009). This can be attributed to the influence and interests of the SEN lobby groups in the national policy arena, where the specific areas of SEN have become more vocal and powerful in promoting their specific interests, such as autism, dyslexia and deafness. The reluctance of the Lamb Inquiry at the end of the Labour period of government to recommend the broadening of the scope of SEN, as in Scotland and Wales, and linking it up with a wider additional needs remit (DCSF, 2009), was also regrettable. The prospects for this wider 'additional needs' concept has become even more remote in England with the Coalition government's Green Paper (DFE, 2011) and the Children and Families 2014 legislation, and moves to narrow the scope of SEN by reducing the number of levels in the graduated approach.

Although there are benefits to the integration of the coordination of provision for pupils with exceptional needs, there are also risks involved. One of the benefits is that pupils do not always fall into neat categories, so the integration of coordination can bring together different forms of knowledge and skills. For example, a pupil may have a SEN and be a child in care or have a specific learning difficulty and be a gifted at mathematics. One kind of risk is that pupils come to be defined predominantly in terms of their area of additional need while their other needs that are common to all pupils and those needs that are unique to them as individuals can be overlooked. To meet these common and individual needs requires the sharing of responsibility of all staff in schools. Another risk in integrating the coordination across the range of additional needs is that some specific kinds of additional needs may be overlooked or not given enough attention. This is where outside support services working at local authority or cross-school level might be better able to provide the specific knowledge, skills and consultancy required, but unavailable from school staff, for example, complex SEN, including autistic and severe behaviour difficulties. Being aware of the range of additional needs and identifying where the appropriate knowledge and skills reside and drawing on it depends on economies of scale. The scarcer the knowledge and skills, the fewer people will have them and so the more likely that they may reside outside ordinary schools. This may be why coordination for additional needs may require sharing staff across ordinary schools, for example, jointly employed additional needs coordinators, and why special schools or units, may be a useful source of support, consultancy, knowledge and skills.

4. Focus of the coordination activities

The last aspect to be analysed and discussed is the focus of coordination activities. As discussed above, the areas of activities for coordination have grown since the initial 1994 SEN Code of Practice (DfE, 1994). The scope of coordination activities relates to strategic and middle management as well as coordination with respect to class teachers and teaching assistants, as well as liaising with external services and parents, as shown in Figures 8.1 and 8.4 on p 126. One of the main themes of this chapter is the gap between official models of the SENCo role and responsibilities and what happens in the variety of particular schools. The scope of SEN coordination makes it possible for different interpretations of the role, as shown in a study by Kearns (2005) that identified and typified a range of different roles. Some SENCos operated as 'arbiters' in which they oversaw the rationalising and monitoring of special educational resources, while helping teachers and parents clarify their concerns and supporting them to be positive about Inclusion and provision. Others were portrayed as 'rescuers', who focussed on pupils and undertook close work with specific class teachers. Kearns suggested that these

SENCos created demand for their support and this resulted in time management problems. The 'rescuers' tended not to focus on or influence management, leading to less influence on the staff overall. Some others operated as 'auditors', who focussed more on procedures such as managing IEPs, organising meetings, record keeping, analysing data, etc. A fourth group were 'collaborators' who focussed on sharing practices within and across schools, engaged teachers in curriculum development and tended not to see boundaries between managers and teachers. Interestingly, only a minority of the study sample saw themselves as 'experts'; those who did tended to have relevant qualifications or be in charge of specialist units. That there are such different interpretations of the SENCo role shows the breadth of the role and how general is the official formulation of its functions.

Clearly the focus of coordination activities depends on many contextual factors, such as those identified above, school phase, school size, etc. It is also evident that the official model of SEN coordination is not one that can be effectively fulfilled by a single person, even if this teacher has specialist qualifications, e.g. has the SEN Coordination National Award. In this respect the last government's requirement that SEN coordinators not be Higher Level Teaching Assistants (HTLAs) was an important recognition of the declining importance that was accorded to this role in some schools and the need for appropriately qualified teachers to become involved. The continued requirement in regulations under the new Children and Families 2014 legislation for schools to have appropriately trained SENCos underlines the central role and responsibilities placed on these teachers.

It is evident that the focus of the SEN coordination cannot be separated from the discussion above about SENCo functions and role. SEN coordination with its multiple foci cannot all be located easily in a single role. This becomes all the more necessary if the SEN coordination functions are integrated into other specialist coordination functions for other groups of exceptional pupils. So, the discussion shows how the different aspects discussed in this chapter are interconnected, and this brings us back to the point where the overall argument of the chapter will be summarised and conclusions drawn.

Concluding comments

The main aim of this chapter has been to highlight some of the key tensions and opportunities associated with SENCo roles and responsibilities. The discussion has shown how interconnected are the aspects under analysis: function versus roles, the justification and boundary of a coordination specialism, the coverage of the functions and roles, and the focus of the coordination activities.

In Figure 8.4, I have represented the range of activities that can be associated with what I call additional needs coordination in an organisation where there are shared responsibilities for these needs. Although Figure 8.4 has similarities with Figure 8.1 in terms of setting out the kinds and levels of activities and relationships, it has two major differences from the earlier figure. The first difference is that the arrows show two-way interactions. This is used to represent that the coordination activities at the different levels of school provision (strategic and

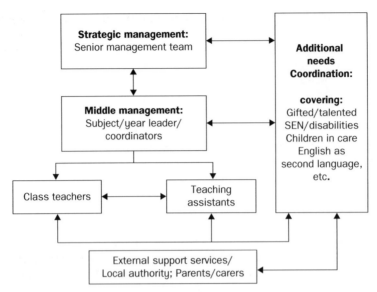

Figure 8.4 Levels of activity relevant to additional need coordination in organisation with shared responsibility for pupils with such needs

middle management and class teaching) are shared between the generic and specialist roles. This is one of the main implications arising from this analysis. I am aware that questions of ownership and responsibility reflect the balance of power and priorities about schooling, but if inclusive education means anything, it is that there is some distribution of specialist coordination roles beyond those in labelled specialist roles. It is also clear that the recommendations of the Lamb Inquiry report (DCSF, 2009), the last expression of the previous Labour government's policy, implied the need for whole-school practical commitments to quality provision for those with SEN. However, the reduced interest in Inclusion as a whole-school commitment as shown by the Coalition government (DFE, 2011) and increased school autonomy and increased focus on parental preferences, through establishing academies and free schools, further undermine the shared responsibilities for 'additional needs'.

Though outside pressures may make it more challenging, finding ways to integrate specialist coordination functions in senior and middle management will continue to be one way forward, so making the residual specialist functions attributed to the coordinator role more manageable and effective. This conclusion is one that also reflects a concept of special educational or additional needs as a 'connective specialistion' (Norwich, 1996). Connective implies that special/ additional is not separated from generic responsibilities in schools, but integral to generic coordination. The second difference between Figures 8.4 and 8.1 is the integration of the various areas of specialist coordination into an additional needs coordination function. This integrates SEN coordination into related areas where the same pupil might come under different systems and titles as well as link coordination for 'vulnerable' pupils with those identified as gifted and talented. Such links might also promote the ownership of responsibilities for 'vulnerable' children and counteract the resistance of some teachers to take on shared responsibilities for them. The new SEN legislation and revised Code of Practice, despite their strategic commitment to inter-service commissioning and collaboration, persist in separating out these aspects of coordination at a school level. Nevertheless, a commitment to adequate provision for all pupils at school level continues to require this kind of integration.

I conclude this chapter with a summary of the implications of the above analysis of the SENCo role and responsibilities. If inclusive provision for pupils with disabilities and difficulties in learning is to be a whole-school matter, then the coordination for these pupils, usually identified in terms of SEN/disabilities, is best integrated under a broader 'additional needs' title. It has been argued that this broader category would specify the range of overlapping areas of additional need and also not only cover pupils identified as 'vulnerable' in various ways. The Inclusion of those with very high abilities and attainments, currently identified as gifted and talented, makes administrative sense and will also contribute to the positive connotation of the 'needs' term in 'additional needs'. It has also been argued that additional needs might also be associated with a learning support function, but not learning support without a specific focus. The specific focus on additional needs, despite its risks, preserves the principle of protected coordination for a minority, whether the term 'need' is used or replaced by another term. Inclusive provision, it has also been argued, requires some shared responsibility and collaboration between generic and specialist roles. This implies that generic senior and middle management roles take on explicit aspects of coordination for pupils with additional needs. Were this to happen, the additional needs coordination role will become more manageable than it has been since its inception. However, as argued above, central government models need to be flexible enough to take account of school particularities. The challenge of defining an inclusive concept of coordination for pupils with additional needs requires an examination and redefinition of generic school management and teaching in the context of a clearer national and school-level commitment to adequate provision for all pupils.

References

Booth, T. and Ainscow, M. (2011) *Index for Inclusion: Developing Learning and Participation in Schools* (Third edition). Bristol: CSIE.

Cheminais, R. (2005) *Every Child Matters: A New Role for SENCOs*. London: David Fulton.

Cole, B.A. (2005) Mission impossible? Special educational needs, Inclusion and the reconceptualization of the role of the SENCO in England and Wales. *European Journal of Special Needs Education*, 20(3): 287–307.

DCSF (2008) *Children and Young Persons Act*. London: TSO.

DCSF (2009) *Lamb Inquiry: Special Educational Needs and Parental Confidence*. London: DCSF.

DfE (1994) *Code of Practice on the Identification and Assessment of Special Educational Needs*. London: DfE.

DfE (2011) *Support and Aspiration: A New Approach to Special Educational Needs*. London: DFE.

DfE (2014a) *Children and Families Act*. London: TSO.

DfE (2014b) *Draft Special Educational Needs and Disability Code of Practice: 0 to 25 Years. Statutory Guidance for Organisations Who Work with and Support Children and Young People with Special Educational Needs and Disabilities*. London: DfE.

DfES (1981) *Education Act*. London: HMSO.

DfES (1988) *Education Reform Act*. London: HMSO.

DfES (2001) *SEN Code of Practice*. Nottingham: DfES.

DfES (2004) *Removing Barriers to Achievement: The Government's Strategy for Inclusion*. Nottingham: DfES Publications.

Dyson, A. (1990) Effective learning consultancy: a future role for special needs coordinators? *Support for Learning*, 5(3): 16–27.

Ellis, S., Tod, J. and Graham-Matheson, L. (2012) *Special Educational Needs and Inclusion: Reflection, Renewal and Reality*. Birmingham: NASUWT.

Frankl, C. (2005) Managing individual educational plans: reducing the workload of the SEN coordinator. *Support for Learning*, 20(2): 77–82.

Garner, P. (2001) What is the weight of a badger?, in J. Wearmouth (ed.) *Special Educational Needs in the Context of Inclusion*. London: David Fulton.

Humphrey, N. and Squires, G. (2011) *Achievement for All: National Evaluation Final Report*. London: DfE.

Kearns, H. (2005) Exploring the experiential learning of special educational needs coordinators. *Journal of In-Service Education*, 31(1): 131–150.

Lewis, A. and Norwich, B. (2004) *Special Teaching for Special Children?: Pedagogies for Inclusion*. Maidenhead: Open University Press.

MacBeath, J., Galton, M., Steward, S., MacBeath, A. and Page, C. (2006) *The Cost of Inclusion*. Cambridge: Victoire Press.

McKenzie, S. (2007) A review of recent developments in the role of the SENCo in the UK. *Support for Learning*, 34(4): 212–218.

NCTL (2014a) *National Award for SEN Coordination: Learning Outcomes*. London: DfE.

NCTL (2014b) National Professional Qualification for Middle Leadership (NPQML). Retrieved 15 July 2014 from: https://www.gov.uk/national-professional-qualification-for-middle-leadership-npqml.

NCTL (2014c) National Professional Qualification for Senior Leadership (NPQSL). Retrieved 15 July 2014 from: https://www.gov.uk/national-professional-qualification-for-senior-leadership-npqsl.

NCTL (2014d) National Professional Qualification for Headship (NPQH). Retrieved 15 July 2014 from: https://www.gov.uk/national-professional-qualification-for-headship-npqh.

Norwich, B. (1996) Special needs education or education for all: connective specialization or ideological impurity. *British Journal of Special Education*, 23(3): 100–104.

Norwich, B. (2008) *Dilemmas of Difference: Inclusion and Disability*. London: Routledge.

Norwich, B. (2013) *Addressing Tensions and Dilemmas in Inclusive Education: Living with Uncertainty*. London: Routledge.

QCA (2001) *Planning, Teaching and Assessing the Curriculum for Pupils with Learning Difficulties*. London: QCA/DfES.

Runswick-Cole, K. and Hodge, N. (2009) Needs or rights? A challenge to the discourse of special education. *British Journal of Special Education*, 36(40): 189–203.

Special Educational Needs Policy Options Group (2009) Has SEN outlived its usefulness?: a debate. NASEN website (accessed 5 March 2010).

TDA (2004) *National Standards for Headteachers*. London: TDA.

TDA (2009) *Standards for National Award for SEN Coordination*. London: TDA.

Terzi, L (2007) Beyond the dilemma of difference: the capability approach to disability and special educational needs, in L. Florian and M. McClaughlin (eds) *Categories in Special Education*. London: Sage.

Thomas, G. and Feiler, A. (1988) *Planning for Special Need: A Whole School Approach.* Oxford: Blackwell.

Thomas, G. and Loxley, A. (2007) *Deconstructing Special Education and Constructing Inclusion* (Second edition). Buckingham: Open University Press.

TTA (1998) *National Standards for SEN Coordinators.* London: TTA.

Warnock, M. and Norwich, B. (2010) *Special Educational Needs: A New Look.* London: Continuum Publishers.

Wedell, K. (1988) Special educational needs and the Educational Reform Act. *Forum,* 31(1): 19–21.

9 The concept of inclusive pedagogy

Lani Florian

Introduction

Beginning with the 1997 Green Paper, *Excellence for All Children*, and continuing in more recent policy documents, the government has acknowledged that there is no single best route to Inclusion for students identified as having special educational needs (SEN) in England and Wales. Although Scotland and Northern Ireland maintain separate education systems, and the devolution of political power within the UK has led to the emergence of a distinct system of education in Wales, education policy and practice in all four countries have many features in common. In particular, the conceptual, philosophical and practical problems of inclusive and special education are shared concerns. As is the case in many countries, national special needs policies tend to retain traditional approaches (i.e. identification and assessment of individual need, individualised education plans (IEPs), and specialist facilities for those who choose them) while also supporting more inclusive approaches without specifying what such approaches might look like or how they might be achieved. Consequently, there are numerous interpretations of inclusive education and a great deal of variability in practice.

Recent research in England has documented an increase in variability associated with educational reform policies that have encouraged new types of schools, notably free schools and academies (Black and Norwich, 2014). This trend is set to continue as the current government's action plan to improve systems of support for children with special educational needs and disabilities (SEND) include ensuring that all forms of state-funded schools and colleges are part of the support system for children with SEND while expanding parental choice by introducing personal budgets for those with an EHC (education, health and care) Plan (DfE, 2014). These actions imply that the long-standing tradition of separate support will continue to operate within a system that also values personal choice. In such a system, variability is not necessarily a bad thing: for choices to exist, options must be available. However, while variability can mean increased choice, it is important to understand that not all options are positive. As the 2009 *Lamb Inquiry: Special Educational Needs and Parental Confidence* noted:

> In talking with parents of disabled children and children with special educational needs (SEN), we met some of the happiest parents in the country and some of the angriest. Many had children who are well-supported and making good progress. But we also met parents for whom the education system represents a battle to get the needs of their child identified and for these to be met. The crucial issue is that both experiences happen within the same system.

While the aims of the SEN framework remain relevant, implementation has too often failed to live up to them.

(DCSF, 2009 2)

Here variability raises important questions about the nature and quality of provision in schools. As Lamb has shown, how schools as organisations, and individual teachers within those organisations, respond to students identified as having special educational needs is of paramount importance. This will be reflected in the culture of the school, including its admission, behaviour and exclusion policies and practices. It is also reflected in the approaches that teachers take and the responses that they make when students encounter difficulties in learning. Ensuring that the aims of the SEN framework are implemented in ways that support the social and academic well-being and progress of all students is a key responsibility of the SENCo.

The aim of this chapter is to introduce the concept of inclusive pedagogy (also referred to as the inclusive pedagogical approach) as a way of responding to individual differences between learners that transcend the limitations inherent in approaches to inclusive practice that are based on scaling-up or transferring individualised special education practices to mainstream classrooms. As will be discussed, the inclusive pedagogical approach has emerged from a programme of research that involves studying the practice of classroom teachers whose classes comprise a diverse range of learners (including disabled students and others identified as having additional support needs), and who are committed to raising the achievements of all learners while safeguarding the Inclusion of those who may be vulnerable to exclusion and other forms of marginalisation. A key driver for this research was to find a way to represent these teachers' craft knowledge of inclusive practice so that it would have meaning for, and be supportive of, the professional learning and practice of others. Although the term craft knowledge is sometimes used by policymakers to denote teaching as a craft that can be learned on the job, here it refers to 'the knowledge that teachers develop through the processes of reflection and practical problem-solving that they engage in to carry out the demands of their jobs' (Cooper and McIntyre, 1996: 76). Craft knowledge is a concept used in research that focusses on recognising, valuing and exploring the complexity of teachers' daily work (Black-Hawkins and Florian, 2012).

Background to the approach

Early efforts to include students with disabilities in mainstream classes focussed on preparing them to fit into an unchanged mainstream. When this proved limited, subsequent efforts sought to change the mainstream by shifting focus from the problem of the child to the problem of the school. Scholars in the UK began to argue for a re-conceptualisation of what they termed the 'special needs task' as part of the process of school improvement (Ainscow, 1991). Consequently, researchers interested in special and inclusive education have focussed on the influence of school factors in learning and in student outcomes. Research in the 1980s explored how school structures could create special educational needs (Tomlinson, 1982). Moses, Hegarty and Jowett (1987) described how special needs teams in mainstream schools might develop a whole-school approach to intervention. As researchers began to study how schools were implementing the ideal of Inclusion, a series of case studies, and action research projects, many of book length, documented the efforts that schools were making to become more inclusive (i.e. Thomas, Walker and Webb, 1998; Allan 1999; Dyson and Milward, 2000; Benjamin, 2002; O'Hanlon, 2003, to name but a few). This work showed that inclusive education was a complex endeavour, characterised by dilemmas (Norwich 1993, 2008) that could be mediated (Rouse and Florian, 1997) as part of a process of increasing participation and reducing exclusion (Booth and Ainscow, 2002). Such work was theoretically principled (Thomas and Loxley, 2001) and required imagination (Hart, 1996, 2000).

Subsequently tools based on individualised approaches such as the *SEN Toolkit* (DfES, 2001), and whole-school approaches such as *Leading on Inclusion* (DfES, 2005), and the *Index for Inclusion* (Booth and Ainscow, 2002) were developed. Today, as new codes of practice come into effect in the countries of the UK, these dual-track developments continue to be reflected in policy. This phenomenon is not unique to the UK but reflects international policy as well (Florian, 2014). The problem is that while the dual-track approach to policy is intended to support individuals as well as improve systems, it also maintains the status quo. Consequently, further advances in developing practice that reduces marginalisation by being inclusive of all learners will require new ways of thinking about long-standing issues and problems. To this end, a change in focus is needed.

Why a change in focus?

There are five interrelated reasons why a change in focus is needed, and all of them can be linked to the intractable problems of individualisation. First, a focus on individual difference has been shown to be more likely to reinforce than solve what has been called the dilemma of difference. That is, as Minow (1990) has shown, when remedies that are put in place to protect vulnerable groups depend on the identification of difference, they are likely to reinforce the very difference that the remedy is intended to redress. Such has been the case with special needs education, where polices intended to ensure access to education have paradoxically created problems of equity within it (for example, students from particular minority groups are more likely to be identified as having special educational needs). Although notions of inclusive education have challenged the concept of special educational needs as 'different' or 'additional' to that which is provided to the majority of children, much of the provision associated with inclusive education reproduces the problems of marginalisation that occur when students who experience difficulties in learning are identified as needing something different. This is because many conceptualisations of Inclusion have done little more in practical terms than replace the phrase 'special needs education' with 'inclusive education'.

This is problematic because of the historical presumption that the identification of individual students who need something different has direct implications for educational interventions. The idea of matching child characteristics with interventions remains popular despite the knowledge that different teaching strategies are not differentially effective with different types of learners (Ysseldyke, 2001).

This is the second reason a change in focus is needed. To date, efforts to define what is special about special needs education have concluded that the teaching strategies used in mainstream education can be adapted to assist students identified as having additional needs in learning (Vaughn and Linan-Thompson, 2003; Davis and Florian, 2004; Lewis and Norwich, 2005; Kavale, 2007). The process of making an accommodation is an important element of any pedagogical approach but does not constitute pedagogy in itself. As will be argued, knowledge about human differences is important (a student who is an English language learner is different from a student who has been diagnosed as having autism; a 6-year-old is different from a 10-year-old, and so on), but the relationship between cognitive processing and learning is still too crude to be directly helpful in educational assessment or intervention (Howard-Jones, 2007). In practice teachers use strategies that are matched to the purpose of the learning, and they adapt these strategies in response to differences between learners.

Moreover, and this is the third reason a change in focus is needed, teachers themselves have reported that they do not differentiate among types of students when planning lessons. For example, Florian and Rouse (2001) studied the extent to which classroom practice in the various subjects of the National Curriculum was consistent with that which is promoted as effective by the literature on Inclusion. A questionnaire designed to examine possible relationships between subject taught and teaching strategy used included an open-ended comments section to aid the interpretation of the data. Teachers commented that the use of some strategies was resource-dependent (e.g. use of computer-assisted instruction) while others depend on administrative arrangements and support (e.g. 'team teaching and co-teaching are difficult to organise but they work'). Some teachers went out of their way to comment that they made no distinction between pupils with SEN and others when it comes to teaching strategy although others made very specific comments about how they included pupils with SEN in terms of behavioural strategies (i.e. 'give the pupil a responsibility vital to the lesson'). These findings suggested that the ways in which the teachers were responding to individual differences were not dependent on, or specific to, the identification of special educational need.

Fourth, while inclusive education is based on the principle that local schools should provide for *all* children, some way of determining 'all' has to be established. In England, Ofsted (2000) guidance specifies that inspectors attend 'to the provision made for and the achievement of different groups of pupils within a school'. A focus on groups of learners as a way of determining 'all' is problematic because of the many sources of variation within and between any identified groups of learners. Yet provision is often organised in this way (for example, according to year groups, students with SEN, EAL, and so forth) despite the fact that individual learners usually fit into more than one category. Even seemingly discrete categories like year groups are not straightforward because each one will contain learners of different ages who will vary considerably. Whatever can be known about a particular category of learners will be limited in the educational purposes it can serve, because the variations between members of a group make it difficult to predict or evaluate provision for each of the individuals within it.

Nevertheless schools are organised by grouping pupils according to commonly agreed categories, and the utilitarian principle of the greatest good for the greatest number (e.g. statistical norms of ability distributed according to a bell-shaped curve). In this way, what is ordinarily provided will meet the needs of most learners, while a few at the tail ends of the distribution may require something 'additional to' or 'different from' that which is ordinarily available. Indeed this is the definition of special needs education and additional support in many countries, and this is the fifth problem: when students who encounter difficulties in learning are identified as having 'special educational needs' an intractable cycle is formed – students are assigned membership of the group because they are judged to possess the attributes of group membership, and they are believed to have the attributes of the group because they are members of it. The problem is that identification of 'special educational needs' can also lower a teacher's expectations about what it is possible for a student to achieve.

One example is that of autism spectrum disorder (ASD). For this rapidly growing group, identification depends on a clinical assessment of a 'triad of impairments' associated with difficulties in social communication, social understanding, and flexibility of thought and imagination (Wing and Gould, 1979). The National Autistic Society (NAS) in the UK defines ASD as:

> A complex lifelong developmental disability that affects the way a person communicates and relates to people around them. The autism spectrum includes the syndromes described by Kanner and by Asperger but is wider than these two subgroups.
>
> (Wing and Gould, 1979)

> Many people have a mixture of features from these two syndromes but do not fit neatly into either. The whole spectrum is defined by the presence of impairments affecting social interaction, social communication and social imagination, known as the triad of impairments. This is always accompanied by a narrow, repetitive range of activities.

> A range of other problems is also commonly found in association with the triad but the three basic impairments are the defining criteria.

> Individuals who are considered to be on the autism spectrum are all very different. The range of intellectual ability extends from severely learning disabled right up to normal or even above average levels of intellect. Similarly, linguistic skills range from those who are mute to those who display complex, grammatically correct speech.
>
> (NAS, http://www.nas.org.uk/nas/jsp/polopoly.jsp?d=1048anda=2224)

Clearly this definition describes a condition that contains many sources of variation. As the definition itself specifies, 'many people have a mixture of features . . . but do not fit neatly into either'. Here, variation between the individuals within the ASD group suggests that there will be degrees of difference between members with regard to the many characteristics thought to affect learning. And yet, tacit judgments are often made about learners based on assumptions that they possess all the characteristics of group membership to the same degree. Moreover, the identification of the difficulties in learning associated with ASD is often assumed to require specialist teaching. Questions about the nature of such teaching are often answered with information about ASD itself, including what learners on the ASD spectrum can *not* do by virtue of their impairments, rather than focussing on the learning that might be possible. In this way, the categorisation of ASD, and the assumed cognitive impairments that are associated with it, arguably put a ceiling on learning and achievement.

As this example shows, a focus on learner types is problematic because of the many sources of variation within and between identified groups of learners that make educationally relevant distinctions between them difficult to observe and judge. Thus, whatever can be known about a particular category of learners will be limited in the educational purposes it can serve, because the variations between members of a group make it difficult to predict or evaluate provision for individuals in it. Clearly the limitations and problems of focussing on individual problems suggest that alternative approaches for responding to them are needed.

Theoretical framework for inclusive pedagogy

As noted in the introduction, the inclusive pedagogical approach was developed in part to help reduce variability in the quality of current provision. In so doing, it takes as its starting point a concern with addressing the problems associated with the limitations described above. Inclusive pedagogy sets out to replace traditional approaches to teaching children identified as having special educational needs that are based upon the argument that such children necessarily require something 'different from' or 'additional to' that which is ordinarily available, and that what is needed can be matched to learner characteristics. While it does not deny individual differences between learners, it assumes that differences are an ordinary aspect of the human condition. Consequently, the approach is located within a socio-cultural framework on pedagogy (Alexander, 2004) where the complexities inherent in providing for differences among students are subsumed within a set of interrelated ideas about children, learning, teaching and curriculum, as well as the school and policy contexts by which they are legitimised (for a discussion, see Florian and Kershner, 2009).

A socio-cultural perspective is important because it permits a consideration of individual differences as something to be expected and understood in terms of the *interactions* between many different variables rather than fixed states within individuals. Difference is not the problem; rather understanding that *all* learners differ is the theoretical starting point for inclusive pedagogy. A socio-cultural perspective assumes that 'all children have much in common, including the fact that their individual characteristics and preferences are uniquely interrelated rather than neatly categorisable' (Florian and Kershner, 2009: 174). As such, it offers a productive way of thinking about how to understand and respond to the complexities inherent in educating diverse groups of learners and encourages open-ended views of all children's potential for learning. This is consistent with what Susan Hart and her colleagues (Hart, Dixon, Drummond, et al., 2004) have called the core idea of *transformability* to assert the principled belief that 'children's capacity to learn can change and be changed for the better as a result of what happens and what people do in the present' (ibid.: 166). Their argument is that how teachers respond in the present can affect any child's capacity to learn and in part determines what will be achieved.

In addition, a sociocultural perspective on learning steers the teacher to focus on how to access and use knowledge about how people learn when helping children who are experiencing difficulties. Here it is productive to think about learning in terms of the development of expertise, and how novices differ from experts (Bransford, Brown and Cocking, 2000), rather than to differentiate groups of learners on the basis of perceived limitations. While sociocultural factors produce individual differences, learning occurs through shared activity in social contexts. Thus, the teacher must think about everybody in the class and how they will work together, as opposed to differentiating for some on the basis of judgments about what they cannot do compared to others of similar age.

This is not to suggest that individual differences are unimportant. As Ravet (2011) has noted, a teacher may have two students, both of whom are experiencing similar difficulties in learning (her example is with understanding common idioms), but differences between the students (a learner with English as a second language and a learner on the autism spectrum) mean that the nature of the misunderstanding is different in each case, necessitating different responses to the difficulty in learning. She worries that an inclusive pedagogical approach might lead to 'an over-reliance on generalist teacher practices' at the expense of attention to individual differences. As will be shown below, the inclusive pedagogical approach does not ignore individual differences between students. Rather it encourages the teacher to extend the range of options that are available to *everyone in the community of the classroom*. This is a subtle but important shift in thinking about individual differences between learners that focusses on learning as a shared activity and thereby avoids the potentially negative effects of treating some students as different.

The inclusive pedagogical approach

Inclusive pedagogy is based on a shift in thinking *away* from the idea of special needs education as a specialised response to individual difficulty, *towards* one that focusses on extending what is ordinarily available to everyone in the learning community of the classroom, taking account that there will be individual differences between learners. This shift in thinking represents a subtle difference in perspective with profound implications for practice. It does not suggest that specialist knowledge is irrelevant or unnecessary. To the contrary, supporting class teachers to utilise knowledge of individual differences to extend what is generally available to *everybody* rather than including *all* students by differentiating for *some*, can avoid the negative effects of treating some students as different.

Extending what is generally available

The approach to inclusive pedagogy detailed below builds on research which examined how some schools have developed strategies to raise the achievement of all their children, while safeguarding the Inclusion of those who were vulnerable to exclusion and other forms of marginalisation (Black-Hawkins,

Table 9.1 Contrast of 'additional needs' and inclusive pedagogical approaches

Additional needs approach to Inclusion	Manifest in terms of Inclusion	Manifest in terms of exclusion	Inclusive pedagogical approach
	Most and some		Everybody
A student with autism uses Voice4Me on an iPod Touch to communicate with his teacher and peers during a field trip to an historic airfield. The tool is selected specifically because a visual approach will reduce the 'processing burden' for the student and enhance both his learning and enjoyment of the trip. He selects a sequence of symbols/icons/pictures, which represent words and/or phrases to tell stories about the trip. The student uses an iPhone to collect photos and videos of the trip, assign meta-tags, and upload the content to a website of the group's field trip.	Student participates in the trip. Student works alongside peers. Student participates in learning activities by contributing photographs to a web page, which is created by all the class illustrating selected idioms.	Peers of the student complain it is unfair that they are not allowed to use their digital phones. Student with autism is marked as different because he is getting special treatment.	Focus is on everybody in planning for the school trip, and the building of a web page to document the trip. While a visual approach is likely to be supportive for some students, immersion in the social context of the site will be more relevant for others. All students are involved in planning how to document the trip – types of information (such as narrative accounts, photographs, audio recordings, maps to illustrate where they went, statistical information such as distance travelled). Students then plan how this data could be collected and negotiate who would be responsible for the different tasks. Returning from the trip the class collate their different forms of data to generate stories about the event and develop the website page.

Florian and Rouse, 2007). While this study explored schools as institutions and considered how values and beliefs within a school's culture shape the teaching and learning that takes place, subsequent research focussed on teacher 'craft knowledge' about how they extend what is 'generally available' to all (Florian and Black-Hawkins, 2011). This was supplemented by the findings from further studies of how teachers can be prepared to use inclusive pedagogy (Florian and Linklater, 2010; Florian and Spratt, 2013).

A key finding from these studies suggested that teachers engaged in inclusive pedagogy work out what they can do to support the learner while maintaining a commitment to *everybody* (Hart et al., 2004), and avoiding situations that mark some students as different. This does not rule out the use of specialists or specialist knowledge but it does not require the identification of special educational need *within* individual learners. While this may happen as a result of seeking support, it is often because administrative rules require such identification rather than because of a teacher attribution of a 'problem' within the learner. Where specialists are consulted, it is in support of the teacher's effort to ensure that the learner is meaningfully engaged in the community of the classroom. The phrase 'community of the classroom' is used purposefully to avoid the idea that the approach is merely advocating whole-class teaching. It is in the *ways* that teachers respond to individual differences, the *choices* they make about group work and *how* they utilise specialist knowledge that differentiate inclusive practice from other pedagogical approaches.

Focussing on how teachers extend what is generally available in a classroom lesson or activity offers an alternative perspective from which to consider inclusive educational practice to those used in traditional approaches to teaching children, identified as having special educational needs, that are based upon the argument that such children necessarily require something 'different from' or 'additional to' that which is ordinarily available. This is illustrated in Table 9.1 where the inclusive pedagogical approach is contrasted with a special additional needs approach to inclusive practice. While this approach, also referred to as the 'additional needs' approach to Inclusion, focusses only on the student who has been identified as in need of additional support, the inclusive pedagogical approach focusses on everybody in the community of the classroom.

As is shown, inclusive pedagogy is defined not in the *choice* of strategy but in its *use*. This required the provision of rich learning opportunities that were sufficiently made available for *everyone*, so that all learners are able to participate in the community of the classroom (Florian and Linklater, 2010). For additional examples of this approach, see Florian and Black-Hawkins (2011); Florian and Spratt (2013).

Conclusion

Inclusive pedagogy rejects the idea that it is educationally helpful to base teaching approaches on categories of learners. The approach has been developed in part as a response to the concern that an emphasis on studying human differences perpetuates the belief that they are predictive of difficulties in learning and potential achievement. This is highly problematic because of the well-documented negative effects of marking some students as in need of something 'different', particularly with regard to the lowering of expectations for achievement. It is also concerned with reducing the variability in current practice so that more students with disabilities and special educational needs have a good experience of schooling.

Inclusive pedagogy is concerned with redressing the limitations on learning that are often inadvertently placed on children when they are judged 'less able'. It does not deny differences between learners but moves to accommodate them by extending what is ordinarily available to all rather than by differentiating for some. Here there is a shift in focus away from the idea of Inclusion as a specialised response to some learners that enables them to have access or participate in that which is available to most students. Extending what is ordinarily available to all learners, taking account of the fact that there will be individual differences between them is a subtle but profound difference in approaching teaching and learning for all that is the hallmark of inclusive pedagogy.

The SENCo's work must begin with an understanding of the variability in identification and type of special educational need, and an acknowledgement that the range and forms of provision availalable can lead to important new insights about how teachers are able to be both effective and inclusive in their practice. For example, while some schools exclude, or refuse to include, certain students on the grounds that teachers do not have the requisite knowledge and skills to teach them, teachers in other schools have been able to include students with many different types of special educational needs. This raises questions about what constitutes the necessary knowledge and skills teachers need to learn in order to work with *all* of the members of a classroom community *together*. In answering these questions, the study of individual teachers' successful practice is providing an articulation of inclusive pedagogy as a way of working with all of the members of a classroom community together (*everybody*), as opposed to individualising for each student. By accepting the notion of individual differences among learners without relying predominately on individualised approaches to responding to them, teachers, with the support of SENCos, can help to ensure that the promise of inclusive education to provide good quality educational opportunities and experiences for *all* is less variable and less difficult to secure for those students who experience difficulties in learning and have not had positive experiences of mainstream education.

References

Ainscow, M. (1991) *Effective Schools for All.* London: David Fulton.

Alexander, R. (2004) Still no pedagogy? Principle, pragmatism and compliance in primary education. *Cambridge Journal of Education*, 34(1): 7–33.

Allan, J. (1999) *Actively Seeking Inclusion: Pupils with Special Needs in Mainstream Schools.* London: Falmer Press.

Benjamin, S. (2002) *The Micropolitics of Special Educational Needs: An Ethnography.* Buckingham: Open University Press.

Black, A., and Norwich, B. (2014) *Contrasting Responses to Diversity: School Placement Trends 2007–2013 for All Local Authorities in England.* Bristol: CSIE.

Black-Hawkins, K. and Florian, L. (2012) Classroom teachers' craft knowledge of their inclusive practice. *Teachers and Teaching*, 18(5): 567–584.

Black-Hawkins, K., Florian, L. and Rouse, M. (2007) *Achievement and Inclusion in Schools.* London: Routledge Falmer.

Booth, T. and Ainscow, M. (2002) *The Index for Inclusion: Developing Learning and Participation in Schools*, revised edition. Bristol: CSIE.

Bransford, J.D., Brown, A.L. and Cocking, R. (2000) *How People Learn: Brain, Mind, Experience and School.* Washington, DC: National Academy Press.

Cooper, P. and McIntyre, D. (1996) *Effective Teaching and Learning: Teachers' and Students' Perspectives.* Buckingham: Open University Press.

Davis, P. and Florian, L. (2004) *Teaching Strategies and Approaches for Pupils with Special Educational Needs: A Scoping Study (Research Report 516).* London: DfES.

DCSF (2009) *Lamb Inquiry: Special Educational Needs and Parental Confidence.* London: DCSF. Retrieved 15 February 2010 from: http://www.dcsf.gov.uk/lambinquiry/related.shtml.

DfE (2014) Increasing options and improving provision for children with special educational needs *(SEN).* Retrieved 31 July 2014 from: https://www.gov.uk/government/policies/increasing-options-and-improving-provision-for-children-with-special-educational-needs-sen

DfES (1997) *Excellence for All Children.* London: HMSO.

DfES (2001) *SEN Toolkit.* DfES 0558-2001. Retrieved 15 February 2010 from: http://publications.teachernet.gov.uk/default.aspx?PageFunction=productdetailsandPageMode=publicationsandProductId=DfES+0558+2001.

DfES (2005) *Leading on Inclusion.* DfES 1183-2005 G. London: HMSO.

Dyson, A. and Millward, A. (2000) *Schools and Special Needs: Issues of Innovation and Inclusion.* London: Paul Chapman.

Florian, L. (2014) What counts as evidence of inclusive education? *European Journal of Special Needs Education*, 29(3): 286–294.

Florian, L. and Black-Hawkins, K. (2011) Exploring inclusive pedagogy. *British Educational Research Journal*, 37(5): 813–828.

Florian, L. and Kershner, R. (2009) Inclusive pedagogy, in H. Daniels, H. Lauder and J. Porter (eds) *Knowledge, Values and Educational Policy: A Critical Perspective.* London: Routledge, pp. 173–183.

Florian, L. and Linklater, H. (2010) Preparing teachers for inclusive education: using inclusive pedagogy to enhance teaching and learning for all. *Cambridge Journal of Education*, 40(4): 369–386.

Florian, L. and Rouse, M. (2001) Inclusive practice in English secondary schools: lessons learned. *Cambridge Journal of Education*, 31(3): 399–412.

Florian, L. and Spratt, J. (2013) Enacting inclusion: a framework for interrogating inclusive practice. *European Journal of Special Needs Education*, 28(2): 119–135.

Hart, S. (1996) *Beyond Special Needs: Enhancing Children's Learning through Innovative Thinking.* London: Paul Chapman.

Hart, S. (2000) *Thinking Through Teaching: A Framework for Enhancing Participation and Learning.* London: David Fulton.

Hart, S., Dixon, A., Drummond M. J. and McIntyre, D. (2004) *Learning Without Limits.* Maidenhead: Open University Press.

Howard-Jones, P. (2007) *Neuroscience and Education: Issues and Opportunities. A Commentary by the Teaching and Learning Research Programme.* London: Economic and Social Research Council. Retrieved 22 September 2008 from: http://www.tlrp.org/pub/commentaries.html.

Kavale, K. (2007) Quantitative research synthesis: meta-analysis of research on meeting special educational needs, in L. Florian (ed.) *The Sage Handbook of Special Education.* London: Sage.

Lewis, A. and Norwich, B. (eds) (2005) *Special Teaching for Special Children? Pedagogies for Inclusion.* Maidenhead: Open University Press.

Minow, M. (1990) *Making All the Difference: Inclusion, Exclusion and American Law*. Ithaca, NY: Cornell University Press.

Moses, D., Hegarty, S. and Jowett, S. (1987) *Supporting Ordinary Schools*. Windsor: NfER/Nelson.

National Autism Society, website: http://www.nas.org.uk/nas/jsp/polopoly.jsp?d=1048anda= 2224 (retrieved 9 March 2009).

Norwich, B. (1993) Ideological dilemmas in special needs education: practitioners' views. *Oxford Review of Education*, 19(4): 527–545.

Norwich, B. (2008) *Dilemmas of Difference: International Perspectives and Future Directions*. London: Routledge.

Ofsted (2000) *Evaluating Educational Inclusion Guidance for Inspectors and Schools*, London: Ofsted.

O'Hanlon, C. (2003) *Educational Inclusion as Action Research: An Interpretive Discourse*. Buckingham: Open University Press.

Ravet, J. (2011) Inclusive/exclusive? Contradictory perspectives on autism and Inclusion: the case for an integrative position. *International Journal of Inclusive Education*, 15(6): 667–682.

Rouse, M. and Florian, L. (1997) Inclusive education in the marketplace. *International Journal of Inclusive Education*, 1(4): 323–336.

Thomas, G. and Loxley, A. (2001) *Deconstructing Special Education and Constructing Inclusion*. Buckingham: Open University Press.

Thomas, G., Walker, D. and Webb, J. (1998) *The Making of the Inclusive School*. London: Routledge.

Tomlinson, S. (1982) *A Sociology of Special Education*. London: Routledge and Kegan Paul.

Vaughn, S. and Linan-Thompson, S. (2003) What is special about special education for students with learning disabilities? *The Journal of Special Education*, 37(3): 140–147.

Wing, L. and Gould, J. (1979) Severe impairments of social interaction and associated abnormalities in children: epidemiology and classification. *Journal of Autism and Childhood Schizophrenia*, 9: 11–29.

Ysseldyke, J. E. (2001) Reflections on a research career: generalizations from 25 years of research on assessment and instructional decision making. *Exceptional Children*, 67(3): 295–309.

10 Reflecting on the role of the SENCo

Fiona and Graham Hallett

In the three chapters that conclude Part 1 of this book, Chapters 4–6, there is an attempt to capture the voice of practitioners, and others, reflecting on the experiences, challenges, tensions and difficulties that arise in the way that the role of the SENCo is operationalised in everyday practice. The views, to a large extent, address situations that are representative of the structures and systems that make up the SEND landscape within schools in England, and which will not be unfamiliar to those working in the other constituent parts of the UK. Those with whom we had conversations were drawn from schools in the mainstream sector at both primary and secondary level, and from special schools catering for the whole age range of pupils.

A major area explored within these conversations concerned the debate surrounding the SENCo as a strategic leader. In Chapter 8, Brahm Norwich, in providing an extended critique of this debate, questions the duplication of middle management roles in schools through the idea of the 'connective specialisation'; as a consequence, no further discussion of this area will be offered here.

However, it also became increasingly clear that the role is described in terms of the tensions and conflicts that are inherent in the structures existing within the settings where the role of the SENCo is delivered. That some of these tensions and conflicts derive from the complexity surrounding the nexus of conflicting policy and ideological standpoints at play within the education system became apparent at an early stage; it is also the case that a second layer of complexity emerged, within the operationalisation in practice of systems that are elaborate and multi-layered, perhaps reflecting ideas around what has been described as 'street-level bureaucracy' (Lipsky, 1980).

The first of these levels of complexity will not, perhaps, be surprising. For those who have been involved with the education system for an extended period, and given the time that we spend in schools as pupils, and beyond, in becoming teachers, teaching assistants, lecturers, etc., this probably applies to us all, the changes to that system will be familiar. In terms of what is written in this chapter, perhaps the most significant of those changes include the introduction of markets in the education system deriving from the advent of neo-liberal policies, the reversal of the 'bias towards Inclusion' (DfE, 2011) signalled in *Support and Aspiration*, the Coalition Green Paper of that year, the introduction of the *SEND Code of Practice* (DfE/DoH, 2015), and the increasing influence of school-based training models for teachers, focussed around programmes such as School Direct (NCTL, 2014a).

One of the most obvious effects of these changes has been the fracturing of the school system with the introduction and proliferation of academies, which now make up the majority of schools in England for secondary age pupils. Directly funded, albeit on the basis of a locally derived formula, the growth in the number of academies has reduced the influence of local authorities in the provision of education, something that might be seen to threaten the accountability of the school system to the local electorate, without necessarily replacing this with a centralised oversight other than that provided by organisations such as Ofsted. The more recent introduction of free schools and University Technical Colleges (UTC) has increased the complex nature of the system, in response to the demand for a system that is more responsive to the right of parents to select schools within a market of high performing schools, where that performance is determined within narrow parameters focussing on attainment and performativity.

It should not be forgotten that many special schools have sought and gained academy status; here a slightly more nuanced funding system is in operation, with local authority top-up funding supplementing the notional £10000 per pupil per annum funding that is the basis for provision within non-academy settings (Education Funding Agency [EFA], 2014). While there is likely to still be a close relationship between such a setting and the funding local authority, it is also likely that these links will be weakened in comparison to a setting that remains within the 'family' of Specialist settings formerly seen in most local authorities.

It is also probably the case that the second level of complexity mentioned above, which might be described as being intra-setting, is also familiar. In any organisational system, it is perhaps inevitable that conflicting aims and aspirations will create tensions and challenges for those operating within that system. The contested evolution of the role of the SENCo since its formal inception following the introduction of the first SEN Code of Practice (DfE, 1994) is well documented (Layton, 2008; Cowne, 2008; Zwed, 2011; Robertson, 2012; Griffiths and Dubsky, 2012; Brown and Doveston, 2014), with research noting issues such as how the role should be operationalised, the strategic nature of the role, the time needed to effectively discharge the role, the status of the post holder, etc. More recent research, conducted following the introduction of the National Award for SEN Coordination (Pearson, 2015), suggests that such tensions still exist, although these occur in areas of responsibility that might not have been as relevant prior to the introduction of the National Award.

The inevitable outcome of the changes represented here is the development of an education system that reflects a varied history of policy change based on competing ideological and theoretical standpoints representing 'multiple competing aims' (Rix, 2015). As Rix goes on to point out, this has led to a system that, while meeting the educational ambitions of many students, has consistently failed the educational needs of a significant minority of pupils, a situation that appears to be entrenched, despite the often stated aim of reducing inequality through the promotion of 'Inclusion'.

It is entirely possible, of course, that the system that has evolved is based on such irreconcilable aims and ambitions that a common sense of direction is unlikely to emerge. As an aim, raising standards might seem to be both benign, and oxymoronic; as Robinson suggests, it is unlikely that an educationalist would propose lowering them (Robinson, 2008). However, the way in which we set about achieving the aim of raising standards may well give rise to practices that cement inequality within classroom structures, for example, in the creating of a linear curriculum that emphasises objective-led teaching and the acquisition of know-ledge over other worthwhile learning, particularly where this is narrowed down so that it lends itself easily to the type of testing and assessment that is so evident in current practice. This might well be regarded by a significant number of teachers as an unsuitable way of implementing teaching, learning and assessment within schools, leading to an unsustainable narrowing of the opportunities that might be offered to pupils, particularly those working with children marginalised by these practices. For these practitioners, a broader definition of value might be proposed, valuing achievement over attainment, a conceptualisation that recognises the diversity of learners within our schools, and which seeks to extend opportunities to be successful to all learners, regardless of the learning propensities and abilities that they bring to the classroom.

It is equally likely that the way that systems become entrenched might not simply grow out of policy positions derived from different views of what an education system should seek to secure for those who use it. The development of initial teacher education in recent years has also demonstrated a considerable change of emphasis that seems to have developed within a narrowly prescriptive framework of attributes supportive of the sort of agenda contained within the raising achievement movement; the increased emphasis on competence, measured against a set of Teachers Standards, has seemed to have encouraged training practices that emphasise the learning of classroom routines and procedures, rather than an engagement with theoretical standpoints that require the construction of a teacher identity capable of meeting the learning needs of all children. While the value of school-based practice within teacher education cannot be questioned, there would seem to be considerable value in mediating these experiences through the lens of thoughtful reflection in the kind of environment provided by experience away from placement. Here views opposing the sort of practices that need to be delivered on placement within schools can be considered and discussed, without the perceived interference that characterised the way that the systematic synthetic phonics initiative was promulgated, for example. The opportunity to access and consider a more balanced and nuanced approach to educational innovation and practice might well only be possible in a setting somewhat distanced from placement, where experienced practitioners can offer theoretical insights derived from extensive classroom practice.

There would seem then to be considerable challenges to be overcome if any change of emphasis in our current configuration of schooling, and of the practices that occur within the settings that this configuration gives rise to, is to be put in place, for the benefit of all pupils. It can be argued that the challenge here is not about replacing one system with another, based on the views expressed by protagonists of a more socially equitable system that the current one is irrevocably unjust and unfair. This is an argument that is likely to be countered by reference to the measures that demonstrate a steadily increasing level of attainment within that system, exemplified by the outstanding results obtained in some settings that overturn the expected outcomes for similar young people.

Rather, it would seem to be much more useful to abandon this type of binary thinking and instead to consider ways in which changes and adjustments can be made within current practice, as a way of steadily moving towards a more equitable system. These might be based on educational principles that maximise achievement for all, promote Inclusion, and explore ways of reconsidering teaching and learning so that more pupils are given the opportunity to excel without the need for interventions, withdrawal, or the use of practices that label, or otherwise distinguish and emphasise individual pupils as different. It is clear that this will require a great deal of goodwill and compromise, and this is not likely to be something that will take root in all schools either immediately, or even in the longer term. However, it must be a direction of travel that we should be willing to make. Otherwise we will continue to endorse and support a system that seems to marginalise and categorise far too many pupils, placing them under undue levels of stress for developing and relatively fragile minds. That this system offers the 'glittering prizes' to those fortunate to be possessed of the type of social capital needed to manipulate a system that favours the individual, appears to privilege the exercise of some rights over others (parental choice versus accessibility), and values a sort of competitive preparation for employability as a marker of educational success, also appears unarguable.

It seems to us that the sort of debate that is needed here is one that lies at the heart of the role of the SENCo, or at least is likely to be personified in the professional and moral purpose of those attracted to the role. It is certainly the case that the views expressed by those with whom we have had conversations can be characterised as child-centred and based on the holistic development of all pupils within their settings. The degree to which these views were explored and developed differed, often because of the nature or stage of the setting involved; for example, there seemed to be a clear divide between the primary and secondary sector, in the degree to which ideas could be operationalised, if not in the degree to which teachers in both types of setting articulated their views. It was also the case that there seemed to be a clearer focus on breadth and balance in the curriculum view of those from specialist settings, as opposed to the more narrowly progression-based views expressed by mainstream colleagues. Finally, there were also marked differences within each of these groupings, with some primary settings, for example, being set up to maximise attainment, while others seemed to be much more focussed on practices that celebrated and extended what was seen as suitable types of achievement within the context in which the setting operated.

However, it was also clear that a number of challenges and tensions existed that stood outside these school-level differences, and it is our intention here to consider how these challenges and tensions might be addressed, within the processes and experiences that make up the National Award and within the personal development necessary in holders of the role of the SENCo. The first of these challenges is what seems to be an increasing use of medicalised assessment within the procedures laid down by the SEND Code of Practice (DfE/DoH, 2015).

It is interesting, in the context of this seeming return to a 'medical model' of disability, to consider the words of Warnock (Warnock, Norwich and Terzi, 2010) writing about the eponymous report of the Committee of Inquiry into the Education of Handicapped Children and Young People, 1978. The intention of the report is clearly stated, as an attempt 'to articulate a concept of education that could make sense in the context of any child' (Warnock, Norwich and Terzi, 2010: 16). In setting three goals, of independence, enjoyment and understanding, a position was taken that suggested that reaching these goals was not something that all pupils could be expected to achieve at the same rate or with the same facility. Indeed, the removal of the barriers likely to be experienced by some learners in reaching these common goals was seen as the essence of what was proposed; that is, the provision of what was needed to ensure progress for each child, according to their individual need or needs.

This presupposed a move away from the medical diagnosis of need; indeed, those with long memories will recall the move away from forms and processes that lay within the remit of medical professionals, and their replacement with multi-agency assessment processes moderated through the education system. It also presupposed the abandonment of assessment through specific labels, and the introduction of assessments based on the perceived educational needs of the child or young person. That this ultimately led to an unforeseen explosion in the numbers of pupils assessed as having a special educational needs is a well-rehearsed debate, although it is also useful to recognise that, even at the time, the Warnock Report used figures that suggested as many as 1 in 5 pupils would experience such a need at some stage of their educational journey.

It is also the case that this period marked the opening of a debate not just about the assessment of pupils with special educational needs, but also about where the education of those characterised as needing a Statement of Special Educational Needs should take place. While clearly describing a system that included both mainstream and special schools, the Warnock Report also gave consideration to the need for a more flexible and less separate system. The Report describes three types of integrative setting, that suggest an increasing level of what might be termed Inclusion, by offering locational, social and functional integration (Warnock Report, DES, 1978, Section 7.6). This perhaps reflected ideas of educational equality and opportunity that were part of influential discourse at the time; what is certain is that there was a consistent application of, first, integrative, and later, inclusive practices over the years that followed. The need for segregated provision for pupils with Visual or Hearing Impairment was challenged early on in this debate, alongside the need for many Physically Disabled pupils being placed in settings of this type, particularly as many of these settings were residential, and in attending such settings, pupils were denied the chance to grow up with friends and family from the home neighbourhood. A similar movement saw a reduction in the number of places available in schools for pupils assessed as having Moderate Learning Difficulties, and a significant reappraisal of the educational potential, and therefore placement, of pupils with Down's syndrome. It is unquestionably the case that this resulted in the contraction and closure of a significant number of special schools, something that was countered to a large degree by the need to open new schools or extend existing provision for the increasing number of pupils being assessed with special educational needs such as Social, Emotional and Behavioural Difficulties or Autism Spectrum Disorder.

There is now an almost total acceptance that this process led to a significant and lasting reduction of the number of children being offered special school places, with a consequent burden being placed on mainstream schools to meet the educational requirements of pupils for whom they were often said to be ill-equipped; the so-called 'bias towards academic Inclusion' (DfE, 2011). It is interesting therefore to consider the statistics provided by a Statistical First Release (SFR) published in 2007 (DCSF, 2007), which show a reduction in the percentage of newly Statemented pupils being placed in mainstream school during the preceding year (–1.5 per cent), and a marked decrease in the number of pupils with new Statements being placed in mainstream schools over the 10 years from 1998 to 2007 (74.0 per cent to 61.5 per cent). This suggests that any move towards a fully inclusive education system operating without segregated provision was much less influential than is generally suggested, even prior to the change in policy direction that followed in 2010 with the election of the Coalition government.

What is unarguably the case, however, is that wherever statemented pupils were placed in these years, the assessment process that led to the issuing or otherwise of a Statement of Special Educational Needs, or that supported the other stages of the graduated approach extant at the time, was focussed on the educational needs of the child at the centre of the process, rather than simply offering a medical diagnosis of those needs. Of course, in many cases a specific impairment or disability formed part of the supportive evidential base for the assessment, but this was neither seen to be the focus of the assessment, nor its prime purpose. This no longer seems to be the case, at least in a number of local authorities, and this represents a worrying development in our perception of need and disability.

It is again noteworthy that Mary Warnock (Warnock, Norwich and Terzi, 2010) recognised the difficulties that bedevilled the education system because of the failure of the Warnock Report to provide a definition of special educational need, leading to a marked disparity in rates of assessment and of the reasons offered for assessments. However, it is the case that successive SEND Codes of Practice (DfE, 1994, DfES, 2001, DfE/DoH, 2015) have made it clear that the individual needs of a child should form the basis for any assessment to be carried out under the processes outlined in those Codes, rather than seeking to use a taxonomy or diagnostic framework to link those needs to a specific medically defined condition or disability. Presumably, this was an attempt to acknowledge that the needs of one child with a particular, often contested, condition such as Dyslexia might be very different from that of another child with the same condition, both in degree, and to the extent that the need presents barriers within that child's educational journey. This would seem to be a crucial, if often ignored, part of the changing view of special needs that developed in the aftermath of the Warnock Report, a view that had an undoubted effect on the way that schools responded to pupils identified as having Special Educational Needs. The challenge of offering an entitlement to a broad, balanced, relevant and differentiated curriculum (DES, 1985) as part of the development of ideas around the introduction of the National Curriculum (DES, 1989), encouraged an increasing emphasis on ways of working with pupils at the margins, to provide a more justifiable balancing of the educational and social elements of good practice.

It is this focus on seeing assessment of need as a balanced process, focussing on the identified *educational* needs as much as on any other, that seems to have become diluted, or indeed, to have disappeared altogether, and this is where the danger lies. In examining practice across a limited, but fairly representative, group of local authorities, it seemed that many had adopted policies of channelling assessment procedures into a limited number of pathways associated with definable and diagnosable medical conditions. For example, we heard of students being assigned to 'the Autism pathway' as a means of obtaining an Education, Health and Care Plan (EHCP) (DfE/DoH, 2015); in another example, a referral to CAMHS (Child and Adolescent Mental Health Services) was seen as a necessary precursor to seeking an assessment within current procedures.

There is, of course, an argument here that prior to seeking an assessment, a referral to CAMHS, or to a designated health professional, is an appropriate and important part of the data gathering process needed to comply with the requirement that a local authority, in considering whether a statutory assessment is necessary, 'will need to take into account a wide range of evidence' (DfE/DoH, 2015, Section 9.14: 145). However, it could equally be argued that what is happening is the re-emergence of ideas aligned to the medical model of disability, with the perceived needs of the child being described within the constraints of an identifiable medical condition, rather than in terms of the educational needs displayed by that pupil within the teaching and learning constraints of the curriculum offer in that setting.

The danger here is one of selectivity; a child may display learning characteristics that make progress towards identified targets very difficult, and this lack of progress might well fit within a medical condition such as Attention Deficit/Hyperactivity Disorder (ADHD); another child might demonstrate difficulties of a similar degree but not have such clearly definable 'symptoms'. In this case, one pupil is much more likely to be referred for statutory assessment following the involvement of CAMHS, the other not leaving the school to meet those needs from existing resources, and denying the child a possible entitlement to greater support within the EHCP process; this certainly seemed to reflect the situation described in some of our conversations with practitioners in the field. By extension, it is at least possible that the learning needs element of this scenario will become lost, with a focus on the perceived medical condition or disability replacing any perhaps more desirable focus on how that condition or disability might hinder the educational progress of that child or young person, a focus that should lead to at least a consideration of how those outcomes could be addressed without the need of a potentially damaging label being applied to the child.

There is a sense that this emergent practice results from the financial constraints that many local authorities currently report. That any rationing of funds for meeting the educational needs of those at the margins is regrettable, but it would seem to be a poor response on the part of schools if that rationing leads to internal procedures, implemented by the SENCo, that medicalise pupils as the precursor to referral for statutory assessment, rather than seeing services such as CAMHS as part of a broader process of data gathering that would make the best information available, enabling a local authority to make a balanced judgement based on established educational need.

In addition to any constraints placed on local authorities through financial strictures, there has also been a considerable degree of pressure placed on the system as a whole to reduce the number of children and young people being included within the special needs arena, with substantial reductions year on year since 2010 (21.1 per cent to 15.4 per cent) in the number of pupils with special needs but without a Statement/EHCP being reported (DfE/DoH, 2015). This reflects current policy, of course, and may be the result of a reappraisal of the type of teaching and learning that is being offered to pupils at the margins in many schools, coupled with a greater willingness to address these needs through collaborative practices led by newly trained SENCos.

There may also be a reactive aspect to this situation; in the absence of funding availability, it might be that schools are having to accept a greater responsibility for meeting needs within existing resources, rather than seeking means of external support. However, the lack of any apparent reduction in the percentage of pupils assessed as being in need of a Statement of Special Educational Need or an EHCP, unchanged since 2007 (DfE/DoH, 2015), suggests a continued requirement for the protection and resources afforded by this documentation. It might be seen as an unacceptable development if the nature or character, in the broadest sense of those terms, of those being assessed had become more strongly aligned with medical categories. A further example of this process might be seen in the replacement of the need described as Behaviour, Emotional and Social Development in section 7.60 of the SEN Code of Practice 2001 (DfES, 2001) with the need described as Social, Emotional and Mental Health Difficulties, in section 6.32 in the Special Educational Needs and Disability Code of Practice (DfE/DoH, 2015).

Apart from the loss of any reference to behaviour in this need, and the potentially emotive use of mental health difficulties, the associated description of the area of need shows a considerable degree of difference between the two codes. The 2001 Code, in addition to a general description, which is echoed to a considerable degree in the most recent Code, also contains a series of bullet points that are absent from the SEND Code of Practice 2015. The eight points include a series of steps to be taken to enhance and improve relationships and behaviour within a setting with the aim of improving teaching and learning opportunities for pupils within this area of need. This might be seen as suggesting that behavioural responses are malleable and changeable within well-structured and supportive environments, a view that would seem to sit comfortably within a social model of disability. By contrast, the SEND Code of Practice 2015 seems to be content in only offering a series of 'disease entities' including ADHD, Attachment Disorder or other underlying mental health difficulties (DfE/DoH, 2015: 98). The concern here is that an assessment within this area as specified will follow a diagnostic assessment of need within the medical field, potentially leading to the use of medication or treatment protocols or procedures, rather than being a process of evaluation of educational need, possibly influenced by the presence of symptomatic behaviours, that seeks to produce outcomes compatible with good classroom practice.

The second of these challenges has parallels with those previously discussed. There has always been a degree of uncertainty about funding mechanisms within the special needs arena, and this is something that appears to have had an increasing impact in recent years as the education system has become centralised and fragmented. The reduction of services available to parents, teachers and schools in meeting the requirements of pupils generally, but of those with special needs in particular, is well reported. The increase in available places to park at the offices of a local authority, reported in one of our conversations, is a stark illustration of the reduction of the number of professional support staff, a situation mirrored in several further conversations. In any situation where financial constraints come into play, it is perhaps inevitable that there will be unintended consequences; the lack of available educational psychologists to provide anything other than necessary statutory assessment support became a situation familiar to many of us with the introduction of local funding arrangements that reduced the amount of money that a local authority could hold back from the budget delegated to schools. The continued introduction of further changes to local funding rules, entirely consistent with ideas derived from a prevailing neo-liberal agenda, have included schools being charged for services previously provided within local authority budgets, including those associated with statutory assessment, for example, by an educational psychologist, or for the advice provided by an area SENCo.

However, such charging arrangements are likely to act in an unbalanced way; in part, this will be due to variations in the funding available to individual schools as a result of the rather imprecise proxy measures used to calculate budgets, even allowing for the adjustments that result from an awareness of the changing needs identified by census returns. It is interesting to note that the Education Funding Agency (EFA), detailing funding mechanisms for the school year 2015/2016, states that element 1 funding (based on the age weighted pupil unit, or AWPU) must be at least £2000 for primary schools and £3000 for pupils in Key Stages 3 and 4, suggesting that budgets might not well reach the £4000 per pupil that is part of the notional £10000 per pupil that a school must provide before High Needs funding becomes available (EFA, 2014).

In a system in which funding beyond the basic element accorded to every pupil, for example, through Element 2 funding related to meeting special educational needs, is based largely on measures of social deprivation or social economic status, a situation could easily arise where a small, rural school in a relatively affluent area of the country might find itself in financial difficulties if a recently enrolled student is felt to be in need of statutory assessment. This is exacerbated if the school has developed a reputation of having an ethos particularly well suited to supporting pupils at the margins of the education system, with parents exercising the right to choose a setting that might best be able to meet the suspected or identified special educational needs of their child. This was something that was clearly identified in one of our conversations, and appeared to be of considerable concern for the school and for those who were seeking to do their best for a significant, if relatively small, number of pupils who might not have been expected to have selected this school, given the population characteristics of the area.

There is also an increasing body of research that suggests that provision for pupils with special educational needs shows considerable variation in rates of identification between schools. An example can be found in the annual Statistical First Release published by the Department for Education (DfE, 2016a). Although the percentage of pupils identified as having non-Statemented/EHCP special educational needs is the same for primary academies as it is overall for all state funded school, at 13.4 per cent, and shows little difference for pupils within secondary education, with 12.4 per cent of pupils identified in academies and 12.7 per cent in state-funded secondary schools, further examination of the figures reveals a different and potentially more worrying picture. Within the primary sector, while the average for all academies is 13.4 per cent, there is a variation between 12.5 per cent for converter academies and 15.4 per cent for sponsor-led academies; the comparable figures for secondary academies, against an average of 12.4 per cent, are 11.2 per cent for converter and 15.2 per cent for sponsor-led academies (DfE, 2016a, SFR 29/2016, Table 2a). Converter academies are those that have chosen to become academies, while sponsor-led are those that have become academies generally as a result of being designated as under-performing. While these might not seem to be huge variations, in a fairly typical one form entry primary school of approximately 250 pupils, the average figure above would suggest approximately 33 being assessed as having non-Statemented/EHCP special educational needs, with a variation from 28 pupils in converter academies to more than 38, on average, in sponsor-led academies.

An explanation for these differences might be found in the social and economic status of the school's catchment area, if this is a sustainable correlate of the incidence of special educational need and disability; this would mean that sponsor-led academies are largely located in areas of social deprivation, while the opposite would be the case for converter academies. If this is case, the equalising effect of basing element 2 funding to a large degree on measures sympathetic to these differences (measures such as free school meals [FSM] or the Income Deprivation Affecting Children Index [IDACI]) would serve to protect the funding needed to meet these challenges. However, it might well be that the location of converter and sponsor-led academies does not fit such an explanation; it might be suggested, instead, that an element of covert selection is at work resulting in a variation between the needs being addressed by the school and those that might be expected based on the indicators of social deprivation in the catchment area of the school.

That this might not be surprising is a reflection of the observed differences in referral rates for additional support, which have shown local variations between similar schools, irrespective of the ways that schools have been organised, but which seem to have been maintained despite the markedly different way that schools have been funded in recent years. The EFA acknowledge these differences by stating that the variation in spending on those pupils assessed as having high needs is 'wide', although it goes on to suggest that there is a lack of robust data 'on the degree to which that variation in spending reflects genuine variation in need' (EFA, 2014: 5).

Although the majority of funding delegated to schools through nationally approved arrangements must be largely pupil-led (at least 80 per cent, according to the EFA, 2014), there are at least six elements of funding contained within this percentage, including AWPU, funding for social deprivation (compulsory), prior attainment, mobility, Looked After Children (all optional), and this makes it difficult to identify what might be considered to be a school's budget for meeting special educational needs. While the flexibility afforded by this uncertainty might well be very useful in a time of financial unpredictability, it also has the tendency to render attempts to ensure accountability and transparency in funding to meet additional needs difficult, if not impossible. It is little wonder that very few SEN-Cos, in discussions during sessions within the National Award for SEN Coordination, are able to identify the special needs budget within their school or setting; one wonders how many SEN governors are able to do this, in reporting to parents how well they are meeting these needs.

There is a sense that this unpredictability represents the development of an ever more confusing situation, that makes external, public scrutiny of funding for specific groups of pupils more difficult. This brings us to a third challenge, that of the relationship between school funding and the increasing fragmentation of the schools' system in England. The period since the advent of the role of the SENCo has been one of continued change and reorganisation within the structure of schooling. This would seem to parallel the movement away from a predominantly locally run system to one in which nominal control rests with central government, even where immediate responsibility is vested in structures such as multi-academy trusts. Both mainstream and special academies, mainstream and special free schools, and University Technical Colleges are all examples of this trend for new structures, even where the results of a change in designation might not be immediately obvious in the outcomes observed. There are currently 3359 primary academies, 2059 secondary academics and 60 special academies (DfE, 2016a), in total representing 20 per cent of the provision for primary aged pupils and 65 per cent of the provision for secondary pupils; there are also 427 free schools, UTCs and studio schools. The announced intention to allow the opening of further grammar schools seems to be another extension of this fragmented approach to provision within the education system.

The recently announced plan to require all schools to become academies by 2022, although abandoned fairly quickly, would seem to represent the logical extension of a policy to remove schools from local control. It is probable that this will happen anyway within the secondary sector, although the perceived benefits to primary schools seem much less clear or perhaps less attractive, and it requires a considerable degree of political vision or determination to envisage a situation where all primary provision follows the academy pathway. However this policy direction concludes, there is an inevitable conflict between changes to the structure of schooling stemming from a centrally devolved structure and the requirements that stem from other policies that remain centrally directed, but operationalised through local authorities; a relevant example is the administration of services relating to special educational needs.

The management of placements within this system remains with the local authority, which needs to consider provision for every child within their area, but who may have only a few schools directly under their control. It may be that such an arrangement will offer an enhanced service for pupils with special educational needs, as the quality of mainstream schools and settings improves under the influence of central policies designed to enhance 'support and aspiration' (DfE, 2011). It is inevitable, however, that a concern remains that some schools, despite any requirement imposed centrally to enrol pupils with special educational needs, will be less willing to meet the needs of pupils at the margins, citing the efficient education of other pupils as a reason. This concern must also extend to the increasing number of special schools that have become academies, where the use of terms such as complex needs in the designation of a school can serve to make the educational requirements of the pupils attending a setting less clear, allowing greater flexibility in admissions.

It is understandable that governors, parents, head teachers and other stakeholders will seek to protect the interests of their schools, in providing the best quality of education for their enrolled pupils, of whatever age and need. It is when these particularised interests come into conflict with broader aspirations for, and beliefs in, for example, the perceived right of children with special educational needs to be included within the sort of schooling generally available to all other pupils, or to participate in a similar curriculum to that offered generally to all other pupils, that difficulties become evident. The evolution of an effective special school system has been largely due to the dedication and hard work of the many passionate advocates of providing the best quality education for their pupils, and this has often meant championing specialist, segregated provision. It might not be surprising then if these strongly held beliefs tend towards a maintenance of current practice, in the face of calls for desegregated provision. Although representing what might be seen as a more utilitarian standpoint, it can also be seen that, in defending the attainment and progress of the many pupils within mainstream schools who succeed within the current performativity-oriented system, schools might question their ability to provide for those pupils for whom significant changes in the teaching, learning and assessment practices of the school will be expected.

It is within these conflicting spaces that the implementation of the Inclusion agenda takes place. On one side of these spaces are those seeking to ensure the implementation of greater Inclusion, often within a prevailing central policy direction. Artemi Sakellariades, in her evocative chapter (Chapter 7) revisits this debate, offering a compelling argument for full Inclusion. On the other are those who maintain that a policy such as this is difficult, if not impossible, to achieve given resourcing, teacher expertise, and curriculum needs within current systems. That policy can change is clear; the removal of the 'bias towards academic Inclusion', noted above, is a very relevant example here. However, the rhetoric involved in the sort of debate and arguments that surround policy directions such as these often serves to obscure the evidence about actual practice.

There is a general acceptance that the period following the publication of the Warnock Report, and the 1981 Education Act, which enacted many of its recommendations, was marked by the closure of many special schools and the placement of many pupils with special educational needs within mainstream settings; that is, the acceptance of ideas around integration and Inclusion became the precursor to significant changes within provision. Mary Warnock would seem to share this view; writing in 2005, she notes that, prior to 1980, about 2 per cent of the school population were educated in special schools (Warnock, Norwich and Terzi, 2010: 25); this included a substantial number of pupils for whom such a placement would not now be seen as appropriate, for example, those with visual or hearing impairment, or those whose disability required mobility assistance but who could not be placed in mainstream schools because of their lack of accessibility.

The current figure for pupils with a Statement/EHCP, of 2.8 per cent of the school population is therefore interesting. This figure includes those educated in both mainstream and special schools, so no direct comparison is possible, but it is the case that this figure is stable, and has been so for at least the last 10 years. Warnock goes on to say, 'after 1981, many of these . . . schools (for pupils with moderate learning difficulties and for those assessed as "maladjusted") were closed' (Warnock, Norwich and Terzi, 2010: 6). The data provided by the DfE in

2016 (DfE, 2016b) states that the most common category of need identified in those with Statements/EHCPs was Moderate Learning Difficulty (MLD), with Social, Emotional and Mental Health (SEMH) needs being identified within a group of needs that have a similar level of incidence, albeit significantly lower than that for MLD. What is particularly noticeable about the overall placement of pupils with these needs is the change in where that provision is occurring. Since at least 1998, there has been a steady decline in the percentage of new Statements being written for placement in a mainstream setting; this has been mirrored by a reduction in the overall percentage of pupils with Statements of Special Educational Needs being educated in mainstream schools; data from the SFR mentioned above shows a drop from 54.6 per cent of pupils in mainstream settings in 2010 to a current figure of 49 per cent; the rise in percentage terms of those attending special schools has been from 38.2 per cent to 42.9 per cent. This presents a much more nuanced picture of the 'bias towards academic Inclusion' that suggests a reversal in the direction of inclusive education that long predates the Coalition government in 2010, but might be seen to be consequent on the increasing emphasis placed on educational attainment following the introduction of the National Curriculum in 1989, seemingly intensified by the 'academisation' that underpinned the move away from the 'bog standard' comprehensive schools in the 'Education, Education, Education' agenda introduced by New Labour in 1997.

There would seem to be two important issues here, indicative of practice taking a somewhat different direction to that which might be expected within the stated policy context. The first concerns the use of Statements, and by extrapolation, EHCPs. Given that many Statements can be expected to be maintained throughout the educational journey of the child or young person, it is not unreasonable to assume that many current Statements or EHCPs, where these have been written to replace an existing Statement, predate recent legislation and may have been first written 10 or more years ago. It follows from this that, in order for the percentage of pupils with Statements in mainstream education to have fallen steadily over this period, at some point a situation was reached where special school placement as a result of assessment became the most favoured option, leading to a position echoing the words of Warnock cited above, where most of the children within the 2 per cent of the school population who have identified special needs are educated in segregated provision. When a further statistic is taken into account, that of the movement of pupils with Special Educational Needs between the two sectors, mainstream and segregated provision, the evidence for a long-term growth in the latter sector becomes stronger. In the 2007 SFR (DCSF, 2007), for example, the number of children moving from mainstream school to special school is given as 5670, while movement in the other direction was 890; these Statements would have been written for the sector from which the student moved, and so would tend to obscure the reality of where these students were actually placed in the longer term.

That the reasons given for this segregation are increasingly medicalised has already been discussed; what might be worth considering here is the degree to which this represents a self-perpetuating system, independent of policy. That is, special schools continue to exist partially to serve the needs of the special school system, and partially to serve the mainstream system's inability or unwillingness to expand the breadth of pupil needs that they feel able to meet. This is not to decry the efforts of those working in either sector, nor to question the degree to which each is successful in meeting the needs of the pupils they serve; however, the question that is worth asking is whether there is now a general acceptance at the policy level that a twin-track system represents the best solution within a prevailing view of education that sets seemingly irreconcilable aspirations for the two groups of pupils, rather than continuing to seek ways that offer a more balanced view of the purposes of education within our system.

The second issue here concerns the increasing fragmentation of types of provision available. It might be argued that such a system could become increasingly inflexible, particularly where a group of schools adopt policies supportive of the twin-track approach discussed here. It is certainly worth remembering that processes associated with integration or Inclusion encompassed a broad range of actions; these included the presumption contained with the 1996 Education Act (DfE, 1996) that Statemented pupils must be educated in mainstream provision unless certain specific exemptions applied, for example. It was also the case that a substantial number of students benefitted from the possibility of a reintegration placement following placement in segregated provision, where progress had been made in meeting educational goals. It is hard to see how this sort of situation could continue, particularly where current assessment processes focus on 'disease entities' rather than on the need to meet specific educational difficulties that might arise independently of such a diagnosis. The presence of Pupil Referral Units (PRU) or Short Stay schools goes some way to obscure this situation. Pupils who attend such settings are presumed to return to the mainstream, following a period of intensive input to meet the need that led to their placement in the setting, suggesting a fluidity that is admirable and desirable. It seems unlikely that this is a process that also occurs with those pupils who move to a special school, within a strictly defined regulatory framework, as opposed to those who enter the rather more unfettered PRU system.

The challenges to those for whom meeting the needs of pupils with special educational needs is a priority would seem to be considerable. However, the picture is still varied to a heartening degree. Experience suggests that there have always been settings that have bucked the trend of a prevailing orthodoxy, and these have often been seen to be effective and successful within inspection or advisory regimes. It is certainly the case that academic excellence measured through attainment is a major factor in being seen as successful, but this does not preclude other indicators of the well-being of a school being noticed and appraised, adding to the way the setting is judged. For example, many special schools are judged as Outstanding by Ofsted, with particular mention being made of the holistic nature of the support offered in all aspects of the development of the pupils within that setting. Other schools, where narrow measures of attainment are hard to foster, accept that such a categorisation is unlikely, but continue to develop systems that encourage, inspire and support all pupils in the common endeavour of education, in the broadest sense of that word.

It is here that the role of the SENCo can be seen as hugely influential, particularly where a stated commitment to include all learners fully and equally within the teaching and learning of the setting accords with the direction of travel of the school, stemming from the vision of the head teacher, staff and governors. That the Learning Outcomes of the National Award for SEN Coordination include the idea of challenging senior leaders, colleagues and governors (NCTL, 2014b, Section 6) in the development of best practice suggests a recognition that change can come from within, to ensure the best outcomes for those experiencing barriers to learning.

Two further challenges exist that are closely linked; that of the curriculum, and of the way that support staff are deployed within classroom practice based on choices made within broader curricula ideas. In discussing curriculum practice, some breaking down of the subject area is needed. First, some consideration is needed about structure, given that there appears to be an increasing divergence of curricular requirements between the countries of the UK; a simple example might be the extension of the Foundation Stage curriculum to the age of 7 in Wales, making for very different practice in schools situated either side of an extended border region between Wales and England. It is probable that there would be very little argument that the National Curriculum in England has, through a series of changes, become more narrowly prescriptive and more narrowly focussed on subject matter that accords to a view of what is 'good'. Certainly, the curriculum critique contained within both the Rose Review (DCSF, 2009) and the Cambridge Review (Alexander, 2009) has been overridden by a different ideological perspective that more naturally aligns with the other changes described above.

And yet, it still seems possible to offer a great deal more variety in what happens in the classroom within this structure than what actually happens, and it is here that we must ask questions about the degree to which teachers at all stages of their careers consider matters related to curriculum design and implementation. That there are external drivers that have the potential to limit classroom practice is undeniable; perceptions of Ofsted and the inspection process, and the testing and performativity regime cannot be ignored even if they are not as intractable as many might consider. However, none of this prevents the rigorous and continuous consideration of best classroom practice, based on theoretical principles reinforced by evidence-based practice. This became obvious in our conversations; some schools are taking a stance that moves away from much of the orthodoxy that has become standard practice in classrooms, in particular in the way that pupils are grouped and in the way that lesson materials are made available to pupils. Here it seems to be the case that two distinct and largely opposing forces are at work, that again mirror the utilitarian versus egalitarian positions discussed previously.

On the one hand, there are schools that use teaching and learning approaches designed to maximise attainment, even where this leaves some children behind. The increased use of streaming in primary schools to separate learners in years 5 and 6 for both literacy and numeracy, as an extension of the sort of setting by table often seen within a year group is an example of this sort of process. Another example, and one that seems to be particularly difficult to accept given frequent complaints about workload, is the way that schools have spent a great deal of time replicating levels within a system that is now described as being 'assessment without levels'. On the other, there are schools that seek to explore different approaches; the use of mixed ability teaching in a large primary school formed the basis of one of our conversations, with teaching and learning being seen to stem from shared aims and activities but differentiated outcomes. It was also noticeable that teachers and support staff in this setting seemed to have a comprehensive and full understanding of the learning needs, achievements and progress of their pupils, based on a shared vision of what achievement means in the context in which the school operates. That the situation in secondary schools is different is perhaps obvious. However, there are schools in this sector that seek to replicate the potentially more pupil-focussed environment of the primary school, at least in years 7 and 8, by providing 'home base' mixed ability teaching in the core subjects of English, Mathematics, MFL and the Humanities, to foster a sense of worth for pupils who would be marginalised within the more usual heavily streamed system found in many secondary settings.

The worrying thing here is that there is a lack of debate couched in theoretical terms about this divide. Rather, there is an orthodoxy about the continued move towards a more restrictive curriculum model that is not mirrored within changes in the opposite direction; here the changes are made in the face of opposition and criticism, rather than being seen as a genuine curriculum alternative, supported by evidence. So, a change to a mixed ability approach will be seen as experimental and brave, and only likely to survive as long as good progress for all pupils can be demonstrated within a very narrow range of parameters, while changes of a more 'orthodox' nature are unlikely to be exposed to the same level of critique, even where outcomes might be marginal. This seems to reflect an unwillingness to consider any changes in a balanced and theory-based way, perhaps as a result of teaching demonstrating the lack of a rigorous discourse about best practice.

This might well be one of the (un)intended outcomes of the move towards Initial Teacher Education being school-based. In a one year PGCE course containing upwards of 130 days of class-based work alongside the modules needed to gain a good grasp of the breadth and depth of the curriculum, it is hardly surprising that adequate time for engagement with, and reflection on, educational theory is difficult. As the Carter Review (DfE, 2015) on ITE suggested, giving an acceptable amount of time to learning about SEND and behaviour management seems very difficult to achieve, let alone going beyond that to consider alternative learning strategies or theories of learning. In this sense, learning by experience tends to become learning by example, with reflection becoming something that focusses on the explanation of practice rather than an exploration of that practice set against alternative explanations.

This would seem to lead to a narrowing of the way that things are understood; certainly, talking to practitioners about, for example, scaffolding tends towards a feeling that what is being discussed is a long way away from an understanding of what a social constructivist might mean when talking about the term; straitjacket might be a better rendering of what is meant, rather than ideas around potential and possibilities. This process seems to have been extended to the borrowing of concepts and ideas from a variety of theoretical positions in a sort of eclectic, educational *pot-pourri* of ideas privileging pragmatism over reasoned and thought-through educational practice. That such an approach might be justifiable is accepted, where a coherent justification is given; where it simply grows out of an unthinking acceptance of rhetoric is to be regretted.

It is this rhetoric that would seem to be the most problematic aspect of this discussion. All too often, what is being said evokes a response in the listener that is not reliant on an understanding of what the terminology might mean in practice. In this sense, the defining rhetoric is atheoretical; acceptance is presumed and no reasoned response is required. Increasingly, educational practice is littered with this sort of terminology; in this case, the term to be explored is Quality First teaching, and its derivatives, such as High Quality teaching or High Quality inclusive teaching. In a short chapter in a recently published book, these terms are used 24 times, describing the sort of practice needed to best meet the needs of all pupils. However, there does not seem to be any attempt to fully explore what these terms mean, or to offer a justification for their use within a defined curriculum structure. Most teachers will be aware of Quality First teaching and the Wave model of curriculum delivery but it seems unlikely that any rigorous exemplification of what Quality First means (does the term have an opposite: Quality Second perhaps, or Poor Quality First?), or what leads to such teaching being deemed to be unsuccessful, requiring the introduction of Wave 2 and 3 interventions.

This argument goes beyond semantics, of course; it would seem that Quality First teaching has come to mean that which is offered successfully to many pupils, possibly the majority, while the Wave model accommodates those for whom the Quality First teaching provides neither quality or teaching. This is not, of course, an absolute measure, so it is very likely that the boundary between Quality First teaching and Wave interventions will be set as an artefact of the curriculum ambitions of a school, with a greater use of Waves 2 and 3 in a setting focussing on maximising attainment, rather than as a concept, in itself arguably dubious, that provides support for those pupils whose learning needs are at the margins. The argument often offered for interventions of this type, of narrowing or closing the gap in attainment, might easily be countered by the adoption of an approach that allows children to develop at a pace suited to their learning needs within a context favouring teacher knowledge and expertise; that is, one that moves away from extending what is ordinarily offered to meet perceived special needs.

Elsewhere in this book, Lani Florian offers a compelling argument for the extension of what is ordinarily available through the concept of inclusive pedagogy. This seems to us to be the antithesis of what is offered through Quality First teaching, that is, offering teaching and learning that are additional to what is ordinarily offered; the worry is that it is very difficult for this sort of idea to gain traction in current educational discourse, given the power of the prevailing orthodoxy.

At the centre, this seems to be a debate about teaching and learning that is predicated on the assumption of raising the achievement of all pupils, rather than focussing on the attainment of some children against prescribed standards, often at the expense of those pupils who are now likely to be termed as 'below average' in the context of Key Stage 2 testing. There is little evidence to support any assumption that the situation differs within secondary provision. Indeed, the experiences recounted in our recent conversations suggests that there might well be even less consideration of alternative approaches to teaching and learning in this sector than within primary schools. There was a general acceptance that streaming is needed, and that students with special needs are likely to be concentrated in the lower streams; it also appeared to be the case that even where this was not the case, there was a heavy reliance on support staff working alongside pupils to ensure that their presence in the class was a useful educational experience.

There is a deep-seated concern here about the way that students with special needs, or indeed any that do not fit into the prevailing culture, are perceived and their needs met in secondary education. In terms of perceptions, it seems likely that the idea that teachers are teachers of all children (DfE/DoH, 2015) is not one that has wholehearted acceptance within the sector; certainly, the responses of students undertaking secondary post-graduate training seem to focus much more clearly on subject knowledge and competence, with the 'othering' of students with special needs as being the responsibility of the Inclusion team, or the special needs department; this seems to be particularly the case in relation to pupils with needs that might be characterised as SEMH. In terms of needs, alongside the frequently reported example above involving support staff, a particular example emerged from one of our conversations, concerning an unwillingness of pastoral staff, in this case form tutors, to engage with aspects of special needs. A SENCo working in a secondary setting described a situation where it had not been possible to carry out the termly reviews for pupils with EHCPs/Statements in the way required within the 2015 SEND Code of Practice, due to workload resistance from form tutors; there also seemed to be an assumption that this sort of direct parental involvement fell within the remit of the SENCo, rather than being a more general pastoral role, despite what is said in the Code (DfE/DoH, 2015). The outcome of this situation was that the SENCo completed these reviews, arguably further intensifying the sense that the pupils concerned were only partial members of their classes. That secondary provision might be intrinsically less accommodating for pupils with special needs can be inferred from the SFR cited above, showing movement between the primary and secondary sectors of pupils with Statements; the majority of these transfers take place either in the period prior to transfer, or in the early years of secondary provision, as the growing conflict between the pupils' learning needs and the demands of an increasingly academic curriculum become intractable, seemingly without any discussion of the pedagogical appropriateness of these demands.

There is a sense here of circularity. For some pupils, including many of those with special needs, the demands placed on them by a curriculum model focussing on a narrow attainment-led performativity create a widening gap between what they can do, and what is expected of them. Whether this leads to placement in segregated provision, in a special school, or in a unit, or simply within a class group with low demands and low expectations, the end product is a lack of success that, in turn, justifies the need for practices that are less than inclusive, the sort of self-fulfilling prophecy that has bedevilled attempts to promote equity and social justice over many years.

The final point to be discussed here, as mentioned earlier, is that of support, and how this is operationalised within the classroom. An important element of the changing face of schools has been the employment of an increasing number of support assistants in schools; in 2014, 255,100 fte (full-time equivalents) teaching assistants were employed in schools in England, a 4.7 per cent increase on 2013, following a further 4.9 per cent increase in the previous year (DfE, 2014, SFR 11/2014). Given this continued increase, it would seem to be relevant to consider the benefits of this increased workforce, in terms of teaching and learning, as opposed to diverting some of this resource into the employment of specialist teachers, the option favoured in many European countries, in Scandinavia and Italy, for example.

At one level, these benefits seem to be limited, or non-existent. The extensive research programme into the role, carried out by the Institute of Education, University of London (now Institute of Education, University College, London) suggests that the use of support assistants does not lead to gains in attainment; indeed, there appears to be an inverse effect, in that those pupils who are not supported in a classroom with more support assistants make less progress than pupils in classrooms without support (Blatchford, Bassett, Brown, et al., 2008). Among explanatory suggestions, the report notes that where pupils were frequently supported by support assistants, they spent less time in direct interaction with their teacher '*as an alternative, as much as an additional, form of support*' (Blatchford, Bassett, Brown, et al., 2008: 11). It goes on to suggest that support assistants focus more on task completion than encouraging and facilitating teaching and learning, something that might not be surprising, given the lack of time and support many are offered in preparing for interventions.

The report goes on to note that broadening the scope of analysis showed clear gains in learner focus and behaviour where support was offered; significant reductions in teacher workload and work-related stress as a result of increased support; and significant learning gains where support staff were properly trained, enjoyed role clarity and shared planning and other important teaching and learning decisions.

Rix (2015), in drawing attention to material drawn from The Education Endowment Foundation Teaching and Learning Toolkit, gives consideration to how well decisions made about interventions reflect the efficacy of those practices. The material offers an analysis of the effect size of interventions against the cost of implementing them; here, it seems to be the case that support assistants offer very limited effect sizes and relatively high costs, making their employment of questionable value in individual attainment/achievement terms. By contrast, peer tutoring and feedback are seen as highly effective and low cost, and are therefore seen as preferred choices. Rix suggests that an analysis of this nature is potentially limiting, not least because effect size and cost might not be the most important units of measure when making this sort of choice. This seems to be particularly the case, given the difficulties associated with extrapolating reported effect sizes in small-scale interventions, such as single subject research designs, to the much more complex arena of whole-class teaching or class-based interventions. What would seem to be clear, however, is that, as Rix suggests, research states that the best interventions use practices that are 'relatively accessible to practitioners', while adding the caveat that other research suggests that these practices are in fact rarely seen within the classroom (2015: 67–68).

It is here that our conversations with practitioners offered both potentially more inclusive approaches at the same time as also offering examples of ways of working that appeared to provide little in promoting effective learning for all pupils. On a positive note, approaches were discussed that clearly empowered support staff. These often focussed on procedures that raised the status of support staff through consideration of contracts, working hours and line management allowing, for example, joint planning with teachers, the removal of perceived barriers between class-based and individual support, and career development opportunities. While the development of this sort of working derived from the stated ethos and vision of the school as a whole, it was also the case that the SENCo was often the driving force behind changes in practice that focussed on the enhancement of learning for all pupils. A notable example of this was a class-room model that assumed that all of the adults present in the classroom occupied roles that were interchangeable, meaning that any child might be taught by any member of staff, in a manner reminiscent of continuous provision. Here, there seems to be a situation where practice can be seen to be diverging from current expectations; every teacher is seen as a pedagogical lead within their classroom, teaching all children, and attempting to meet the assessed learning needs of those pupils by adapting and extending the range of learning opportunities within a curriculum offer based on the shared and growing expertise of all adults in the classroom. In this sense, the first requirement of inclusive learning would seem to be the establishment of a community of inclusive learners reminiscent of the sort of community of practice described earlier, rather than in the continued use of hierarchies based on narrowly delineated and prescriptive roles.

This would seem to be in sharp contrast with the sort of support practice that occurs in many primary schools, and in the secondary sector, where a support assistant works with an individual child or group of children with special needs, while the teacher works with the remainder of the class, or where children are withdrawn from the class for some sort of individual or group intervention, or to go to a separate class or facility, often euphemistically called the Inclusion Centre. And yet, the orthodoxy of practice seems to lie still with the latter model, and this represents the negative side to the positivity discussed in the previous paragraph. In one of our conversations, discussed more fully earlier, a SENCo describes the deep sorrow that she felt when sending a child out of the class for an intervention, put in place to try to secure higher scores in the Key Stage 2 assessment. The SENCo recounts how sad she felt, in needing to provide this opportunity as a result of pressures external to the school; it seemed as if deeply held inclusive beliefs were being abandoned for short-term gain. There was also an awareness that the pupil, despite an initial enthusiasm for the withdrawal activity, still recognised the loss of their place in the class. Compare this with many practitioners who would unquestioningly embrace these sort of opportunities from an attainment perspec-tive, without considering the degree to which practices of this sort contradict the development of inclusive practice – and which seem to be less effective than peda-gogical approaches that can easily be developed within the classroom.

It would seem to be prudent to round off this section by considering the degree to which an individual teacher or SENCo can resolve the conflicts and contradic-tions inherent in the dilemmas identified here. It is certainly the case that the degree to which an individual can influence policy and practice within a school setting is dependent on the position they hold within the management structure of that setting, although even here, being a part of the senior leadership team does not guarantee that change can happen, unless other permitting circumstances are also in place. However, it is equally the case that our area of greatest influence is in our own classroom, or in the case of the SENCo, in the area of expertise that falls within this remit. It is here that we can make the greatest changes, in moving towards a more inclusive approach to teaching and learning; a first step must be to ask questions about how we shape teaching and learning in our classroom within the constraints imposed by external requirements, which are often arguably less onerous than we tend to believe them to be. That this will lead inexorably to questions about how we use support staff, how we use assessment information, how we motivate and inspire the aspirations of our pupils, and so on, would seem to be the challenge that needs to be met. Having built our own good practice, then the next step, of changing practice in the setting, might not seem to be so daunting.

References

Alexander, R. (ed.) (2009) *Children, Their World, Their Education: Final Report and Recommendations of the Cambridge Primary Review*. London: Routledge.

Blatchford, P., Bassett, P., Brown, P., Martin, C., Russell, A. and Webster, R. (2008) *Research Report RR027 Deployment and Impact of Support Staff in Schools and the Impact of the National Agreement*. Nottingham: DCSF.

Brown, J. and Doveston, M. (2014) Short sprint or an endurance test: the perceived impact of the National Award for Special Educational Needs Coordination. *Teacher Development*, 18(4): 495–510.

Cowne, E. (2008) What do Special Educational Needs Coordinators think they do?, *Support for Learning*, 20(2): 61–68.

DCSF (2007) Statistical First Release 20/2007. (Retrieved 14 April 2008).

DCSF (2009) *Independent Review of the Primary Curriculum [The Rose Review]*. Nottingham: DCSF.

DES (1978) *Report of the Committee of Enquiry into the Education of Handicapped Children and Young People [The Warnock Report]*. London: HMSO.

DES (1985) *The Curriculum from 5 to 16 [Curriculum Matters No. 2]*. London: HMSO.

DES (1989) *The National Curriculum in England*. London: HMSO.

DfE (1994) *Code of Practice on the Identification and Assessment of Special Educational Needs*. London: DfE.

DfE (1996) *Education Act*. London: HMSO.

DfE (2011) *Support and Aspiration: A New Approach to Special Educational Needs and Disability – A Consultation*. London: TSO.

DfE (2014) *Statistical First Release 11/2014 School Workforce in England*. Retrieved 24 October 2016 from: https://www.gov.uk/government/uploads/system/uploads/attachment_data/file/335413/sfr11_2014_updated_july.pd.

DfE (2015) *Carter Review of Initial Teacher Education*. London: TSO.

DfE (2016a) *Statistical First Release 29/2016 Special Educational Needs in England*. Retrieved 16 October 2016 from: https://www.gov.uk/government/uploads/system/uploads/attachment_data/file/539158/SFR29_2016_Main_Text.pdf.

DfE (2016b) Open academies and academy projects awaiting approval. Retrieved 6 October 2015 from: https://www.gov.uk/government/publications/open-academies-and-academy-projects-in-development.

DfE/DoH (2015) *Special Educational Needs and Disability Code of Practice: 0 to 25 Years.* London: TSO.

DfES (2001) *SEN Code of Practice.* Nottingham: DfES.

Educational Funding Agency [EFA] (2014) *Schools Revenue Funding 2015 to 2016 Operational Guide EFA, 2014.* London: DfE.

Griffiths, D. and Dubsky, R. (2012) Evaluating the impact of the new National Award for SENCos: transforming landscapes or gardening in a gale? *British Journal of Special Education,* 39(4): 164–172.

Layton, L. (2008) Special educational needs coordinators and leadership: a role too far?, *Support for Learning,* 20(2): 53–60.

Lipsky, M. (1980) *Street-level Bureaucracy: Dilemmas of the Individual in Public Services.* New York: Russell Sage Foundation.

National College for Teaching and Leadership (2014a) *School Direct: Guidance for Lead Schools.* London: DfE.

National College for Teaching and Leadership (2014b) *National Award for SEN Co-ordination: Learning Outcomes.* London: DfE.

Pearson, S., Mitchell, R. and Rapti, M. (2015) 'I will be "fighting" even more for pupils with SEN': SENCOs' role predictions in the changing English policy context. *Journal of Research in Special Educational Needs,* 15(1): 48–56.

Rix, J. (2015) *Must Inclusion Be Special? Rethinking Educational Support within a Community of Provision.* London: Routledge.

Robertson, C. (2012) Special educational needs and disability coordination in a changing policy landscape: making sense of policy from a SENCO's perspective. *Support for Learning,* 27(2): 77–83.

Robinson, K. (2008) *Changing Education Paradigms.* London: RSA.

Warnock, M., Norwich, B. and Terzi, L. (2010) *Special Educational Needs: A New Look.* London: Continuum.

Zwed, C. (2011) Reconsidering the role of the primary special educational needs coordinator: policy, practice and future priorities. *British Journal of Special Education,* 34(2): 96–104.

11 Conclusion

Fiona and Graham Hallett

In concluding the previous chapter, some thought was given to the degree of influence an individual SENCo can exert over the development of good practice in a setting, as an extension of the manner in which the role itself has developed over time. The central thesis developed in this book is that the role of the SENCo has been subject to a process of evolution and transformation ever since the need for the post was first recognised, and that this process mirrors the policy direction suggested in documents such as the *SEND Codes of Practice* and those surrounding the National Award for SEN Co-ordination.

Additionally, it can also be suggested that the role is transformative, in the sense that a move from a process style of role management to a much more strategic style has presented the opportunity for post holders to become an integral part of the development of practices that embrace the learning needs of all pupils. This seems to be one of the major changes that has resulted from the introduction of the National Award for SEN Coordination, as both newly appointed SENCos and many of those who have held the post for a considerable period of time have engaged with an extended period of academic study, many for the first time since completing their Initial Teacher Education. Experience of working on the National Award suggests that many participants found this challenging, partly because of workload issues in what has become a very pressurised working environment in many schools, but also partly because of the breadth of knowledge that the National Award assumes. It certainly seemed to be the case that gaining sufficient knowledge to comfortably occupy the position of 'expert' (Kearns, 2005) is daunting; that this might stem from the acknowledged lack of coverage of SEND and behaviour management in many ITE courses (DfE, 2015) would seem to be an unsurprising, if unwelcome, situation.

It also seemed that other areas of the National Award offered a considerable degree of challenge to some participants: four areas in particular might be considered. The first appeared to be a lack of involvement with the theoretical underpinnings of teaching and learning, evidenced through a lack of practical engagement with learning theory, curriculum development, principles of differentiation, and assessment in its widest forms. This seemed to stem, not from a lack of knowledge, but more from a lack of experience of alternative structures in a school system that has become increasingly homogenised around practices that might not best serve the sort of practices a SENCo might wish to implement and develop.

The second centred on leadership; there again seemed to be an acceptance of the practice on offer within the setting where they worked, without considering alternative structures that might empower colleagues to seek, demonstrate and develop practices of greater benefit to their students. It is recognised that the implementation of such structures is not within the direct remit of a SENCo completing the National Award, but this should not, in our view, preclude the consideration of leadership within the Award, as part of the professional development of those who are increasingly likely to already be or who will become senior leaders within schools.

The third challenge was a need to focus much more strongly on the use of reflection as part of the everyday practice involved in teaching and learning. This is not to suggest that participants do not engage in reflection, but it certainly seemed to be the case that much of what did occur did not go much beyond the sort of reflection that focuses on the consideration of immediate practice, such as the use of support staff, the lack of necessary resources or, in the case of the SENCo role, on the everyday practice occurring in their setting and the difficulties inherent in implementing established practice. It certainly seemed that a broader application of theoretical constructs associated with reflection was uncommon, of the type associated with the sort of situation that Tripp (1993) would consider to form the basis of a Critical Incident leading to a structural change in practice.

The fourth area of potential difficulty for participants in the National Award concerns the need to engage with the research process, in particular with educational research. Where participants have carried out small-scale research projects in the past, this presented less of a difficulty, but this was not always the case; for many participants, gaining confidence in this area represented a steep learning curve, encompassing aspects of methodology and ethics, alongside a need to consider a personal view of knowledge and knowledge acquisition.

As the National Award has evolved, it is unquestionably the case that providers have sought to address these issues, to provide a supportive and enabling environment for a group of participants who demand the highest standards of themselves, and seek to achieve the best outcomes in a very pressurised situation.

It might be easy to argue here that a simpler response would be to lower the expectations of the National Award. Indeed, there is evidence to suggest that there are those who do argue for this. For example, Griffiths and Dubsky (2012), in an evaluation of the National Award, report data gathered from head teachers that questions the need for the Award to be compulsory, that suggests the greater utility of workplace learning rather than academic study, and that repudiates the need for the completion of academic work at Master's level, as being 'time-consuming'. This seems to align with other recent policy changes; for example, the removal of the requirement that head teachers have to complete any formal training for their role, or that some types of schools do not have to employ qualified teachers.

Indeed, an approach that removes the need for extended study at a theoretical level seems to have become firmly entrenched in the English education system; the advent of Initial Teacher Training programmes such as School Direct and Teach First privilege apprenticeship approaches over what might be termed mastery learning, implicit in the sort of study offered within an extended academic training leavened by extended periods of *practicum*. Two further points might be made here; the contrast with other, highly successful teacher training systems, for example in Finland, where the achievement of a Master's level qualification is a precursor of classroom practice, is obvious. The second point concerns the National Award; the requirements laid down for providers of the Award demand the completion of a portfolio based on evidence matched against the Learning Outcomes, a practice that can be argued to require the demonstration of practical, school-based knowledge as an adjunct to the formal academic requirements of the Award.

It is our view that there should be no dilution of the academic requirements of the National Award. In our conversations, those participants who had completed the Award acknowledged the many difficulties faced in studying while meeting the requirements of a demanding job. However, there was also a recognition that study at this level was worthwhile. The completion of 60 of the 180 Level 7 credits needed to gain a Master's degree was a major advantage of the Award; the opportunity to study with other post holders, and thus to gain a broader picture of the role of the SENCo was also seen as beneficial. A significant number of participants also talked about the benefits of the sort of reflection encouraged in the Award; the adoption of this type of reflective approach encouraged and facilitated a greater awareness of the needs of students offering thoughtful ways that these needs might be met. It could be argued, indeed, that the practice of thoughtful reflection marked out these practitioners in a way not usually seen in practising teachers. Finally, given the current demands for an evidence-led profession, it would seem to be particularly important that appropriate, rigorous and ethical approaches are adopted by practitioners in fostering relevant and balanced approaches to research that do not simply replicate current practice, but that ask, and seek to answer, important questions about teaching, learning and assessment.

In Chapter 3, we talked about what it is to be a professional; it would seem to be the case that the retention of the requirements for SENCos to be qualified teachers, to hold the National Award, and to have studied at Master's levels are not things that should be questioned, but are attributes that should become part of a different vision of teachers, as members of a thoughtful, theoretically oriented profession dedicated to best practice for all, rather than being little more than classroom technicians implementing dogma and orthodoxy.

References

DfE (2015) *Carter Review of Initial Teacher Education.* London: TSO.

Griffiths, D. and Dubsky, R. (2012) Evaluating the impact of the new National Award for SENCos: Transforming landscapes or gardening in a gale? *British Journal of Special Education,* 39(4): 164–172.

Kearns, H. (2005) Exploring the experiential learning of special educational needs coordinators. *Journal of In-Service Education,* 31(1): 131–150.

Tripp, D. (1993) *Critical Incidents in Teaching: Developing Professional Judgement.* London: Routledge.

Index